i

THE LONG WALK TO COMPOSTELA

LIFE LESSONS LEARNED ON THE CAMINO DE SANTIAGO

ROB LEACHMAN

West Gale Press

ISBN   979-8-9934935-0-3 (paperback)

ISBN   979-8-9934935-1-0 (ebook)

CONTENTS

PROLOGUE

"I WANT TO HIKE THE CAMINO"

IT WAS MAY 11, 2017, my wife Bev's sixtieth birthday. Surrounding our dining room table were members of our family who had gathered in our home in suburban Kansas City to celebrate Bev entering her seventh decade. It was a festive evening, filled with wine and good food, reflection, and memories. In all the merriment, someone asked Bev what big goal she still wanted to attain.

At this point in our lives, we had biked the Katy Trail across the state of Missouri and had completed a rim-to-rim hike of the Grand Canyon. And in less than four months, we were scheduled to begin a cross-country bicycle trip. In answer to this inquiry, she responded quickly and enthusiastically, "I want to hike the Camino."

Six years later, she and I did just that.

BEV'S FASCINATION WITH THE Camino de Santiago dates back several decades. Many years ago, during a time of deep spiritual exploration, she brought home a copy of *The Camino: A Pilgrimage of Courage*, a memoir written by the actress Shirley MacLaine. In this book, MacLaine uses a deeply personal and mystical approach to describe her journey to Santiago de Compostela. And Bev ate it up, with the actress's spiritual tales of completing her pilgrimage reinforcing my wife's desire to do the same. But like our dreams of traversing the Grand Canyon or biking across the United States, career and family obligations at that point in our lives made hiking across northern Spain just one more distant fantasy.

In time, though, career transitions and ultimately retirement made these goals much more attainable. We biked across Missouri in 2013, then hiked across the Grand Canyon in 2015, and finally biked across the southern United States in 2017. We thrived on these adventures, pushing ourselves to prepare for the challenge, immersing ourselves in the experience as we completed each journey, and walking away with a sense of satisfaction that came from dedicating ourselves to and then reaching lofty goals. As we reflected together after we arrived in St. Augustine, Florida, at the end of our long bicycle trip, Bev and I both knew we wanted, and needed, more adventures like that one.

But some relatively minor but still pesky health issues soon arose. And then the world shut down because of the pandemic, an experience that affected our lives in ways that transcended the threat of the virus itself. Through all of this, we maintained our focus on our fitness and well-being, more to maintain our health (and, for a time, our sanity) than to prepare for any adventure trips. But suddenly, or so it seemed, it had been nearly six years since we had dipped our front bike tires in the Atlantic Ocean at the end of our cross-country trip. And though Bev and I have never dwelled on our advancing ages, we both found ourselves in our mid-sixties.

The Camino was calling us, and we had a sense that, if we wanted to reach this longtime goal, we needed to start planning. That process began in the spring of 2023.

The Camino de Santiago, or the Way of St. James, is one of the oldest and most famous pilgrimage routes in the world. Completing a pilgrimage to Santiago de Compostela, Spain, had its origins in the ninth century after the remains of the Apostle James were supposedly discovered in Galicia in northwestern Spain. Since the tenth century, millions of pilgrims, or peregrinos, have made their way to the Cathedral of Santiago de Compostela, where the remains of the apostle are said to be buried.

For the first 1,000 years or so, pilgrims completed the arduous trek on the Camino as a means of gaining a plenary indulgence from the Catholic Church, a way of reducing or eliminating the punishment followers would ultimately receive for their sins. Walking the hundreds of miles under primitive conditions was almost always completed for religious reasons, a sacred and holy journey through which pilgrims showed their devotion to God, Jesus Christ, and the Church. In modern times, there are still many who complete their Camino for religious reasons.

But over the past few decades, there has been an explosion of interest in hiking all or part of the Camino. As an illustration, in 1990, the pilgrim's office in Santiago awarded a Compostela, or certificate signifying official completion of the Camino, to fewer than 5,000 pilgrims. By 2023, that number had increased to nearly half a million.

The bulk of this steady increase resulted not from Catholic Church-related religious fervor, but rather from individuals seeking adventure, a greater spiritual connection, or a combination of both. This was fueled by the depiction of the Camino de Santiago in popular culture. Paulo Coelho's 1987 novel, *The Pilgrimage*, offered a mystical and novelized depiction of the author's journey across Spain. Shirley MacLaine's memoir about her Camino gained considerable readership, particularly in the United States.

But to many individuals, including Bev and me, the most powerful enticement to complete a Camino came from a 2010 film written and directed by Emilio Estevez that was simply titled *The Way*. In this film, Estevez plays a globetrotting young man who dies on his first day on the Camino de Santiago, perishing in an unexpected snowstorm as he hiked across the Pyrenees. Estevez's character's estranged father, played by his real-life dad, Martin Sheen, travels to St. Jean Pied de Port, the French border village at the start of this Camino route, to claim his son's body. Sheen's character has the body cremated and then carries the remains as he completes the Camino his son had just started. This journey, and the father's interactions with a whimsical group of hiking mates, form the basis for the movie.

Filmed on location in northern Spain, *The Way* is a poignant and beautiful film that Bev and I have watched countless times. Though Bev's dream of hiking the Camino de Santiago predated mine, I found this simple film to be a source of great fascination and motivation to tackle this adventure. I suspect countless others share this same reaction.

Regardless, what had started over a thousand years ago as a simple, primitive, and purely religious rite of passage has become a popular, at times commercialized, often crowded, but still beautiful and meaningful journey.

THE CAMINO DE SANTIAGO is actually made up of several routes, all starting somewhere on the European continent but ending at the Cathedral of Santiago de Compostela. These various routes are used by a limited but growing number of peregrinos, and on each is slowly being built adequate infrastructure (i.e., lodging and eating establishments) to service the increasing numbers of pilgrims.

But by far the most popular route is the Camino Francés, the path on which most pilgrims travel to Santiago. The route travels in a westerly direction, beginning in the small French village of St. Jean Pied de Port. From there, the path crosses over the Pyrenees mountains into Spain, through the major cities of Pamplona, Burgos, and León, over innumerable hills and through countless small towns, across the relatively barren plateau region called the Meseta, and into Santiago de Compostela. The entire route is around 800 kilometers or nearly 500 miles. The trail encompasses long stretches of "natural path" of gravel and dirt, paved sidewalks and paths through towns and cities, and sometimes roads shared with motor vehicles.

Though the distance traveled each day on the Camino Francés can be a personal preference, some of that decision is dictated by the availability of lodging. As a result, it is common for peregrinos to follow a fairly standard schedule as they cross northern Spain on this route. As Bev and I completed our Camino, we experienced several days of eighteen, nineteen, and twenty miles, but averaged around fourteen miles each day. The challenge is not only being able to hike over varied terrain (with a loaded pack, no less) for such long distances, but to do so day after day with only a few rest days. To hike the entire 500 miles of the Camino Francés, one must be prepared to handle the physical (and mental) toll such an arduous journey can place on the body.

With around six months until our desired Camino start date, we had a great deal of preparation ahead of us.

As our hike approached, the three most pressing areas we needed to address as we prepared for our Camino included personal development, most notably gaining knowledge and proficiency related to the Spanish language and culture; travel planning, including flights, ground transportation, and lodging; and training for the physical rigors of the hike.

My greatest apprehension as we pondered hiking by ourselves across northern Spain was our inability to speak the language. Over the years, I have read countless accounts of individuals completing treks across the Camino Francés, with all but the first ten miles or so taking place in Spain. Most of these authors suggested that many of the native people they encountered spoke English and that they had been able to communicate with those who did not. We found that outside of the major cities, relatively few people spoke English, but we were able to communicate with most of those with whom we didn't share a language. Still, I remained apprehensive and believed our journey would be enhanced by being able to communicate in the local language.

I had completed two years of high school Spanish, earning solid grades, though never really approaching proficiency. But whatever I learned during those two years was seldom used, and in the fifty years that had passed, I had apparently forgotten everything. Bev, who had no formal training in Spanish, was less concerned about the language barrier than I was.

An accomplished speech and language pathologist, in retirement, she has volunteered to work with individuals who have recently immigrated to the Chicago area. To her, deciphering conversations in different languages and dialects just comes more easily.

So, for the next few months, I devoted twenty to thirty minutes each day to completing online Spanish lessons. I signed up for Babbel and diligently completed the daily lessons, but soon found that I was not internalizing what I was learning. I could translate words and phrases when spoken slowly and distinctly, but using them in a conversation continued to confound me. But I plodded on.

In time, I supplemented the Babbel training with online lessons offered through our local library. This helped, and though I could recall more and longer phrases, being able to follow a conversation completed at a regular pace continued to elude me. I finally started watching YouTube videos featuring a Ph.D.-level college Spanish instructor with a southern accent, writing the various words and phrases so I could engage my visual learning style.

But with just a few weeks before we were to depart for a month-and-a-half in Spain, I felt only slightly better prepared to engage with native Spanish speakers than I had when I started. I was just never able to make things click in my mind.

There is a body of research suggesting that it is far more challenging for older individuals to learn a foreign language. As we departed for Spain, I represented additional confirmation of those research findings.

Regardless, we were getting ready to travel to the European continent for the first time, we were still unfamiliar with the culture, we couldn't converse in the native language, and we would be completely on our own. What did we have to be apprehensive about?

A MAJOR STEP IN our preparation involved completing our Camino travel plans. But before we could make those plans, we had to decide what kind of

Camino we wanted to complete. And that decision was more complicated than we had expected.

We originally had an almost idyllic view of how we wanted to trek across the Camino Francés. The traditional approach, the one peregrinos have been following for centuries, the one Camino purists suggest is the only way to truly experience this journey, is fairly simple. One departs from St. Jean Pied de Port when ready, hikes as far as they want each day, and when they arrive at the city or village in which they would spend the night, seeks a bed in an albergue, or pilgrim hostel. Albergues offer the quintessential Camino experience, often large, barrack-style rooms with rows of bunk beds and communal bathrooms in which groups of pilgrims, most strangers to one another, spend the night close to each other.

But with those large rooms come smells, snores, burps, and other bodily noises, and occasionally unsavory challenges like uncleanliness and bed bugs. Albergues are relatively inexpensive and provide the camaraderie that comes with a diverse group of peregrinos sleeping in a confined space. To be fair, albergues have evolved in recent years, and some are modern, very clean, and designed to offer more privacy than what I have described. Still, we were concerned that such lodging would not provide our aging bodies with what was needed at the end of each long hike.

Camaraderie and fellowship are noble and certainly desirable, and we admired the many pilgrims who followed such a communal approach to completing their Camino. But for Bev and me, at sixty-six, we needed sleep and rest more than we needed camaraderie. Early in our research, we decided to seek a travel company that would book in advance a private room at each stop along a pre-determined route with daily distances that would be, for us, challenging but doable. Such a company would book our lodging in advance, schedule any transfers from the trail to and from the inn if needed (they were), and assist us if we ran into difficulty along the way.

Camino purists would likely cringe at following such a pre-determined schedule. Where's the spontaneity? What if you want to go longer one day? Shorter the next? What if you get injured and need to take a few days off the trail? These are valid questions, and we pondered them in depth as we made this decision. But finally, we decided that peace of mind (and sleep) was ultimately more important than spontaneity. Ultimately, based on our approach that not every inch of the Camino had to be traveled on foot, we found we had a lot more flexibility than we had anticipated.

AFTER SOME EXTENSIVE RESEARCH, we learned that several travel companies offered full, self-supported trips across the Camino Francés. Bev found a company based in Scotland, but with a presence in the United States, that offered services we needed and for which customer reviews were very positive. We soon were talking with a US-based representative for Macs Adventure and ultimately purchased a travel package with that company. It was a good choice.

We would begin our Camino in St. Jean Pied de Port on September 2nd and arrive in Santiago de Compostela on October 8th, with two rest days built into the schedule. For our thirty-five hiking days, we would average just over fourteen miles each day. We would have rest days to explore the cities of Burgos and León and an extra day in Santiago de Compostela before returning home. We would have a guaranteed reservation each night in an inn or hotel with a private room and bathroom. Sometimes, the lodging would be rather primitive, but the best available in the city or village in which we would be staying. And though we understood and though it was not ideal, because of a lack of available lodging at the endpoint of a few of our hikes, there would be instances in which we would be taxied to and from the trail to an inn or hotel in another town. It seemed to be just another moving part that could go wrong, but the back-and-forth shuttling ended up being far less of a hassle than we had expected.

Once the itinerary was finalized and our sizable deposit had been paid, this notion of walking across northern Spain, which had previously been a mere dream, suddenly became quite real.

One idyllic Camino practice we were hesitant to eliminate, at least at first, was carrying all our possessions in our packs as we hiked from one town to the next. A component of the "traditional" Camino experience, whatever that means, is for peregrinos to be self-sufficient as they travel toward Santiago, much like travelers of ancient times. And to reduce the weight on their backs, pilgrims often whittled their travel possessions down to a bare minimum. I recall reading a memoir of a hiker who maintained one hiking outfit he walked in each day and one evening outfit he wore every night after showering and getting settled in the albergue, with a few extra garments to be worn when he regularly washed his primary outfits. While I admire the tenacity of folks like this, I'm not sure my preparedness instincts would allow such a spartan existence. (What if one of us ripped out our only pair of hiking shorts?) Still, we toyed with the idea of carrying all our possessions instead of having our luggage transported from one inn to the next.

This issue arose because the travel package we purchased included the daily transfer of one suitcase per traveler from one lodging establishment to the next, so we were paying for this service already. As we were speaking with Dan, our contact with the travel company, I mentioned we were considering not using the luggage transfer service. The phone was quiet for a moment, and then he said calmly but with authority, "Oh, you don't want to do that." Unstated but still clear from his tone, Dan was intimating, "Why would you not want to take advantage of this service?" It was a reasonable question and one for which we didn't have a valid answer. Maybe we wanted to have a more authentic Camino experience. But also, perhaps we were concerned about what other peregrinos might think about two people not carrying all their clothing and equipment as they trekked across Spain.

That was the last time the issue was discussed, and we ended up using the luggage transport service. Each morning, we dutifully placed our suitcases at the designated drop-off point. And every evening, without exception, those same suitcases were waiting for us when we walked into our next inn. We found that as many pilgrims used such a service as did not, with luggage transfers seeming to be more popular among the older folks on the trail. Though we ended up taking more clothing and other items than we needed, we were glad we opted, again, to "walk our own Camino."

On the trail, Bev and I each carried a daypack that was heavier than we might have expected. For example, in my pack, I placed a jacket, a poncho, an extra set of clothes, sunscreen, and a pair of hiking sandals in case I encountered untimely blisters. (Really, any blisters would be "untimely.") But simply out of caution, I also carried my iPad, a small bag of prescription medications, and my travel documents, items that, for different reasons, were vitally important to me. We each also had in our daypacks a hydration bladder, basically a bag of drinking water we could access through a little tube that attached to the front of our packs. Wanting to be over- rather than under-prepared, I almost always filled my hydration bladder to its three-liter limit. With all of this, my daypack at the start of each day weighed at least twenty pounds, lighter than a full pack with all our belongings, but still a substantial weight to lug around for six to eight hours a day.

WITH OUR START AND end dates confirmed, we began searching for flights. And it was a bit of a shock, very expensive fares that largely constituted one-way flights to and from Spain. We had long wanted to visit Barcelona, known for its unique culture, odd architecture, and the 1992 Summer Olympics. So, we decided to fly into Barcelona and spend two nights in that amazing city, time to do some exploring, but also to work through some of the inevitable jet lag we would experience. We would then take the train to Pamplona and then be shuttled to St. Jean Pied de Port, where we would begin our Camino. After we finished, because flights from Santiago de Compostela to the United States are both limited and very pricey, we planned to fly to Madrid, stay overnight, and then return to the United States.

We would be away for a month and a half. As we confirmed all our travel arrangements and posted each flight or train trip on our calendars, it all seemed like an odd combination of surreal and blatantly real. On the one hand, it still didn't seem possible we were actually going to complete this long-imagined trip. But with payment confirmations from travel companies, airlines, and Renfe, the Spanish rail system, it was suddenly clear we were going to walk the Camino. And by the time we had completed all these travel arrangements, our departure was just a couple of months away.

By this time, we had been seriously training for months. Compared to most people in their mid-sixties, Bev and I are in reasonably good physical condition. For the past decade, in an average week, we have typically walked four miles two or three times, pushing ourselves to maintain a pace of around four miles an hour. We have usually biked either outside or on an indoor trainer twice each week, with a target distance of around fifteen miles for each ride. We had gone to a fitness center two times most weeks, completing hard elliptical workouts of thirty-five to forty minutes, followed by a weight workout. While we couldn't claim to be in stellar physical condition, we had a solid base from which to start our Camino preparations.

As Bev and I have prepared for these adventure travel trips in the past, our goal has not been to simply be able to finish the trip, but to be in good enough condition to enjoy the journey. As a result, whether biking across Missouri on the Katy Trail, hiking across the Grand Canyon, or biking across the southern United States, we worked hard enough that we felt surprisingly fresh each time as we reached our destination.

But the Camino posed unique challenges, some of which would be difficult to prepare for. In Spain, we would complete long walks that averaged over fourteen miles almost every day, making our four-mile power walks seem far less significant. And while just six years earlier we had completed a cross-country bicycle tour in which we averaged over seventy miles each day, cycling places far less stress on the body, particularly the knees and hips, than even walking. While Bev's joints were relatively healthy, I had some mild arthritis in my knees and had undergone a hip replacement just three years earlier.

Adding to the constant stress on our legs and joints, we would carry packs weighing fifteen to twenty pounds. Plus, we would hike over varied terrain, with some significant climbing, including a steep twelve-mile ascent over the Pyrenees on the first day. To prepare for such conditions, we would logically start climbing some long hills. Our challenge, though, was that we lived outside of Chicago where there are very few short hills and almost no long ones.

BEGINNING A YEAR AHEAD of when we hoped to start our hike, we began increasing the length and frequency of our walks. The Chicago suburbs offer many "forest preserves," large blocks of open land on which there are walking and biking trails. In the months leading up to our Camino, we frequented many of these large natural areas. Additionally, there are lengthy walking trails near our home. With these options, we could regularly complete long hikes without getting bored (at least with our surroundings).

As our departure approached, we were walking six to eight miles, six days a week. Our longest walk before we left for Spain was twelve miles along a river trail, a hike that was characterized not by its physical difficulty but rather by the mental challenge of walking for four hours through terrain we had experienced countless times in the preceding months.

But all these trails were largely flat, unlike the Camino Francés with its mountains and undulating terrain. To build up climbing strength, Bev focused on bumping up the resistance on her elliptical workouts. I shifted some of my workouts to a stair climber machine, climbing 120 to 150 floors at a pace fast enough to raise my heart rate and generate copious amounts of sweat. I also shifted some of my walking sessions onto our treadmill, going three to four miles at inclines of up to ten percent in workouts I found to be physically and mentally challenging. And whenever we traveled in the months before our departure, to Missouri, Tennessee, and Wisconsin, we found hilly areas to hike.

When we started our Camino, we quickly found that we were relatively well-prepared, at least physically, for the rigors of the trail.

DURING THIS TIME, THOUGH, I faced two physical challenges, one of which threatened to derail our Camino before it even started. During our past hiking adventures, especially as we traversed the Grand Canyon, we found that hiking poles were helpful as we climbed and took some of the strain off our knees and hips as we descended the very steep trails. For the past few years, I had noticed increasing numbness in my right hand as I grasped items like bicycle handlebars and elliptical handles, and occasionally at night while I was sleeping. As I used my hiking poles for long stretches as we trained for our Camino, I noticed my right hand going numb, often preventing me from using that pole.

The doctors diagnosed the problem as carpal tunnel syndrome. They prescribed some exercises that I dutifully completed each day, but the problem persisted. I had a cortisone shot in that wrist, but that, too, failed to stop the persistent numbness. Finally, I began working with an occupational therapist who specializes in hand issues. Though that didn't eliminate the problem, the wrist exercise routine I followed made the condition a little more manageable.

The wrist issue plagued me on our Camino with my thumb and forefinger going numb, occasionally forcing me to grip the right pole with just the last three fingers on my hand. However, I experienced fewer issues than I might have expected from an issue that would eventually require surgery.

THE SECOND PHYSICAL ISSUE was potentially much more critical but ultimately had a positive resolution. Around two months before we were to depart for Barcelona, on a warm and muggy Saturday afternoon, Bev and I completed a long hike along a river trail not far from our home. Just a couple of hours before we started walking, we had eaten some spicy Mediterranean food, something I normally didn't consume before exercising. About halfway through our six-mile walk, I started to experience some slight "burning" in my chest. It was like indigestion or heartburn, but somehow different.

Believing this issue to be a simple case of heartburn, I didn't mention it to Bev, and when I got home, I took some antacid. But after some time, the burning sensation was still there. I took my blood pressure and it was elevated, as was my resting heart rate, all no doubt made worse by my mild panicking. I have been treated for some mild heart issues over the past few years, so different scenarios were racing through my head. Adding to the situation was the constant realization that, in just a couple of months, we would hike an average of fourteen miles a day in a foreign country in which we didn't understand the language, much less the healthcare system. And here I was experiencing what could be the beginning of a heart attack... or, more likely, just a bad case of heartburn.

Out of an abundance of caution, Bev took me to the emergency room.

If you have ever experienced a modern emergency room, you know that once you're hooked up to the requisite monitors and the doctors determine you are stable and not at significant risk of a sudden bad outcome, everything moves slowly. The nurses hooked me up to the monitors, inserted an IV, and took several samples of blood. The ER doctor, who was likely more used to dealing with car accident injuries and actual cardiac events rather than what I was presenting, came in and asked a series of questions. He seemed skeptical but still determined to rule out any cardiac issues.

After a variety of tests had been completed, and around four hours had passed, the ER doctor returned and told us that all the tests had ruled out that a heart attack had occurred. He suggested it was likely I had suffered a bout of what he called GERD, which I later learned stood for gastroesophageal reflux disease. He did, however, suggest that I talk with my primary care physician about scheduling a stress test.

I made an appointment with our family doctor early the next week, and a basic stress test was scheduled for the following week, around six weeks before we were to leave for Spain. I wasn't particularly concerned, as I have completed these procedures in the past and the results have never uncovered any cardiac issues. The greatest challenge as I completed this stress test was walking fast enough and on a steep enough incline to get me to the target heart rate, which was 130 beats per minute. Finally, I reached that level of intensity, and the test ended shortly thereafter.

The cardiologist on duty at the imaging center came into the exam room to discuss the results. He indicated the test showed evidence of some abnormalities, and he suggested that I likely had some blockages in and around my heart. Blockages like this are a precursor to a heart attack, and again, we were scheduled to begin our Camino in a month and a half.

Also, if I had some cardiac blockage, as the cardiologist suggested, there would likely be procedures and treatments available to control that condition. But there would never be a "cure" that would eliminate the heightened risk of a heart attack. With that possibility unexpectedly hanging over us, our Camino trip was likely not going to be simply postponed; at that point in time, it seemed likely it would never happen.

Because of an unrelated cardiac condition, I have been under the care of a cardiologist for the past several years. When we moved to the Chicago area in 2022, I needed to find another specialist to monitor my cardiac issues. I had only seen this new cardiologist one time, just a few months earlier, and I was impressed by his patient-friendly manner. Though he was out of the office, the day after I had completed the stress test, he sent me a message suggesting he thought the result might have been a "false positive," or an indication of abnormalities when none actually existed. He suggested his office would be in contact with me the following week.

The next Monday, the cardiologist called me. "Rob, this is…" sharing his first and last name when I answered the phone. As I had never received a phone call from a specialist, it took me a moment to get my bearings and realize who I was talking with. He expanded on his text message from the previous week and briefly explained why he thought the results might be misleading. He suggested that a more expansive stress test could provide more information and that the results would dictate what other tests might be warranted. When I explained we were scheduled to start a long hike in Spain in a month, he recommended I complete a cardiac catheterization procedure that would not only determine if there were any blockages but would also allow for any obstructions to be treated with a stent. Given the ambiguity of the original stress test, it was perhaps an aggressive approach, but the results would be instantaneous and conclusive. Our rollercoaster of emotions was continuing, and now our expected journey *might* still happen.

The following week, we reported to the hospital for my early morning procedure. We were three weeks from our scheduled departure for Spain, and we had continued our near-daily long walks, though there was a cloud of uncertainty hovering over our planned Camino. For the cardiac catheterization, I was given a general anesthetic and then a scope was inserted into my arm that was moved up and through my heart; pretty amazing stuff! Based on the results of the original stress test, and despite the uncertainty expressed by my cardiologist, when I went to sleep on the gurney, I fully expected that I would wake up after having had one or more stents inserted during the procedure.

The next thing I remembered, I was in a recovery area and Bev was at my side. Though my memory of the conversation remains a little fuzzy, I recall the cardiologist telling us he found very little "disease," and certainly none that needed to be addressed. It was largely a clean cardiac bill of health.

After all that uncertainty, our journey on the Camino de Santiago was, amazingly, still on schedule. Ready or not, we were leaving for Spain in three weeks.

Chapter One

Our Introduction to Spain (and France)

As we boarded the plane for the eight-hour flight to Barcelona, Bev and I had a strange blend of interrelated emotions. We were excited almost to the point of exhilaration, but those positive feelings were colliding with the countless nervous thoughts coursing through our heads. We were relieved to be undertaking a journey that, just three weeks earlier, seemed doomed not to occur. But we were still uncertain that, at our age, we had not made a huge mistake in undertaking the trip to begin with. Nonetheless, we were beyond grateful we had the opportunity to have what we anticipated would be an amazing experience.

We left O'Hare International Airport at 6:30 p.m. on a Boeing 777, the largest plane on which I had ever flown. With a capacity that approached 300 passengers, most of the wide-body plane on our sold-out flight had three aisles of three seats, nine across through the vast economy section. Bev and I had selected seats near the back of the plane on a side aisle with only two seats, allowing us a bit more freedom and privacy on this long, non-stop, trans-Atlantic flight. After taking off (often a lengthy process at O'Hare) and reaching cruising altitude, we had an adult beverage and then a light dinner before most of the passengers settled in to get a little sleep. Never one to sleep much under these circumstances, I dozed for around forty-five minutes and Bev a little more before the cabin got active again, a couple of hours before we were scheduled to land. After a light breakfast and coffee, we started our approach into Barcelona.

With a seven-hour time difference, we landed in Spain at around 9:30 a.m. at the end of a flight that had been more pleasant than we might have anticipated. After a long walk through the terminal, we arrived at customs only to find a long line of travelers, a by-product of hundreds needing to be processed and Bev and me de-boarding from the back of the plane. The Spanish customs agents were very efficient, however, and we were soon granted entry into Spain, our home for the next month and a half.

We picked up our suitcases and then ordered a taxi through the Uber app, our first of many transactions made with euros. Barcelona is a very Western city, and much of the signage in the airport included translations in English. But even though we were directed to what we believed was the correct pickup point in the adjacent parking garage, we were unprepared for the organized (sort of) chaos that greeted us as we waited for our cab. Finally, we located our ride, and the friendly driver helped us as we loaded our bags into the trunk.

It was a thirty-minute ride to our hotel, a scenic drive that offered our first look at the Mediterranean Sea, the Barcelona skyline, and the famous Sagrada Família Basilica in the distance. We had booked three nights in a boutique hotel in the Gothic Quarter, an ancient section of the city close to the Cathedral of Barcelona. This part of the city is known for alleyways diverging in different directions, all lined with shops and restaurants. We would find the Gothic Quarter to be both fascinating and confusing, and we got lost there on several occasions.

The Hotel Barcelona Catedral is prominently located, but its location in the Gothic Quarter requires restricted access for motor vehicles, including taxis. We were informed by the driver that he could not drop us off at the hotel, but rather a short distance away, requiring us to find our way to its entrance. He pulled over to the side of a very busy thoroughfare, removed our two suitcases, and with the cacophonous sounds of this vibrant city making it even more difficult to understand his broken English, he quickly gave us directions to our hotel. As he pulled away, I looked at Bev, who hadn't understood the directions either. So, for the first of countless times we would do so on this trip, we pulled out our phones and found our way to the entrance of our hotel.

The Hotel Barcelona Catedral is a fairly modern establishment with a restaurant and bar and complimentary wine and snacks each evening. It was around noon when we arrived and were greeted by a nice young man who spoke impeccable English. Luckily, at this early hour, our room was available. When we arrived at our room on the third floor, we found it small but clean and updated, except we couldn't get the lights to work. As we played with the various switches, we finally assumed that the power was turned off just in our room, as the hallway was brightly lit. I finally went back down to speak to the same nice young man at the front desk. After I explained our issue, he tried to describe a special slot where we needed to place our key card. Seeing the befuddled look on the face of this old American guy, he decided to simply come to our room and show us. As we would find in most of the over thirty rooms we would stay in over the next six weeks, there was a special slot where the key card had to be inserted to turn on the power to the room. Whenever we left the room and needed to take our key card with us, we had to turn off the power to the room. With no lights left on when no one was in the room, it is a logical energy-saving strategy we had never experienced in the United States, but which is common in Spain. We thanked this nice young man, again, and settled into our room.

We were exhausted, having slept little in the past thirty-six hours. But we knew that taking a nap in the middle of the day would throw off our biological clocks just as we were preparing to begin our Camino in a few days. So, instead of taking a nap and risking being awake that night, we sought a diversion.

We walked the short distance from the hotel to the Catedral de Barcelona, the primary cathedral serving the city. While we would tour several huge churches during our time in Spain, this was the first. And it was magnificent. Construction on this most recent iteration of the cathedral began in 1498 after an earlier version had been destroyed; it wasn't completed until over a century later. As we toured the main sanctuary and the different wings of the church, we were struck by the ancient artwork, paintings, and sculptures that permeated the facility. The main sanctuary is enormous, with a towering ceiling and parts of the edifice flaked in gold. Not for the last time, we were struck by what these over-the-top cathedrals must have cost nearly a thousand years ago when so much of the Spanish populace was mired in poverty. Even so, it was impressive.

BEFORE WE LEFT HOME, we met with our next-door neighbors who had visited Spain and whose daughter had studied in the country while in college. They had some restaurant recommendations for us. After we visited the cathedral, we were hungry and still wanted to remain active as we tried to ward off sleep. One restaurant on the list of recommendations was called Cal Pep, and though it was a considerable distance from our hotel, we walked there for lunch. What followed was one of the most memorable meals we have ever had.

Unknown to us, this restaurant with an unassuming façade has been named one of the fifty best restaurants in the world. This would be our first meal in Spain, and we didn't know what to expect when we walked through the entrance. We were greeted by a server standing behind the counter, and he motioned for us to sit in two available bar seats at the counter with two chefs cooking right in front of us. There was no menu offered to us, but the amiable gentleman who had seated us asked us in very good English if we knew what we wanted. We kind of played dumb (which really wasn't "playing" in this setting), which caused the server to take charge. On a notepad, he started listing what he would suggest in this famous restaurant known for tapas, which are small plates of appetizers or snacks that can be combined to make a meal. When he had finished listing his recommendations, we naturally said it sounded great (it did). We each added a glass of vino blanco, and he brought us each a glass of Rioja white wine. Then, one by one, the server brought us delectable menu items that we shared. We enjoyed fried calamari and prawns, a Spanish omelet made with eggs and potatoes, steamed clams served with a white wine sauce, and tuna tartare served with house-made crackers. It was all amazing. And while we had little idea of what our meal would cost, we soon found that we had experienced the first of many reasonably priced meals we would enjoy during our time in Spain.

We wandered through the Gothic Quarter on our way back to the hotel, trying to better orient ourselves to this bustling city. Later that afternoon, after enjoying our complimentary glass of wine at the hotel and still kind of full from lunch, we found a Spanish chain sandwich shop and had a small, nondescript sandwich for dinner. As we made our way back to the Hotel Barcelona Catedral, we savored the end of what had been a good, albeit very long, day.

I AM A NOTORIOUS short sleeper, with six hours representing a pretty good night of sleep. Bone tired the previous evening, we had gone to bed at our normal times. I woke up after around six and a half hours, a good night for me. I got up, read some e-mails, but then went back to sleep for another hour and a half. It had to have been the first time I slept for eight hours in one night in years. Bev slept even longer than she typically sleeps, so, with both of us much better rested, we were ready for a good day exploring Barcelona.

Our first task was to find some breakfast. This would be the first time we would experience how Spain follows a different schedule than the United States, especially as it relates to when meals are typically eaten. We left the hotel at around 7:30 a.m. and simply couldn't find a restaurant that was serving coffee at that hour, much less breakfast. Finally, we found a little shop that served bread, pastries, and coffee beginning at 8:30 a.m.

When we visit a new city, Bev and I often look for any noteworthy art museums that may be available, and Barcelona was no different. We toured the Museu Picasso, which featured works created by the artist during his time in Barcelona. As impressive as the artwork, which showed the developmental years of Picasso's career, was the setting. The collection was housed in five adjoining medieval palaces, interconnected buildings that had been fully restored while maintaining their ancient appearance. It was an impressive display of some of the early works of one of the city's most famous residents.

After a quick lunch, we walked to the beach on the Mediterranean Sea. The sky was overcast on this late August day, and the breezes coming off the water were, as we have so often found, restorative. We sat on a bench and watched couples and families enjoy the small urban beach and individuals seemingly on their break from work as they sought a brief, calm reprieve in this fast-moving, modern city.

ON OUR WAY BACK to the hotel, we toured the Moco Museum (Modern Contemporary Museum), which showcased a small but impressive collection that included works by Warhol, Basquiat, Koons, and my favorite, Banksy. It was housed in a building constructed in the 1500s that formerly served as the residence of a prominent Barcelona family. And like in the Museu Picasso, the ancient vibe of the facility could be felt as we looked at very contemporary works of art.

That evening, we followed another recommendation from our neighbors and dined at a very famous and classic restaurant called 7 Portes, which has been serving delectable meals since 1836. Knowing we were in for an elegant dining experience (our server wore a formal white dinner jacket), we chose from our limited hiking wardrobe the nicest outfits we could put together. It didn't much matter, as at our early dining hour (for Spain), we were among only a handful of customers.

With a bottle of Spanish white wine, we started our meal by sharing a large tureen of steaming monkfish soup, one of the house specialties. Then we each had the seafood paella with lobster, large portions of this classic Spanish dish. From the service to the food to the ambiance of the restaurant, it was a memorable meal.

On our last full day in Barcelona, we took a bus tour that included stops in all the major areas of the city. From our seats on the top of the double-decker bus, we had a great view of the many sights of this amazing city, from the waterfront to the business district to the main stadium and other venues used in the 1992 Barcelona Olympics. And with the provided headphones, we heard a steady stream of English-language information regarding what we were seeing.

But in many respects, Barcelona is the city of Antoni Gaudí, the Catalan architect whose whimsically weird buildings are on prominent display. Known for buildings designed with wavy and undulating lines, we drove by famous structures like Casa Milá, Casa Batlló, and buildings near Park Güell. Built in a style that became known as Catalan Modernism, viewing these designs had an almost dizzying effect on us.

But by far the most famous of Gaudí's building projects, and one that is only now nearing completion after over 140 years of construction, is Sagrada Família. With its towering spires, the huge cathedral is the most prominent building in Barcelona and the most visited monument in Spain.

We enjoyed our time in Barcelona, but our focus in the weeks before our trip had been on the upcoming Camino. As a result, other than making a hotel reservation and getting dining recommendations from our neighbors, we had done relatively little research to prepare for our time in the city. So, when our tour bus pulled up to the enormous edifice of Sagrada Família, we were struck as much by the throngs of people as by the structure itself. As we weaved our way toward the entrance, we saw signs in English suggesting that tour tickets should be pre-ordered online. We wanted to enter the cathedral to view the nearly finished interior, but when we tried to purchase tickets, we were informed that the next available tour would be in five hours. Only mildly disappointed given the immense crowd, we opted to walk around the outer perimeter of the structure, which took some time given the size of its footprint. It was huge, oddly impressive, imposing, and just a little weird.

Antoni Gaudí died in 1926 when construction of the cathedral was less than one-fourth completed. The foundation tasked with completing

Gaudí's vision and plans recently announced that this amazing structure would be completed in 2026, 100 years after the death of its designer.

WHEN WE CLIMBED OFF the tour bus for the last time at the stop at which we had started, we sensed a subtle change in our attitudes. Our three days in Barcelona had been great, a memorable experience. But we were in Spain for another, much more important reason. When we returned to our hotel, our focus shifted to preparing for the next day, when we would travel to the starting point of our Camino. We had gotten more relaxed the longer we were in Barcelona, becoming more acclimated to being in this major city in a foreign country. But in our room, as we sorted through our clothes and equipment and returned to studying our Camino de Santiago guidebooks and materials, I felt a subtle nervousness settle into my psyche, likely a by-product of the healthy respect I had for what we were about to tackle.

We were up early the next morning as we prepared to depart Barcelona on a train bound for Pamplona. From there, we would be driven across the border into France to St. Jean Pied de Port. Our time in Barcelona had been like a holiday; on this day, we would begin what, at least for us, would be purposeful travel.

As taxis called by the hotel were allowed to pick up riders at this location, we were waiting outside as the cab arrived. It was a fairly short ride to the train station, and as is typical for us given my desire not to have to rush at airports and now rail terminals, we arrived about an hour and a half before our departure. There was a café open inside the train station, so, lugging our suitcases and backpacks with us, we nervously enjoyed large coffees and breakfast sandwiches. Afterward, we tried to enter the departure area. While the areas of the city we had visited had been English-language friendly, the announcements in the station were in Spanish and little of the signage had translations into other languages. We had no reason to complain (we were in Spain, after all), but for the first time on this trip, we felt particularly challenged by the language barrier (and I felt my apprehension increasing). As we approached the entrance to the departure area, which included a security screening for each passenger, we were met by a woman who, while polite, was sternly all business. When we asked her where we needed to go to catch our train, she shared in serviceable English that we were not to enter the departure area for another half hour. Or at least that's what we thought she said. It's possible much of this was explained on the abundant signage that was ever-present. Still, she smoothly transitioned from us to the next clueless traveler, unaffected by these two older American travelers who clearly didn't know what they were doing.

With still more time to kill, we found a bench on the side of the terminal where we could wait and keep track of our suitcases and backpacks. As we had prepared for this trip, we learned the Camino was considered largely safe from criminal activity, as was most of Spain. It was emphasized, however, that particularly in the larger cities, care should be taken to thwart being victimized by pickpockets.

As we were waiting in this train station, we heard a commotion and then saw a young man run by clutching a backpack to his chest. A few seconds later, we watched as three uniformed officers ran by. Shortly thereafter, we saw those same police officers walk back in the other direction, two escorting the young man and the other officer holding the backpack the young man had been carrying. It was like watching a scene from a movie. Though we had been protective of our possessions before witnessing this altercation, we suddenly moved our suitcases and backpacks just a little closer to us.

In time, we entered the departure area and quickly worked our way through the security screening, which didn't amount to much; we apparently didn't fit the criminal demographic they were looking for. From the screening area, we took an elevator down to the lower level where we would board the train. We got in the line designated for our train, but we continued to feel some nagging uncertainty. After a while, as we were still waiting to move outside to the boarding area, Bev eyed a friendly-looking Renfe official (the railway service in Spain), and she confirmed we were in the correct line that would lead us to the correct train.

The line eventually started working its way outside and toward a sleek, modern, clean, and fast train that would take us to Pamplona. With assigned seats, we entered our car, placed our bags in an overhead bin, and settled in for what would be around a four-hour ride. We soon departed, smoothly and quietly on this high-speed train, and sat back and watched the countryside and small towns of eastern Spain pass by.

Bev had booked this train trip, and every indication, from the reservation confirmation to our tickets, confirmed we were headed to Pamplona. But the signage at the Barcelona train station had listed Salamanca as the destination for this train. And now, on the train, the conductor had on multiple occasions stated in Spanish I could decipher that the train was bound for Salamanca. After hearing this a few times, we got a bit concerned we had possibly boarded the wrong train. Not knowing the location of Salamanca, I took my phone and pulled up a map of Spain to compare the location of the two cities relative to Barcelona. Salamanca is due west of Barcelona, while Pamplona is north and west of the city. Pamplona had not been mentioned and a route through this city in the northeast section of Spain seemed out of place on a route to Salamanca, in the western part of the country. Finally, an hour or so after our departure, I asked the conductor to confirm we were headed to Pamplona. He gave me a sort of pitying look and then said in English, "Yes, we're going to Pamplona." With that, we settled in for the last few hours of our train ride.

Having experienced Amtrak train travel in the United States, we were impressed with the Renfe service in Spain, the modern components, the cleanliness and comfort, and the overall efficiency of the system. That last couple of hours as we headed toward Pamplona included time for some reflective thoughts. I was admittedly still a little nervous about all the "moving parts" of this trip and about the arduous hiking journey we were to begin the next morning. But as I sat in that Spanish train next to my partner in life and adventure, the scope of what we were doing began to dawn on me. Here we were, two sixty-six-year-olds from the midwestern United States, without a grasp of the local language and completely on our own. We have traveled extensively, but this was the first time we felt like world travelers. I hoped that positive feeling would continue.

We arrived in Pamplona at 1:30 p.m. but were still a good distance from St. Jean Pied de Port, where we would stay that evening before beginning our Camino the next morning. There are no trains from Pamplona to St. Jean, and the one bus that traveled that route had departed earlier that morning. Bev had scheduled a shared taxi ride that would have significantly reduced the cost. But she had received an email while we were in Barcelona stating that the cab company could not fulfill our order. We surmised that the company had been unable to find another traveler to share the ride. We were in a quandary, as you can't begin a hike if you can't get to the starting point. Though much more expensive, Bev had found a car service with positive reviews and had scheduled a pickup at 2:00 p.m. After de-boarding the train, we got a quick lunch at the train station snack bar, and as we were waiting for our food to arrive, we saw a young woman we suspected was our driver. I asked if she was, and she introduced herself, pointed out her vehicle, and told us to take our time. Ready to get to St. Jean, we quickly downed our food and were soon loading our bags into this young French woman's SUV. In no time, we were driving through the gorgeous Pyrenees Mountains on our way to France. It was a relaxing hour-and-a-half drive, and we arrived in St. Jean Pied de Port at around 3:30 p.m.

Our travel company, Macs Adventure, had worked with a Spanish company, Tee Travel, to reserve all our lodging as we traversed the Camino Francés. We had not previously worked with either of these companies, and this would be the first time on this trip we would rely on their planning. We had been booked into the Hotel des Pyrenees, a beautiful hotel right in the middle of this quaint and historic village. And as we would find at each stop on our way to Santiago de Compostela, everything worked exactly as planned and promised.

We were checked in by a nice young lady who spoke excellent English. She gave us our key, told us about breakfast, which was included in our travel package, and explained where we should place our luggage to be picked up the next morning. Then she gave us a large folder from our travel company that included maps, guidebooks, and hotel information we would rely on for the next six weeks. We took our luggage and materials to our room on the second floor, a surprisingly large and elegant room with a view of the village and surrounding mountains. We thought that if all our rooms were like this one as we hiked across Spain, we would live quite well. (They were not, but we still lived well.)

We soon left our hotel to explore this charming village. On the meandering Nive River and just five miles from the Spanish border, St. Jean is a small town of around 1,500 inhabitants that was rebuilt in the 1200s after the original village was destroyed by troops loyal to Richard the Lionheart. The core of the village consists of one street enclosed by walls that give it a fortress-like feel, which was no doubt the original intent.

As we walked up and down the main street of this ancient town, it was oddly calm and quiet on this late summer, Friday afternoon. Many of the businesses were Camino-focused, albergues and restaurants, small shops offering hiking-related gear, and several stores offering Camino souvenirs and memorabilia. We had received our "pilgrim's passport" from the travel company, and we would have this document stamped in each city and village in which we stayed. At the end of our journey, we would use this verified passport as documentation that we had completed the Camino de Santiago and thus receive our official Compostela, or certificate of completion. But first, we had to get our pilgrims' passports officially stamped at the starting point of our trek.

We located the pilgrim's office and quickly found the lines were divided by language. There were just a few in line to speak with the English-speaking volunteer, so she directed all six of us to gather around her as she provided important information about what we should expect during the first few days of our Camino. It was rather noisy in the small confines of the office, and much of what she shared was difficult to hear. When she was finished, she stamped each of our passports and gave us a little Ziploc bag in which to keep them dry. Little did we realize how important these little baggies would be as soon as the next day.

A primary symbol of the Camino de Santiago is the scallop shell. Depictions of this shell are ubiquitous on the trail, with lines on the shell all converging at the same point, just like how all the different Camino routes lead to Santiago de Compostela. As we traversed the 500 miles of our hike, we would see thousands of these shells on signs and roads signifying the direction peregrinos should follow on the trail. Other than backpacks and the fact they are walking on the trail, the most prominent symbol signifying that an individual is completing a Camino is one of these white scallop shells attached to their backpack. As we headed back to our hotel, we stopped in a little gift shop and purchased two of these shells. Though we ultimately found them difficult to attach to our packs and ended up simply keeping them in our suitcases, we still value these shells for what they symbolize.

ON OUR WAY BACK to our hotel, we encountered an issue that would plague us all the way to Santiago. We hoped to get an early start the next morning for what we anticipated would be the most challenging section of the entire Camino, a long hike over the Pyrenees and into Spain. But as we walked by the many restaurants in the late afternoon, we found that virtually all of them were closed or were simply serving drinks. The restaurant in our hotel is rather famous, but besides being very pricey, it didn't open until 7:45 p.m. Hoping to get a good night of sleep before our challenging first day, we considered this too late. Other restaurants began serving dinner even later. We finally found an open-air establishment in which the owner, who seemed less than enthused about having to deal with foreign-speaking patrons, tersely told us the kitchen opened at 6:30 p.m. With no better options available, we were back precisely at the opening time and had a glass of wine and a non-memorable meal served by a surly waiter. But we were back in our room at an early hour, giving us time to review the route for the next day, sort through the gear we would take with us in our daypacks (for the umpteenth time), and finish an email update about our trip that I would send to family and friends.

As we settled in for the night, we were nervous but ready to get started. We had no clue what would unfold on the epic first day of our Camino.

Two issues were adding to our apprehension and sense of uncertainty as we prepared to begin the longest walk of our lives. The next morning, we would leave St. Jean Pied de Port and begin climbing, a steady incline of twelve miles before completing a steep downhill section into Roncesvalles, Spain, our destination for the evening. This would be a formidable feat for us under ideal conditions, but the weather forecasts consistently called for rain to begin in the morning and then taper off in the afternoon. We believed we had the apparel and equipment needed to tackle the inevitable wet conditions we would encounter as we walked across Spain. (We were wrong.) And we were confident we had trained long enough and hard enough to complete this most challenging of Camino segments. (We were a little wrong.) As a result, we weren't nearly as concerned about finishing this first day as we likely should have been.

The second issue was just as problematic. While in Barcelona, I had developed some chest congestion and a scratchy throat, and I was feeling run down. It didn't seem to be anything major, but still a concern at the beginning of a 500-mile hike, with the first day taking us over a mountain range. We ruled out Covid, and I suspected it was a cold or related malady that I have often contracted at this time of the year. But it was affecting my breathing, and we had the ever-present concern that this illness would worsen, perhaps as we were climbing across the Pyrenees the next day.

Bev and I discussed whether we should forego walking on that first day and just take a taxi to our inn in Roncesvalles. Another option was to avoid the worst of the climbing and complete a less strenuous alternative route to Roncesvalles. The guidebook we were following, written by the legendary Camino expert John Brierley, suggested this less strenuous path should be taken by hikers with questionable fitness or when the weather is forecast to be inclement or expected to deteriorate in the mountains. The alternate route, which historically was used by Charlemagne and his army to enter and depart Spain in the eighth century, is shorter than the main path, not as steep, and never reaches the high elevation of the primary route. But though this alternative route is considered easier, it follows a main road and lacks the stunning vistas available on the traditional path. As we would learn, it was the path we should have taken, were we to take any path at all.

But despite the weather forecast and whatever illness I was experiencing, the lure of what was called the "Route of Napoleon" was very strong. In addition to being arguably the most challenging section of the entire Camino Francés, this trail over the Pyrenees is considered the most beautiful and spectacular section, offering stunning vistas from its relatively high elevation. We had looked forward to tackling this challenging start to our Camino for years.

In the various adventure trips we have completed, Bev and I have each shown some resiliency and the ability to overcome obstacles to reach the destination of each trip. That resilience would be put to the test the next day.

Given the forecast for rain, warnings from a respected and revered author who had walked the Camino countless times, and the illness I was experiencing, we had no business attempting this most difficult section. But we discussed our options and decided we would tackle the more challenging Napoleon route, confident we could make it to Roncesvalles.

By the following afternoon, we would realize just how foolhardy this decision had been.

"NOT TACKLING A CHALLENGING GOAL SIMPLY BECAUSE OF SELF-DOUBT IS A UNIQUE FORM OF FAILURE."

"It is hard to fail, but it is worse never to have tried to succeed."
Theodore Roosevelt

As BEV AND I departed from St. Jean Pied de Port, France, the traditional start of the Camino Francés route of the Camino de Santiago, we knew we would face mountains and cities, wilderness and the barren Meseta, and unknown difficulties that, at that point, we could not predict. We were sixty-six, had in the past dealt with different medical issues, had no first-hand knowledge of the Spanish culture, and were not conversant in the local language. Yet we were planning to traipse across the Spanish countryside on our own and with little outside support. Realistically, we had no business even attempting such a demanding journey.

But in many respects, the greatest challenge associated with our Camino journey wasn't walking 500 miles across Spain, but rather simply committing to the tour. If we accomplished anything of significance on this trip, it wasn't that we *finished*… it was that we *started*.

To clarify, trekking fourteen miles a day over difficult terrain was challenging, even tougher than we had expected. But what most distinguished Bev and me (and the many others who completed their own Camino that year) from the countless individuals who had the interest, time, and resources needed for such a journey but never turned their dreams into action wasn't a matter of ability. Rather, it was gumption, the willingness to tackle a challenge we weren't positively sure we could complete.

Beyond family members, we told very few about our upcoming trip. And after completing a 3,000-mile bicycle ride across the southern United States just six years earlier, no one with whom we shared this information expressed any skepticism (at least to us) that we might not be able to pull this off.

No, the skepticism about our ability to successfully meet this challenge was internal. We had devoted most of the past year to Camino preparation, spending hours each day on training and logistical planning. Long before our departure, we had committed a significant amount of resources to cover the cost of this tour. We had, in a limited sense, staked our reputation on an adventure we weren't convinced we could complete. What if we failed? What if I failed?

WHAT IF I FAILED? What an incredibly powerful question, one that can limit, much more powerfully than we realize, the scope of our lives and the realm of our accomplishments. When we base our endeavors solely on the surety of success, we artificially limit the breadth of our experiences. This type of thinking doesn't necessarily lead to an unfulfilled life, though it can. What it can do, though, is prevent us from spreading our wings, broadening our horizons, and, sometimes, learning the valuable life lessons that come from failure.

Fear of failure has been studied enough by psychological researchers that it has its own name ("atychiphobia"), and symptoms of this phobia can range from subtle to profound. It may manifest itself with a reluctance to try new things or take on difficult projects, procrastination in taking steps that might lead to success, and a level of perfectionism that impedes individuals from tackling challenges that don't guarantee success. From my perspective, our fears in this area often manifest themselves more covertly, gently but still forcefully nudging us away from activities that push us out of our comfort zones and in which we may not ultimately be successful. Whether we are even aware of these fears, the effects can be long-lasting.

One of my early memories of fearing failure is one that many can likely appreciate. In junior high school, I was a geeky, bookish, husky kid with unruly curly hair and thick black athletic glasses. Like many adolescents, I didn't have the most positive self-image. Each year in seventh and eighth grade, the student council, of which I served as vice president, sponsored three dances. I felt compelled to attend these events, and not just because my involvement in student government dictated my participation. Though young for my grade, my interest in girls was in full bloom, and I longed to dance with as many of them as I could, preferably the slow variety, but even a fast dance that would showcase my likely dorky, spastic moves. But I was too terrified to ask girls to dance with me, not out of fear they would say yes, but that they would say no. That fear of rejection, of failure, was palpable and a sensation I can still recall to this day.

The social trepidations of a young teenager in the early 1970s notwithstanding, these limiting thoughts can extend to even more important issues throughout one's life. Fear of failure, whether rational or ego-driven, that leads to inaction can impact career decisions, relationships, and an individual's willingness to pursue his or her dreams. As I reflect on my life, and particularly my career, though some might disagree with this assessment, I don't believe I ever experienced a *major* failure. This doesn't include bad decisions or examples of poor judgment, of which I certainly had my share, but rather failures of a life-altering, career-impacting nature. Conversely, there have been times in which I (and Bev and I) have stuck my neck out when failure seemed to be a legitimate possibility. While these may not have been *Profiles in Courage*-level decisions, they surely caused some significant consternation at the time.

But if I am honest and transparent in my life reflections, I have to wonder if there have been instances in which my aversion to risk, which in some respects is related to the previously discussed fear of failure, has played a role in decisions to not "spread my wings." A good student and a self-professed bookish scholar, the valedictorian of my high school graduating class, I attended college at a good but academically undistinguished university because it was close and convenient. An above-average athlete, I opted out of participation in collegiate sports in part to focus on my studies. Considered a good high school history teacher and a successful coach, I was content to complete my teaching/coaching career at the same high school where I had started rather than pursue opportunities at larger schools. Similarly, I spent the last twenty years of my career in that same school district, progressing through various administrative positions until ultimately retiring as superintendent. In the process, I never considered entertaining opportunities to move to larger, more lucrative settings. In retrospect, I regret virtually none of these decisions, any of which might have altered the trajectory of my life and career, as well as that of Bev and our children. And in most of these instances, there was a clear rationale for not following the more traditional path of career progression.

But a part of me wonders whether a subconscious factor in some of these decisions was actually a latent resistance to getting out of my comfort zone, and even a subconscious fear of failing, that impeded what might be considered the career advancement version of "spreading my wings." But I was as comfortable as I was competent in each of these challenging positions, and my contentment, as well as that of Bev and our two children, served to tamp down any impulse to further advance my career. I have the luxury of hindsight and the ability to judge the happiness that resulted from the career choices I made. Even if risk aversion played a minor role in this decision-making process, I still look back at that career with much contentment and great satisfaction.

Which brings us back to our 500-mile trek across Spain, yet another example of Bev and me putting our doubts and fears behind us and pursuing a tough but ultimately attainable long-held goal. We are both incredibly proud that we were able to hike the Camino de Santiago, an accomplishment that will help to define us for the rest of our lives. But many individuals possess the desire, ability, and resources to tackle such a challenge and would be successful if they tried. What differentiated us from most of these other adventurers was our willingness to commit to and begin such a trip; in simply beginning, we conquered what was perhaps the real challenge in this endeavor.

Chapter Two

An Auspicious (and Dangerous) Beginning

St. Jean Pied de Port to Pamplona

It started raining before we made it out of St. Jean Pied de Port. It would still be raining when we arrived in Roncesvalles over eight hours later.

We had slept better than we might have expected, given what was ahead of us this first Saturday in September, and I was up at my usual early hour. As I lay in bed waiting for Bev to wake up, I reviewed the information about the route we would follow and pondered my physical well-being. While I still had chest congestion and a scratchy throat and didn't feel any better than I had the day before, I didn't feel any worse. At this point, I took that as progress and had no second thoughts about our decision to proceed with our plan to tackle the more challenging route over the Pyrenees.

I again checked, for at least the tenth time, the weather forecast for St. Jean Pied de Port and Roncesvalles. As in the past few days, the forecast called for rain to begin in the morning, not become overly heavy, and taper off in the afternoon. Two factors, though, would take on critical importance as the day progressed. First, weather forecasts aren't always accurate. Second, between St. Jean and Roncesvalles were mountain passes at a much higher elevation where the weather can be much more unpredictable.

An important decision involved the apparel we would wear on this critical first day of our Camino. Based on the weather forecast of seasonal temperatures and intermittent rain in the morning, we opted for shorts and t-shirts, both made of quick-drying synthetic materials. If and when it rained, we had in our packs Gore-Tex jackets that we could quickly put on, garments made of a breathable material that would repel the rain. We also had vinyl ponchos, purchased almost as an afterthought. Because we did not bring waterproof pants, our rationale for wearing shorts on this expected wet day was simple. If it rained long and hard enough, the long pants we did bring would become saturated, would provide limited protection once wet, and would take longer to dry than would our bare legs. That was our reasoning on the morning of our hike into the Pyrenees, flawed as it might have been. In retrospect, the rain was falling hard enough, and the wind was blowing strongly enough that we would have ended up drenched regardless of the apparel we were wearing.

Our packs ready and our intentions set for the day, we went down to the dining room of the Hotel des Pyrenees for breakfast. It was a good and hearty meal, similar to what we would experience many times as we made our way to Santiago de Compostela. The very congenial and professional server brought us each a small cup of coffee with steamed milk. He also poured for each of us a small glass of orange juice. He then brought us large chunks of bread, along with butter, different jams, and slices of ham and fresh cheese. No bacon and eggs, no biscuits and gravy, no pancakes or cereals, like we might have back in the United States. But delicious and filling, and no doubt, much healthier.

There was a group of ladies at an adjacent table eating their breakfast and speaking with what seemed to be Australian accents. We surmised from their attire that they, too, were beginning their Camino that morning. After we finished eating and were walking by their table, I said to them,

"Buen Camino." This is the standard greeting for peregrinos, or pilgrims, who are completing a trek to Santiago de Compostela. It was the first time I had offered this greeting to another pilgrim. Judging from the smiles on the faces of these ladies from Down Under, it was likely the first time they had received this salutation. We would offer, and receive, this greeting thousands of times in the next thirty-seven days.

AFTER DEPOSITING OUR TWO suitcases among the several that would be transported to the next place of lodging, we began our Camino. Or at least tried to. Donned in t-shirts and shorts at around 8:30 a.m. on a warm and overcast, but still dry, September morning, we left the hotel. The Camino Francés is typically well-marked, with yellow scallop shells and directional arrows placed prominently along the route. But the start of the trail on the other side of the village from our hotel was difficult to locate, at least for us. After studying our maps and the GPS-powered app the travel company had provided, we found what we thought was the start of our path to Santiago de Compostela. We were surprised there weren't more pilgrims headed in that direction, but we weren't sure of the route until we spotted several hikers with backpacks striding confidently in the direction we had identified.

Then, just as we were ready to leave St. Jean, it began to rain. It wasn't a hard rain to start but it would increase in intensity over the next few hours. We found a little alcove, took off our packs, fished out our jackets, and put them on; we would not remove them until we were in our hotel rooms over nine hours later. And then we were off, our Camino officially underway.

In all our research about this trip, we had read little about the makeup of the path on this first day. As we left this quaint little village behind us, we started to climb as we walked on a paved village street that soon became a rural road. The precipitation at this point was merely a nuisance, and we used our hiking poles to assist us in maintaining a steady pace up the mountain.

Above St. Jean Pied de Port

The incline was not particularly steep in most places, but we would climb almost continuously for the next several hours. We passed homes and sheds and long stretches with no structures around us. We were soon walking through vast pastureland, with large herds of sheep and cattle grazing on the surrounding hillsides.

Many of these cows and sheep grazing across the open countryside had bells around their necks. These bells were most often made of copper, and those of each herd had a distinctive sound. Some of the sheep or cows in these large herds had a greater tendency to wander off, and the distinctive sound of the bells allowed the shepherds to more easily locate the roaming animals. These shepherds, most often older gentlemen, were fascinating to watch, their calm and peaceful demeanor as they walked along the hillside having a soothing effect on their animals. We would see many of these individuals as we walked across Spain, and we seldom gave them more than a quick, glancing look. But the presence of these sheep and cattle herders seemed to have a calming effect on us, too. We observed none of them get upset, raise their voice, or get too excited, though I'm confident that occurs occasionally. But when a shepherd noticed one of his herd missing, he calmly walked toward the bell or sent his dog to coax the aberrant sheep back into the fold.

The sound of the bells during the early stages of our first day on the Camino was memorable, not musical but still almost melodic. As our journey across Spain continued, we paid less attention to the clanging sounds coming from these animals, much like an inhabitant of a home near a highway notices the sounds of traffic less and less over time. But on that first day, the incessant sounds of these clanging bells were quickly etched in our minds.

THE RAIN CONTINUED, STEADY and now more intense, and the incline was steeper in places and still unrelenting. But despite the challenging terrain and conditions, we were making good progress and enjoying the beauty of our surroundings, still visible at this lower elevation.

The road wasn't as crowded as we had expected, and we only occasionally passed, or were passed by, other pilgrims. But we found many of the characters we encountered in the first few miles of our Camino to be quite interesting. It reminded me of *The Canterbury Tales*, the classic story by Geoffrey Chaucer about a group of pilgrims traveling together from London to visit a shrine in Canterbury. Just like in that tale from the 14th century, we encountered some memorable personalities.

There was the older Irish gentleman we met early on who was carrying everything in a huge and unwieldy backpack. He had quickly realized he had brought too much clothing and gear and told us in a deep Irish brogue that he might need to "jettison" some of that clothing at the end of the day. There was the young man with a full pack who wordlessly passed us at a much quicker pace than ours. It was after he was a few strides ahead of us that we noticed he was barefoot, something unfathomable to us for only a short distance, much less a 500-mile trek across challenging terrain. We never saw him again.

Then there were the two older Dutch gentlemen who were riding their bikes to Santiago. The one who spoke the most English told us he had walked the Camino three times, but that this was the first time he was biking it. His fellow rider said little, but we interacted with them countless times throughout the day, taking photos of the two of them and having them take photos of Bev and me. The less talkative gentleman, we eventually realized, was riding an e-bike, which provided a needed boost on the never-ending inclines. So, as his partner struggled to walk and push his bike up the hills, the guy with the e-bike just pedaled effortlessly and then waited for his partner to catch up with him. It was like a cartoon playing over and over on a loop. But the e-bike guy seemed to wait patiently for his travel mate to catch up with him, and the other didn't seem at all irritated by the advantage afforded to his partner.

Just like in *The Canterbury Tales*, there was an inn, or in this case, an albergue, where everyone gathered for a meal (and some spent the night). There are very few places of business between St. Jean Pied de Port and Roncesvalles, and the last one is located around five miles up the mountain in the tiny village of Orisson. Refuge Orisson is a beautifully restored albergue that offers warm meals and snacks and, for those with the forethought to secure a reservation, dormitory-style housing. For those pilgrims wanting to divide the challenging Napoleon route between two days, this albergue is the primary choice. On this day, that choice would have been a wise one.

By the time we arrived, we had been on the trail for around three hours, and in the last hour, the rain had increased dramatically. We were soaked, and though we wanted to get some food, more than anything, we wanted to dry out a little.

Though the rain and increasing fog impaired our view, this mountainous albergue provided a beautiful image. On days with no rain, most peregrinos ordered their food from inside the building but ate it outside on tables overlooking a gorgeous vista of valleys below and lush, green, rolling mountains in the foreground. But on this day, with the rain pouring down, no one was staying outside. The rustic dining room of the Refuge Orisson was packed, and we were fortunate to find a couple of chairs at the end of a communal table in the back of the room. Everyone was dripping wet, and for most, the excitement that accompanied the start of their Camino had been tempered by the constant precipitation and the effort required to get this far up the mountain. Most took the conditions in stride, but some were downright surly. We fit mainly in the former category, though, admittedly, with at least a touch of surliness.

A character worthy of *The Canterbury Tales*, the surliest of all, was one of the innkeepers. This young lady walked around the dining room chastising people for getting the floor wet (how could you not?), for placing their packs in the wrong location (like I did), and for not following the rules, whatever they were. Like most in that dining room, we wanted to be respectful of the property but struggled to follow unknown guidelines. And if on this wettest of days, the innkeeper didn't want her floors to get wet, she probably should have closed for the day. We were glad she did not, because the sandwich we each ate was tasty and much needed as we prepared to tackle the most challenging parts of the route.

WE STAYED AT THE Refuge Orisson for around forty-five minutes, getting warmer but never really dry. Despite the chaotic atmosphere and the incessant patrolling of the innkeeper, we didn't want to leave. As we walked out the front door, we quickly realized that the intensity of the rain had significantly increased; it was pouring. And whether because of a weather front or just the increasing elevation, it was noticeably colder, not a positive development given the precipitation and the shorts we were both wearing. Bev and I looked at each other but said nothing; we knew that, despite the deteriorating conditions, we had no choice but to plod on.

So, we continued up the mountain, steady inclines that were, in places, very steep. But we were still walking on a paved road that had not been impacted by the inches of rain that had fallen. As we climbed higher on the mountain and the rain continued, fog set in and limited our visibility. The panoramic vistas that had, at least in part, led us to tackle this challenging route under trying climatic and personal conditions would not be visible for the remainder of the day. In time, we came to a series of signs located just off the paved road on which we had been walking. The signs pointed toward Roncesvalles, sort of, and in the rain and fog, it was confusing whether the signs referred to the paved road or to a field on which we could see no discernible path. We were in a quandary, standing in the rain with no other pilgrims in sight, trying to figure out which route to take.

Around that time, a large man with a huge backpack appeared out of the fog. He was walking on the paved road, never wavered as he walked by the Roncesvalles signs, and confidently continued walking on the pavement. He seemed to know where he was going. There was no one else around, we weren't sure where to go, and this guy seemed to be sure of himself. So, we decided to follow him. What could go wrong?

The road followed a subtle but steady downhill, the first easy walking we had experienced since leaving St. Jean. The man with the enormous pack continued to walk several hundred yards in front of us. Every few steps, he would shift his pack to center it on his back. This should have told us his backpack didn't really fit him, he was carrying an excessive amount of clothing and equipment, and thus, perhaps he didn't know as much about walking the Camino as we had given him credit for. But we were following blindly, almost literally.

As we saw no other pilgrims on this isolated road, we got suspicious about our route decision. The tour company that arranged our trip provided an app for our phones with maps that showed the route and our precise location relative to the route. After we had gone around a mile and had seen no one other than the man with the large backpack, we stopped and checked the app. We were off-route, a potentially dangerous mistake given the conditions we were experiencing. So, we backtracked the mile or so, subtly but steadily uphill, costing us probably forty-five minutes or so, time that would become more valuable as the day continued. In those worsening conditions, it was heart-wrenching. But we truly had no choice but to walk the mile or so, uphill, back to the "Roncesvalles" arrow signs where we had gone off course.

When we got back to where he had diverged from the route, in the cold rain and eerily foggy conditions, several hikers were approaching, including the Irish "jettison" fellow. ("So we meet again," he warily greeted us.) We had an interesting but intense conversation with these gentlemen. One, with a German-sounding accent, argued with us that the road had to be the route; after a few moments, without additional comment, he turned and headed out on what would prove to be the correct path. Another younger man, seeing the rather modest sign suggesting that Roncesvalles was in the direction of a nondescript trail through rocks and mud, suggested that anyone could have turned the sign in any direction. So much for "trusting the Camino," I thought at the time, as if a prankster or disgruntled peregrino would go to the trouble of altering this sign just to wreak havoc on the trail. For us, there had been enough havoc already.

We shared our experience with the paved road and showed the others the GPS map on our phone and how the trail veered away from that road. After some discussion, and despite their skepticism, the group headed in the direction the signs vaguely suggested, though there was no clearly defined path to be found (which was surprising given that pilgrims have been following this route for centuries). We took off through the rocks and mud in the direction of (we hoped) Roncesvalles. Though we left together, the group quickly dispersed, and soon it was again Bev and me walking largely alone. It was wet, rocky, and muddy in places, a "trail" that was difficult to follow. And as we got higher on the mountain, it got colder and the rain increased in intensity.

THE RAIN, FOG, FALLING temperatures, and increasing winds made for an almost spooky atmosphere as we continued up the mountain, like a scene from a Stephen King novel or an episode of the "Twilight Zone." But unlike a book or TV show, this was surreally real, and for us, increasingly dangerous.

It would be difficult to describe the conditions we experienced that day after leaving the paved road. For the next five miles or so, while we were still climbing, we encountered standing water and little streams that had become much more treacherous with the heavy rain. And rocks, lots of rocks, rocks that were made slick and dangerous by the wet conditions. We had to pass through a ravine that had turned into a bog of some strange black mud that tried to swallow our shoes with every step. There was no way of moving forward without going through this black mess, so the going was frustratingly slow. As we worked our way through, we came to a young man who said he was from Baltimore. He seemed to be enjoying himself about as much as we were, and as we passed him, he asked, "Is this what you were expecting?" Lacking a wise-ass response that might lighten the mood, I simply replied, "Not exactly." We never saw him again, and hoped he wasn't swallowed by that muddy black bog.

Bev and I had to carefully work our way through herds of large work-horses standing in the middle of the path, not wanting to startle or provoke them. We encountered an agitated cow with horns that threatened us as we tried to get past her. We soon realized she had a calf she was protecting, and we finally climbed a short hill around a tree that allowed us to get past the cow and calf and continue down the trail, the mother's eyes never leaving us.

We passed a man pushing a bicycle (a nice, multi-speed road bike) up a very muddy and rocky section of the trail. Traversing the Camino Francés on a bicycle has become increasingly popular, though reputable guide-books direct bikers to roads and trails separate from these primitive sections. This young man was wearing a short-sleeved cycling jersey, padded cycling shorts, and cleated cycling shoes, which were being engulfed by the mud. We were questioning our selection of attire on this dismal day, but this young biker's outfit made us look almost knowledgeable. Almost.

It WAS GETTING MUCH colder as we approached the top of the mountain, the wind was howling, and the rain now felt almost like sleet. Bev and I were still wearing short-sleeved synthetic shirts, synthetic shorts, and Gore-Tex jackets, very appropriate clothing under less severe conditions. And the problems we were experiencing were nearly inevitable, regardless of what we were wearing. We had been working hard all day, working up a sweat as we climbed this mountain. As a result, though our jackets kept out moisture while allowing in ventilating air, our shirts were getting soaked from the inside out. So, we were dripping wet, and now, we were facing wind that created almost horizontal precipitation that no jacket could fully seal out. We were terribly cold and absolutely miserable.

There was a small concrete building near the top of the peak, designed to provide shelter in emergency conditions. A few miles back, Bev had put on her poncho over her jacket, and that was providing some additional protection from the wind and rain. For reasons I cannot recall, I had not. By now, it was not an option to stop, dig in my pack until I found the poncho, and struggle to put it on in the blustery, rainy wind. Similarly, we had each brought a set of dry clothes, but changing apparel in the middle of a rainstorm made no sense. I suggested to Bev that we needed to increase our pace simply to stay warm. We tried, though conditions and the terrain made that very difficult.

The entire plot of the Emilio Estevez movie, *The Way*, is based on his character perishing in the Pyrenees on the first day of his Camino when he was confronted by unexpected weather conditions. Without that death, the Martin Sheen character wouldn't have traveled to St. Jean Pied de Port to claim his son's body, and he wouldn't have walked the Camino Francés in his son's place. I had always believed that plotline to be rather shaky, a very unlikely and convenient event that would probably almost never happen in real life.

After our first day on the Camino, facing falling temperatures and sleet-like rain, that plotline now seems much more plausible, and all too realistic.

I don't know that we were ever in danger as we topped the Col de Lepoeder in the Pyrenees. But as we stood in the limited shelter provided by that small, concrete building, I was cold enough to be shaking, with whatever illness I had contracted likely making things even worse. But we didn't feel like we had time to ponder how bad things were, as it seemed imperative that we keep moving.

We learned the next day that conditions in the Pyrenees had been historically bad for an early September afternoon and that some pilgrims had been evacuated off the mountain. This could have been a by-product of the pipeline of information on the Camino, some of which is more reliable than others. However, having experienced what was likely the worst of those conditions that day, we can believe all of this. At the time, though, we simply needed to keep going, get to Roncesvalles, and get warm. Still more challenges stood in our way.

We finally reached the peak of this small mountain, unaware we had unceremoniously crossed from France into Spain. Given the fog and rain, as well as our mental state at the time, we had missed the inauspicious marker denoting the border. While we were happy to be descending after a day of climbing, the path was very primitive and not well-defined, and the signage was inconsistent. We knew we weren't more than a couple of miles from Roncesvalles. But as we tried to find and follow the path and with no one else around, we looked at the app on our phones and realized we were again off the route. Given the day we had already experienced, the miserable weather, and my declining physical condition as whatever illness I was experiencing was really starting to kick in, it would be difficult to overstate the disheartening effect this latest mistake had on us.

But as we were trying to figure out what to do, our hands numb and our bodies getting progressively colder, two ladies with whom we had hiked off and on all that afternoon arrived at where we were trying to figure out our next steps. We had introduced ourselves to each other earlier in the day, one lady from Pennsylvania and the other from Colorado. They were using the same travel company as we were and were clearly more experienced with and prepared for these conditions.

We discussed our situation for a few moments, and I assumed we would simply backtrack to where we had lost the route. We noticed one of the ladies looking down the mountain at Roncesvalles, which we could tantalizingly see in the distance but didn't know how to get to. Then the other lady pointed in another direction and said, "See down there? I think that's our road." They then started heading down a lightly worn alternative path that wasn't clearly defined and had no clear destination. It seemed counterintuitive to head off in this direction, literally away from the town, but we decided to trust the Camino, and more importantly, these two ladies, and followed them. We were glad we did.

BUT FOLLOWING THIS TRAIL wasn't without mishaps. It was a rough, muddy, and rocky trail, and I know that by now I wasn't thinking straight; my sickness would peak shortly after we arrived at the inn at which we stayed that night. No doubt wet, cold, and tired like we were, these ladies started moving. As we were struggling to keep up, my right foot lost traction, and I did an awkward (and rather painful) set of splits. A short distance later, I slipped on a rock and did a crude somersault, my pack helping to protect me from much injury. Bev asked me if I was okay after this last awkward move. As I tried to quickly get back up and moving, I said, "We just need to keep up with these ladies." By this point, with the heavy cloud cover creating odd, dusk-like conditions, we had no idea where we were or where we were headed. And without our two navigators leading the way, we would have been completely lost.

To this day, I don't know how these ladies from Colorado and Pennsylvania found this alternative route into town. But we eventually reached a paved road that led us to a highway. Just before we reached that busy traffic way, we saw a yellow arrow signifying a Camino route into Roncesvalles.

Had we been on our own, when we realized we were off route, we would have gone back to find the original route and then tried to follow that path to our inn. We likely would have made it into town, eventually. But with these two ladies leading the way, we followed a nice riverside trail into town and soon found ourselves at an albergue in Roncesvalles, just a short walk to our inn.

THOUGH OURS HAD BEEN made worse by some of our mistakes and boneheaded decisions, it had been a brutal day for everyone. When we stepped into La Posada Inn, a small hotel and restaurant in a building originally constructed in the sixteenth century, the small lobby was filled with wet and cold hikers, many of whom seemed to be in a daze after what they had experienced. The inn wasn't luxurious, and the floor was covered with pools of water brought in by soaked peregrinos, but it was otherwise dry and warm. We had made it.

By now, I was starting to physically feel quite bad. As I stood by our packs, Bev went to stand in line to check in, a process that seemed to take forever. I suspect I was having a mild case of hypothermia because as I stood there, and especially as I sat on a nearby bench, I started to shiver uncontrollably. I had sat down on a bench next to a young lady who seemed less than enthused by my presence. But it was the one place in that entrance hall where you could get off your feet, and though I didn't want to infringe on this young woman's space, I was struggling and needed to sit down.

I don't believe I was thinking clearly as we waited to get into our room. I was wearing a pair of special waterproof hiking shoes, designed for individuals with wide feet, like me. The challenge with waterproof footwear on a day like today quickly became apparent. While they might have done a credible job of keeping water from permeating the shoe, with hours of incessant rain, copious amounts of moisture flowed into the shoe from above. And once in the shoe, it had nowhere to go.

My memory of this time remains a little foggy. But at one point while sitting on that bench, I recall taking off each of my shoes and emptying them onto the floor, kind of like pouring water from a pitcher. I would never do something like that when I'm in my normal frame of mind, but the young lady glanced at me while I did this as if I was absolutely crazy. At that moment, her perception might have been accurate.

When Bev reached the front of the check-in line and began conversing with the clerk, she motioned for me to come over and show my passport. As I stood there waiting while my passport information was recorded, Bev noticed how furiously I was shaking and realized we had a problem that needed to be quickly addressed.

We soon got our room key, and when we got to our room with our packs and our suitcases, which had been delivered as promised, Bev took over. Once in the room, she started the shower, helped me get into the shower, and then readied our clothes for the evening as I allowed the water to slowly get me warmer. Once out of the shower and dried off, I crawled into bed and lay there cuddled in the blankets while Bev took her shower. The warmth was restorative, and I was soon feeling much better. By the next day, my throat was feeling less scratchy and my chest less congested.

After the most trying of days, we were exhausted and our bodies felt beat up, but we were slowly getting back to normal.

La Posada Inn was known as much for its restaurant as for its lodging options. When she checked us into the inn, Bev had made a reservation for dinner, and by that time, we were famished and ready to eat. It would be our first "pilgrim's meal," a sort of prix fixe meal that was economically priced to be affordable for peregrinos. I was feeling markedly better, and the shower and brief rest had revitalized Bev, as well. When we reached our table, there was a bottle of local wine ready for us. Then, for fifteen euros for each of us, around sixteen dollars, wine included, we each had large salads, the Basque chicken for Bev and a grilled beef filet for me, and a dessert of some sort of ice cream cake. It was a wonderful meal that helped restore our spirits and fuel us for the next day.

We knew the second day would be difficult, with challenges we had not expected. As we headed back to our room for some much-needed sleep, we each reflected on what we had experienced since leaving St. Jean Pied de Port. It had been an incredibly challenging day for everyone on that mountain, one that will be remembered for a lifetime and that likely offered countless lessons for those wise enough to learn them. And for a brief period later in the day, it had been a dangerous time.

AFTER A RELATIVELY GOOD night of sleep for both of us, we woke up feeling refreshed and in a little better frame of mind about the challenging day ahead of us. My illness seemed to have peaked, suggesting I had hopefully dodged a more serious illness. Bev, however, was starting to experience some of the same symptoms I had.

Moving slowly as we started our day, we went down to the dining room and had a traditional Spanish breakfast of toast with butter and jelly, fresh yogurt, fruit, sliced ham and cheese, and a croissant, all with some excellent café con leche. It was a lot of food, but we figured we would need it during the coming long day. The route to the tiny village of Akeretta was listed as 16.7 miles, a couple of miles longer than the previous day. But there was far less climbing, with much of the route downhill. And, at least according to the forecast, there would be no rain. (At one point, it started to sprinkle lightly; those few raindrops caused a brief, minor PTSD-like response.) We were a little slow getting started and left the hotel at around 8:40 a.m., later than we had hoped.

The trail was located just across the road from La Posada Inn, and just down that path is an iconic sign that reads, "Santiago de Compostela – 790 (kilometers)." Like us, everyone stopped for a photo at the sign, though the notion that we were 491 miles from our destination was a little daunting. At this point, though, we just wanted to get to Akeretta, from which we would be shuttled to our hotel in Pamplona.

It was a much better day. The natural surface of the trail was surprisingly dry after the heavy rains of the previous day. We only missed the trail twice, never going a great distance out of our way, a vast improvement from our misguided adventures in the Pyrenees. Still, our distance for the day ended up at almost eighteen miles, significantly more than expected.

AFTER AN HOUR OR so on a smooth, level, and shady trail, we started looking for a café for coffee and a mid-morning snack. As we entered a little village, we came across a man standing by a swing set in a playground, talking with another man wearing a backpack. As we walked by him, he engaged with us in fluent English and told us we should stop at the *second* café in town, where he was the owner and chef. He suggested his café served different foods not typically found in this part of Spain. As we walked away, we thought he was perhaps a better marketing representative than a chef. We walked past the first café and then came to the second, where we enjoyed scrambled eggs and bacon, not a typical Spanish breakfast staple, and café con leches. It was, as advertised, very good, and we were fortified to continue down the trail.

These were just the latest of the excellent cups of coffee we would enjoy on our Camino, café con leche, or strong espresso with steamed milk. The cups were seldom very large, but they packed a punch.

The first part of the day was uneventful as the trail followed a slight, steady downhill grade. The highlight of the day was our walking for several miles with the two ladies who had led us into Roncesvalles the previous evening. (Our "Camino Angels," as we called them) It was great to interact with some very nice, like-minded people. We learned that they had attended college together and then remained friends after pursuing careers in different parts of the country. They continued traveling together, hiking in different parts of the world and biking across most of the United States. Just a little older than us, though you wouldn't know it by watching them hike, they were scheduled to continue on the Camino Francés for a few more days, then transfer to another Camino route before ultimately finishing in Santiago de Compostela. Very interesting people.

While the morning was uneventful and pleasant, we operated under a deadline the entire day. The tour company had mapped a route for that day that ended in Akeretta, which had only one hotel. Because that hotel had no availability, we were scheduled to be picked up by taxi at 4:00 p.m. and shuttled to our hotel in Pamplona. After getting a later start, we pushed all day to make that time. The terrain and weather made it impossible.

DURING THE AFTERNOON, AS the heat was building and the sun was starting to bear down, we encountered parts of the trail that seemed barely passable. Over the centuries the Camino Francés has been used by peregrinos, parts of the trail have been worn down by footsteps, wind, and rain, resulting in exposed rock formations that are unavoidable. This section of the trail is known in Camino lore as "dragon's teeth" for the slate-like rocks that protrude out of the ground. You couldn't step on them because they were too sharp and slick. There was typically just a narrow space between them, so you had to slowly and carefully take one step at a time as you navigated through these surprisingly dangerous rock formations. And they went on, off and on, for miles. It was very tough terrain.

A lady from the United States we had met in passing slipped and fell as she tried to descend through one of these "dragon's teeth" sections, banging and cutting her forehead. There were countless times when we slipped or stumbled on these pesky formations, and we were lucky to have avoided an injury like this woman's. With a 4:00 p.m. taxi to catch, we tried to move faster, but the "dragon's teeth" slowed us to a virtual crawl.

Finally, we came to a smoother section of the trail. But the day was getting longer and hotter as we approached the village of Zubiri, where most pilgrims stayed at the end of this stage. But we still had three-and-a-half miles remaining on our route to Akerreta. We were tired from a long and trying day, the stress of the previous day, my lingering illness, and Bev's developing symptoms.

So, as most of the pilgrims veered away from the main trail toward their lodging in Zubiri, we plodded on, still pushing to meet our 4:00 p.m. pickup time. It was a lonely stretch of trail, undulating hills with odd, tall grasses lining either side of the path but offering little sustained shade. We were hot and tired and were not enjoying ourselves at all. We finally accepted what we had suspected since we entered the "dragon's teeth" section, that we could never reach Akerreta by 4:00 p.m. This would be the first time we would be shuttled to or from a hotel, and we didn't know how flexible those pickup times listed in our itinerary would be. Bev called the travel company and informed them of our dilemma. While she waited, the representative called the taxi service and then came back on the line to let us know she had moved the pickup time to 5:00 p.m. No problem, though we still had to get to Akerreta.

What a difference twenty-four hours can make! The previous day during our sojourn into the Pyrenees, we had been soaked from rain and cold to the point of being concerned about hypothermia. As we trudged along the path from Zubiri to Akerreta, we were soaked from sweat and getting hotter, the sun intense and unrelenting. Still a little concerned we might miss our revised pickup time, we pushed on, reaching the Hotel Akerreta at 4:40 p.m. after an eighteen-mile day.

As we walked down the steps to the courtyard of this old, restored Basque inn, I strangely recognized the surroundings. In the movie *The Way*, early on his Camino, Martin Sheen's character comes upon a group of pilgrims having a spirited discussion around a large table in the courtyard of an old inn; that scene was filmed at the Hotel Akerreta.

With a little time until the 5:00 p.m. taxi was scheduled to arrive, we went into the hotel for a cold drink. We ordered two cans of regular Coca-Cola. (None of that diet stuff for these two peregrinos.) The clerk who served us wasn't effusively outgoing but compensated with great efficiency. He soon brought out two cold cans of soda as well as two glasses, each with *two* ice cubes. During our time in Spain, we learned that ice is a far rarer commodity in that country than back in the United States. So, after toiling in the afternoon heat, we had the first regular Coke we had had in years. As I poured that amber liquid over those two ice cubes, waited for the foam to subside, and then took my first sip, it tasted amazing.

The Cokes and ice disappeared rather quickly, and we walked back up to the driveway to wait for our taxi. At 5:10 p.m., a small van with taxi-like markings pulled up to the hotel. While we had assumed that the driver had come solely to pick us up and ferry us to Pamplona, we were surprised when two people with backpacks stepped out of the van. We were even more surprised to see the two ladies from the previous afternoon and with whom we had hiked earlier that day, our "Camino Angels." They had aggravated knee conditions as they descended the "dragon's teeth" section and didn't want to risk the remainder of their trip. As such, they had called the same travel company, which called the same taxi service. They got out of the van, we said our surprise greetings, then we got in and we headed to Pamplona.

We quickly realized that the taxi service, which was widely used in this part of Spain by pilgrims and other hikers, was a bigger operation than it appeared at first glance. The driver was very pleasant but spoke very little English. In the front passenger seat was a younger man who spoke passable English and worked the phone as he spoke with potential riders, other drivers, and representatives of travel companies like ours. Our drive took around twenty-five minutes and allowed us to see parts of Pamplona we had not seen on our train ride into the city or on our drive to St. Jean Pied de Port.

We thanked both gentlemen for being so flexible in changing our pickup time and then settled back to enjoy the beautiful Spanish countryside. Partway through the drive, the young man with the phone took a call from a woman from the United States. She had found this phone number and, though she had no reservation, wanted her and her partner to be picked up from some location on the trail and shuttled to Pamplona. All of this conversation was conducted on speakerphone, and this hiker was openly irritated that the young man didn't speak English more fluently (we were in Spain, after all). She wanted to be picked up immediately, and when the young man told her they had this fare and then another before they could get to her and her partner, she openly questioned why they couldn't "move some things around" so she could be picked up when she wanted. The driver told the young man to tell the woman he would call her back. They then consulted their computer and called other drivers to check their availability. They ultimately called the woman back and told her she would be picked up just a little later than she had originally requested. Having largely gotten her way, she seemed happy.

Talk about the "ugly American." We were a little embarrassed to have overheard such a childish display from one of our compatriots. But the two taxi guys seemed unfazed and continued to try to find a way to meet this individual's needs. I might not have been able to show such patience. But the attitude exhibited by the driver and his colleague was emblematic of what we saw time after time from service workers in Spain. Not all were this way, but most, like these two men, were polite, unrushed, largely unflappable, and wanted to meet the customers' needs.

As we were scheduled to be shuttled back to Akerreta the next morning, we were booked for two nights at the Hotel Tres Reyes ("Three Kings," named for the three "wise men" of the Biblical story of the birth of Christ) in the heart of Pamplona, one of the nicest hotels in the city. We quickly showered and prepared for what we suspected would be a short evening. As we headed out to dinner, we noticed that each side of the walkway outside of the main hotel entrance was lined with a large throng of people, most sporting soccer jerseys. With a corridor created by barriers and enforced by several police officers, at the end of this walkway was a large bus. Not wanting to inject ourselves into this enthusiastic crowd, we went back to the nice young woman at the front desk who had checked us in and asked her what all the excitement was about. In impeccable English, she told us the Pamplona professional men's soccer team, CA Osasuna, was playing FC Barcelona that evening, and that the team was staying in this hotel. I know virtually nothing about international professional soccer, but it was obvious this was a big deal. I suggested to the young lady that we had thought that perhaps these people were here for us; she gave me a smile that suggested she was tolerating me and told us we could certainly walk out the front doors and through the crowd. And we did, resisting the urge to wave to the crowd of fans. Actually, we tried to pass through as inconspicuously as possible.

We found it difficult, again, to find a restaurant open for an earlier dinner—most didn't start serving food until 8:00 or 8:30 p.m. We finally found a bar where a friendly bartender helped us each order a large salad (which, as is typical in Spain, came with a bunch of unique ingredients [at least to us] like tuna and corn) and a huge burger with goat cheese, bacon, aioli, and a bunch of other stuff I can't remember, all on a brioche bun. It was an excellent meal that provided needed calories and allowed us to get to bed at our normal time.

Though getting better, I was still not feeling up to par, and Bev was starting to feel worse as we had completed our second-day hike. We were scheduled to be picked up at 8:45 a.m. the next morning and driven back to Akerreta so we could hike the ten miles back to the hotel we were staying in. Under the circumstances, with both of us still a little battered by the first two days and both feeling the effects of whatever lingering bug we had contracted, it made no sense to do that. We would have little time to explore this historic city, and more importantly, we would have little time to rest and get well. So, we called and canceled our shuttle for the next day. It was the perfect decision for us, as it allowed us to do a little sightseeing, visit a pharmacy where Bev could find some medicine for her scratchy throat and chest congestion, and otherwise just rest.

On these long trips on foot or bicycle, some are driven to make sure they walk or cycle every inch of the route. In line with the reasoning of many of these people, not doing the entire route is tantamount to not doing any of the route. Bravo to these dedicated and driven folks, though such attitudes seem to border on being obsessive. Bev and I are not like that, as we wanted to have a good experience more than to claim we walked every step of the Camino. There would be other times when we would use alternative means to travel along the Camino and our experience was enhanced rather than lessened as a result. As the saying goes, you must "walk your own Camino." We're glad we did.

We slept well in our bright, clean, and modern hotel room. Breakfast was served in a large room that offered a buffet of different breads, meats, cheeses, fruits, and juices. With nowhere to hike on this impromptu rest day, we took our time and enjoyed the variety of offerings. A highlight that we would find a few times in hotels in larger cities was a coffee machine. Much of the coffee we had consumed had been amazing, café con leches of strong espresso served with rich, steamed milk. But though they were included as part of the breakfast, we typically had to order the coffee from a server who then made each small cup individually. As a result, each morning, we seldom had more than one of those small cups. With a coffee machine, we simply pushed a button and the machine would create the café con leche. Not as good as those that were individually crafted, but much more convenient. Perhaps too convenient, as I ended up drinking several, the resulting buzz being a bit much for this grandpa.

Our first order of business was visiting a pharmacy for some medicine for Bev. "Farmácias," as they are called in Spain, differ from the drugstores and pharmacies now common in the United States. Spanish pharmacists are considered a more vital cog in the healthcare system in that country. Though a physician's prescription is required for most drugs, Spanish pharmacists often offer advice, guide sick and injured individuals to needed treatments, and are the first line in treating many common illnesses and injuries.

With a large neon cross signifying its location, we found a farmácia near the hotel. The pharmacist, who spoke fluent English, listened to Bev as she described her symptoms and then recommended a series of herbal and homeopathic treatments. Bev purchased these recommended medicines, used only some of them over the next couple of days, and saw her symptoms continue to improve.

We did some exploring of this beautiful and historic city of around 200,000. We toured the Ciudadela, a huge ancient fort that was never the site of any warfare and was eventually converted into a beautiful urban park. We walked down streets that, during the San Fermín Festival, are used for the "running of the bulls." Walking down these streets among other human beings is as close as I would ever want to come to this famous tradition. We were struck by the narrowness of the alley-like streets and how, with the rush of the bulls and other runners, it would be nearly impossible to get out of the way of these stampeding animals. We followed these narrow streets down to the Plaza de Toros, the large circular stadium into which the bulls were herded to be killed in "bullfights." Outside of the stadium, we saw a famous statue of Ernest Hemingway, who wrote *The Sun Also Rises* while living in Pamplona.

Given the challenges of finding an early dinner offering, we found the Spanish lunchtime typically extends into the late afternoon, which could allow us to have our large meal of the day in the afternoon (just like the Spaniards). We found a restaurant with outdoor seating that offered the "menu del día," or menu of the day. It's a multi-course, prix fixe meal, much like a "pilgrim's meal." We each had a large salad, a grilled pork steak for Bev and a beef steak for me, each thinly sliced and grilled with unique spices, all served with fries and croquettes filled with ham and cheese. It was excellent, a large meal that alleviated the pressure of finding a full-service restaurant that evening.

For the remainder of the day, we just rested on a park bench watching people walk by and in our hotel room. By the time we departed Pamplona the next morning, we weren't back to feeling normal, but the rest day had been very beneficial.

During the cross-country bicycle tour Bev and I completed in 2017, we had four rest days built into the forty-six-day schedule. We always looked forward to these respites from riding. But each time, by the end of the non-biking day, we were a little fidgety, itching to get back on the road. As we settled in for our last night in Pamplona, we were ready to get back on the trail, wanting to get into a groove and routine we had not yet established in our first two challenging days of walking. It would be during this next stretch of the Camino that we came to feel like true peregrinos.

Life Lesson # 2

"The Camino Is Not About You."

"In the whole expanse of time, a single human life is no more than a fleeting moment. Remember this when you act, speak, or think."

Marcus Aurelius

WE WERE JUST A few hours into our Camino experience, and we were miserable. It had rained since we had left St. Jean Pied de Port, we were soaked, and the dropping temperatures brought further attention to the poor clothing decisions that would continue to haunt us for the remainder of this epoch first day. We had followed a paved road until reaching a confusing (at least to us) set of signs that led us to erroneously continue on that same thoroughfare. Dealing with illness, dripping clothes, fatigue, and frustration, we lost an hour of precious time as we followed the wrong route and then backtracked to the same confounding set of directional signs. As we stood in the cold, foggy rain and discussed route options with several other pilgrims, I thought to myself, "Why don't *they* do a better job of marking the route?"

Then, just twenty-four hours later, still dealing with the fatigue and illness that had plagued us the previous day, we came to the infamous "dragon's teeth" section of the Camino Francés. Long stretches of the trail were dominated by exposed, sharp, slate-like rock, hard "teeth" too pointed and dangerous to step on. Frustrated and just wanting the day to end, we painstakingly edged our way down the steep trail, moving slowly as we sought a stepping spot between the rocks that would not cause a fall or a twisted ankle. Lucky to reach a speed of a mile an hour on these treacherous sections, I similarly thought to myself, "Why don't *they* make this trail smoother and safer?"

I LOOK BACK ON these aberrant thoughts with a bit of embarrassment. For starters, who are *they* whose job it is to ease my brief time on the Camino de Santiago? The Spanish government? Some not-for-profit organization created to make my journey easier? And why should it be *easier* to begin with? To be truly transcendent, trekking the entire Camino Francés should be challenging and should push you out of your comfort zone. Much of the meaning of completing a Camino comes from overcoming the challenges, from dealing with the difficulties you face, and from adapting yourself to the path rather than vice versa.

In our modern world, we are constantly seeking ways of making our lives easier, often expecting others to clear the way if not carry us to our destination. What can *they* do to make my life easier? I know I am certainly guilty of this reliance on the efforts of others to make things better for me. All of this has made life easier and more efficient, and in some instances, society has benefited in the process. But our overreliance on others to ease our way has decreased our self-reliance and, in some respects, diminished our well-being. On the Camino, luggage shuttles, taxis, lodging reservations, sophisticated equipment, and other recent advances have admittedly made life easier on the path to Santiago de Compostela. But a pilgrim still must put one foot in front of the other for 500 miles to complete the entire route.

But of greater significance, lamenting the inherent difficulty of this historic 500-mile trail and hoping that, somehow, our path could be eased seems to shortchange the accomplishments of the the many who have walked over this same trail during the past millennium. So many of these peregrinos completed their trek with great humility and without the aid of GPS, cellphones, fitted backpacks, and special hiking shoes. In fact, many were fortunate to have any shoes at all.

On the evening after our dangerous encounter atop the Pyrenees, the same day I lamented the lack of effective trail signage, I overcame my illness and fatigue with a long, hot shower, a nap in a warm bed, and a wonderful pilgrim's meal in the hotel restaurant. My predecessors, what some might call the "true pilgrims," would have been fortunate to spend the night out of the rain. The evening after navigating the "dragon's teeth" section, after an eighteen-mile day that seemed to never end, we were shuttled (yes, shuttled) to a wonderful modern hotel in Pamplona. My point in this is that we had no justification for griping about anything as we experienced the absolute blessing of being able to complete our Camino.

In our egocentric society, we tend to think we are the focus of whatever is happening in the world. In almost every instance, we are not. As we completed our hike on the Camino Francés, I often tried to remember the countless pilgrims who had preceded us, who had stepped on the same section of trail I was passing through at that time. I can be as egocentric as the next person, but I tried to remember that my brief time on the Camino de Santiago was like a minuscule piece of dust on the trail, an inconsequential blip in time in the history of this iconic pilgrimage route. My impact on the path was virtually nonexistent. Its impact on me… well, that was yet to be determined.

Chapter Three

Finding Our Stride on "The Way"

Puente La Reina to Logroño

Our impromptu rest day in Pamplona had been the elixir we needed after our ordeal crossing the Pyrenees and as we recovered from whatever illness we had contracted. As we prepared to leave the bustling confines of the city and the comfortable Hotel Tres Reyes, both Bev and I were feeling much better and ready to resume our Camino.

But as we started our fourth day since leaving St. Jean Pied de Port, we had yet to get into a routine, to feel like true pilgrims. Our first day had been a struggle to survive, our second simply a struggle, and our third a day to recover. We hadn't yet felt the natural flow of the Camino; we had yet to find our stride.

That began to change on the fifteen-mile route from Pamplona to the little town of Puente La Reina.

After another hearty breakfast in the dining room of the Hotel Tres Reyes, we departed at around 7:45 a.m. We quickly found the trail, and as we passed by the Ciudadela at this relatively early hour, Pamplona wasn't congested but still felt busy. It was cool and overcast to start, but the sky would clear and it would get intensely hot as the day continued.

Just as we were transitioning from the city into a more suburban/rural setting, we saw up the trail a police van and three individuals in police-like uniforms. Unsure of their purpose, we approached them cautiously, expecting we might be asked to show our passports and justify our presence in Spain. Instead, a nice young man approached us and, after inquiring about where we were from, welcomed us with very good English. He was an officer with Guardia Civil, a national law enforcement agency in Spain tasked with, in part, protecting pilgrims on the Camino de Santiago. Very cordial and polite, he provided us with a pamphlet describing the agency's role, what to do if we had any difficulty, and the number to call if we needed help (062). The Camino is considered a relatively safe place for hikers, though crimes occasionally occur. Still, our brief and pleasant conversation with this officer was reassuring.

The trail was clearly marked, on smooth pavement for the first three miles as we approached the growing suburb of Cizur Menor. This early part of the day's hike brought focus to an occasional issue when walking through developed (i.e., non-rural) areas. Particularly early in the day after getting fully hydrated with coffee, water, juice, etc., the need for a toilet can become critical. For perhaps ninety percent of the Camino Francés, through secluded areas with ample trees and other natural barriers and with long stretches with few other pilgrims, toilet options are virtually unlimited. As we left Cizur Menor, after having no luck in locating a restroom, we came across a local police officer standing next to his patrol car just off the trail. I approached him and, in muddled Spanish, tried to ask him where we might find a "baño," or toilet. He spoke serviceable English and told us there were no public restrooms available in the little town. But then he smiled and made a sweeping gesture with his right arm, indicating that the area we were hiking into would provide ample options for where we might take care of our business. It was kind of funny, this officer of the law "sanctioning" our completing these bodily functions out in nature, something we would have done anyway, though with a minute amount of lingering guilt. Within the next couple of miles, we dutifully followed this officer's guidance.

Though our destination was Puente La Reina, our focus for most of the day was a ridge halfway into our hike. As we left Pamplona, we could look in the distance and see a hill lined with wind turbines. It seemed to be a great distance to these huge, spinning machines, though they were just eight miles away. Just after Cizur Menor, we started climbing, a steady incline that got steeper as we approached the peak of Alto del Perdón, the iconic ridge on which the wind turbines had been placed. A few miles out of Pamplona, we had transitioned from sidewalks to a paved trail and finally to what Camino sages call a "natural path" of gravel, dirt, and rocks. But as we climbed to the top of this ridge, the rocks on the trail got larger, looser, and thus, more treacherous.

"Alto del Perdón" in English is "hill of forgiveness," and Camino lore suggests that with each step up this long incline, pilgrims ask for forgiveness. On this warm and sunny September day, Bev and I were mainly just wanting to get to the top of that hill.

Of course, we did, and we were rewarded by spectacular views of Pamplona and the Pyrenees behind us and the lush and beautiful valley of the Río Arga ahead of us, with Puente La Reina in the distance. In 1996, a large metal sculpture had been installed along the ridgeline that quickly became one of the most iconic spots on the Camino Francés. The sculpture depicts the evolution of Camino pilgrims, from medieval times to the present. With this huge work of art, the amazing views, and the warm wind threatening to blow our hats off our heads, this made for a surreal experience. A group of Scandinavian hikers asked us to take their photo in front of the sculpture, and they reciprocated by taking ours. It was a memorable moment, but the most striking part about being on this ridge was not the sculpture or the impressive views, but rather the constant, loud droning sound from all those wind turbines.

On the Alto del Perdón

A steep and challenging ascent is almost always followed by an equally challenging downhill section. After reaching the top of the Alto del Perdón, we began descending a mile-long section of rough, loose rocks that posed a much greater challenge than we had experienced climbing to the top. We had been warned about the hazards of this steep descent, loose rocks posing a constant threat to our footing. Very concerned about slipping and falling, we slowly and gingerly made our way down the hill as we used our hiking poles to help us maintain our footing. Another American hiker we had met earlier in the week, part of a trio of interesting ladies from Wisconsin, fell on these rocks and injured her head. We talked to her at breakfast the next morning, a large bandage on her head; she would not hike for the next few days.

In time, we reached the bottom of the hill, and the trail leveled into a much gentler descent into Puente La Reina. But it was hot and getting hotter, temperatures in the upper eighties but with intense sunshine that made it feel much warmer. To help us get to our destination, we stopped at a bar in the little village of Muruzábal where we each had a large bottle of Coca-Cola, served with lemon and a glass of ice. It was glorious, an icy cold beverage we had unconsciously consumed so many times in the past. Admittedly, we were sleeping in inns, having our bags transported, and consuming any food and drink we wanted. Even so, we were living a relatively simple existence, walking from one town to the next with far fewer possessions than in our regular lives. And as a by-product, we were feeling much greater gratitude for what we had. Though for the entire Camino we struggled to find restaurants with earlier dinner service, and though many of the meals were less than spectacular, they were enjoyed and appreciated. And when we could score a "pilgrim's meal," the menu del día that was priced less than we could afford and was seldom culinarily exceptional, our appreciation was heightened even more. And on this day in this setting, a cold soft drink with ice and lemon was considered a blessing.

Reinforcing a lesson we had learned on our cross-country bicycle ride, the fewer your possessions, the more you seem to appreciate what you do have.

WE EVENTUALLY MADE OUR way into Puente La Reina, a rather run-down little town of 2,500 on the banks of the Río Arga. Our lodging for the evening was in the Hotel Rural El Cerco, described in the materials from our travel company as a "delightfully restored house." Given the dreariness of this village, our hopes were not high as we reached this little inn. It was much nicer than we had anticipated. Our room was tidy and clean but, as we had been experiencing, minuscule. With two suitcases, two daypacks, and us, we had to crawl over the bed to get from one side of the room to the other.

After showering and rinsing out some clothes, we left the hotel to explore this ancient village. We stopped at a little bar where I had a beer (Estella Dramm, a local favorite) and Bev, a glass of Rioja vino tinto, or red wine. Fortified and rehydrated, we visited a farmácia where we picked up a couple of items for some minor aches and pains. We then started looking for a restaurant that opened for dinner service earlier than 8:00 or 8:30 p.m. We walked by a hotel and noticed diners eating dinner on a terrace just outside the front door. Some tables were available, so we sat down and started perusing the menu. As we were doing so, we noticed our "Camino Angels," the two ladies we had met on the first day, walking toward the entrance to the hotel where they were staying that night. Bev got their attention, and they ended up joining us for a very nice dinner. Bev and I each had a large salad and paella with chicken and shrimp. The food and wine were good, but the best part of this enjoyable meal was getting to know more about these two interesting ladies.

Despite the challenges we faced, it had been a good day, a day of putting miles behind us and getting into a groove and a routine. This was the day we started to feel like true peregrinos.

THE NEXT DAY'S ROUTE to the small city of Estella was a little shorter at thirteen miles, with fewer obstacles and better terrain. It would be one of the best walking days we experienced, with cooler temperatures in the morning before getting blistering hot and sunny in the afternoon.

Puente La Reina translates as "the bridge of the queen," and as we left this village, we crossed over the Río Arga on the stunning namesake bridge, a long, Romanesque span of six arches. Compared to where we live in the Midwest, virtually everything in Spain is ancient. And like so many landmarks we passed, we crossed over this eleventh-century bridge not realizing its historical and architectural significance.

After around four miles of hiking, we were approaching the hilltop village of Cirauqui when we were passed by an Italian gentleman, probably a few years younger than us, who was hiking with two young people we assumed were his daughter and son. We had seen this trio several times since leaving Pamplona, and the older man seemed very vocal and energetic. As he passed us, this older gentleman was saying repeatedly, "bocadillo and cerveza, bocadillo and cerveza." It was around 10:30 a.m. when we got to a small café in the village, and as we walked in, that same Italian gentleman was eating a sandwich with a glass of beer waiting for him. When I saw him, I said, "bocadillo and cerveza." His mouth full of bocadillo, he just gave me a thumbs up. It was an entertaining encounter with a character we never saw again.

Bev and I had a wonderful café con leche and a glazed croissant with chocolate filling that was becoming our go-to treat on the Camino. It was a perfect mid-morning snack that provided the energy we needed to get to the next village.

It was a stunningly beautiful day for walking as we passed olive groves and stands of almond trees. But the most striking feature of this part of the Camino Francés was the vast array of vineyards. We were in La Rioja, the most prominent winemaking region in Spain, and vineyards seemed to be everywhere. The trail passed through these immense fields of grapevines, and at almost any time, you could reach out and grab a cluster. Respecting the rights of the owners, we did not, but we witnessed many pilgrims who did. And as we were now well into September with harvest time just around the corner, the grapes were ripe and the heat and intense sunshine were making the aromas tantalizingly pungent. It was a memorable setting that fed our affinity for Rioja wine, a passion that continued after our return home.

The terrain we were walking through featured rolling hills and little lush vegetation. Centuries ago, many Spanish villages were built on the top of some of those hills to provide them with an obvious strategic advantage in the event they were attacked. One of many such villages we passed through was Lorca, which we started seeing in the distance as we left Cirauqui and tracked our progress in getting there over the three or four miles between the two villages. Lorca is a neat little town, with every street seemingly on a very steep pitch leading to the center of the village at the top of the hill. It was lunchtime when we got there, so we stopped at a bar and had a bocadillo; no cerveza for us this early in the day, but we each did have a cold can of Coca-Cola.

Leaving Lorca, we descended the gentle slope of a road constructed over 2,000 years ago during the time of the Roman Empire. This short stretch of rock road is considered one of the best examples of a "Roman road" on the entire Camino Francés. The surface felt rough to us, but in its day, this paved rock road was the ancient version of a superhighway. It was humbling to be walking on a surface with such a storied past.

WE FINALLY MADE IT into Estella, a small, historic city of 14,000. Like so many of the Spanish towns and villages we visited, the old center of Estella had narrow, alley-like streets lined with ancient buildings. In one of those old structures, we found our hotel for the evening, the Hotel Hospedería Chapitel, which our materials suggested offered "a unique artistic yet classic charm." We weren't sure what that meant, but we found the Chapitel to be a modern hotel in an ancient section of the city that offered clean, but small, rooms. It served our needs very well.

We found a restaurant that offered early dinner service, and Bev and I each had a large salad served with large fried prawns. With thirteen miles ahead of us the next day, on the way back to the hotel, we stopped for ice cream. It had been another good day.

With a forecast for more intense heat, we left Estella at 8:00 a.m., early for us, as we made our way to the little town of Los Arcos. Bev and I were both dealing with some minor foot issues, little hot spots we didn't want to become blisters. We had visited a farmácia in Estella for some special bandages, and those and different shoes for me seemed to help. In time, we started applying duct tape to those areas, and we had few problems with our feet for the remainder of the trip.

Bodegas Irache "wine spigot"

A highlight of the morning was a stop at one of the most iconic spots on the entire Camino Francés. Bodegas Irache is a winery outside of Estella that, like countless others in this region, specializes in Rioja wines. For decades, the winery has offered Camino pilgrims (and, I assume, anyone else who wanders by) complementary wine that flows from a spigot. On this ornately decorated wall just off the Camino trail are actually two spigots, one labeled "vino" and the other "agua." Later in the day, the supply of free wine was often depleted, but when we arrived before 9:00 a.m., it was still flowing. Bev poured some of the free wine into an empty water bottle, which we then shared. Let's just say that, at least on this day, the friendly folks at Irache didn't offer their "good stuff" through the complimentary tap. From my perspective, it was rather nasty. But a memorable part of the Camino experience, nonetheless.

The day was calm and rather pleasant, though we again got hot and tired as we approached Los Arcos. We climbed Monjardín, a famous mountain/hill on the Camino Francés, though the trees and other foliage were too lush at the top to see much of anything. It was a reminder that, though we had left the Pyrenees behind us, we were still in mountainous terrain. We stopped at the only town we came to on the route and had an omelet on big chunks of white toast and a large slice of potato, egg, and cheese casserole, all with a couple of cans of Coca-Cola.

We still had six miles to go, suspected there was little between there and Los Arcos, and didn't want to "bonk," or run out of fuel/energy, before we got there. The rest of the afternoon was routine: long, sunny, and hot. We had plenty of water and a few snacks, so we were confident we could make it to the next hotel. But six miles in those conditions with no stops or respite would be physically and mentally draining.

There is a saying suggesting that, in some sense, whatever you need on the Camino, the Camino provides. A few miles after we had left our lunch spot, as we were dragging and a little dejected, we rounded a curve, and in front of us was a large food truck that offered virtually anything you might want on the trail. I walked up to order ice cream for Bev and me, and the older gentleman working in the truck was talking with a distinct American accent. When I asked him where he was from, he replied, "Tampa," and asked me the same question. When I said, "Chicago," he said, "Well, you probably want some Lou Malnati's (deep-dish pizza), maybe some Portillo's (Italian beef)." It brought a huge, unexpected smile to my face, something I needed at that time. The ice cream bars we purchased worked just fine and were quite amazing in that setting.

THE REST OF THE route involved long stretches of smooth walking surface. When you don't have to concentrate on "dragon's teeth," or loose rocks, or muddy trails, or long inclines, your mind can naturally wander. And on this long, scorching afternoon, mine certainly did just that. I thought about the stream of lessons in humility that seemed to be constantly available on the Camino. Every stretch of this trail has been used by countless pilgrims over the past thousand years, most of whom had far fewer advantages than we did. And when those lessons in humility are offered, one can either learn from them or be annoyed by them; I think I did some of both as we made our way to Santiago de Compostela. This trip, our efforts, and what we were doing were certainly important to Bev and me, a potentially life-altering experience. But really, our Camino represented just a minuscule blip in time in the history of this amazing pilgrimage route. And the realization of the relative insignificance of my experience was itself a powerful lesson in humility.

WE FINALLY ARRIVED IN Los Arcos a little after 2:00 p.m. and made our way to the Hotel Monaco, which, as far as we could see, was the only hotel in this rather decrepit small town. After getting cleaned up, we went downstairs to the hotel bar where we had a beer and watched the end of a stage of the Vuelta de España, the three-week bicycle race that is the Spanish version of the Tour de France. Just six years earlier, around this time of year, we were preparing to begin a bicycle ride across the southern United States, a 3,000-mile journey that, to that point, was the most amazing experience of our lives. Watching some of the greatest cyclists in the world complete that day's stage of the race caused us to reminisce about our earlier trip. Few people have the opportunity to complete one major adventure like that one. Now, just a few years later and at sixty-six, we were walking across Spain, attempting to reach another of the goals we had established for ourselves. Drinking that cold beer and watching a bicycle race with commentary we couldn't translate but largely understood, a wave of gratitude washed over both of us.

The word on the street in Los Arcos was that the best place to eat was the Mavi Restaurant, a nondescript but very functional establishment located across from the hotel. The restaurant didn't start serving dinner until 7:00 p.m., early by Spanish standards but very workable by ours. We were standing in line when the doors opened, and we were treated to a pilgrim's meal, the menu del día of a three-course dinner with wine for fourteen euros, around fifteen dollars. Bev ordered the lentil soup, Trout

Navarre, and cake while I had a large salad (with tuna and corn, which I was surprisingly coming to like), thin slices of grilled pork, and an ice cream cone. It was a good meal, the end of what had been a good day. We continued to hit our stride, and when we left Los Arcos the next morning, we were around 80 miles into our Camino, 420 miles from Santiago.

WE WERE IN THE middle of a stretch of hot weather, and high temperatures and intense sunshine made the afternoons challenging. Particularly given our age, if we weren't careful, such conditions could be dangerous. On this Friday in early September, as we were scheduled to travel seventeen miles to Logroño, the forecast high was in the upper 80s with few clouds. As a precaution, we decided to cut the route short. We asked the hotel clerk about scheduling a cab to take us to the next small town on the route, Torres del Río. He told us a bus headed in that direction would arrive soon. We hurried to the bus stop where several backpack-wearing hikers were waiting. As we stood around longer than we had expected, we noticed on a sign at the bus stop that the aforementioned bus was scheduled to arrive at 8:50 a.m., which by this point was forty-five minutes later. We panicked a little, as we were losing the cool morning temperatures as we waited for this phantom bus. Then, just as we were calling to schedule a taxi, the bus arrived a half-hour earlier than the listed time. We boarded the bus, and the driver seemed to be one who was used to dealing with foreign hikers who didn't know what they were doing (like us). He politely and positively responded when we asked if the bus stopped in Torres del Río, informing us of the fare for such a brief ride on a bus that would ultimately travel to Logroño. A bit relieved, we boarded the bus and soon arrived at the next little town, cutting four critical miles off a long, hot hike.

In a little village of just a few buildings, we quickly found the trail and were soon moving toward Logroño. We had adopted the notion on this trip that "we didn't *have* to do anything," and we firmly agreed with the idea that everyone needs to "walk their own Camino." And conditions were forecast to become very hot as the day continued. Still, as we started walking for the day in Torres del Río, I had a subtle feeling of guilt because we would not be walking the entire route that day. As the temperature continued to rise and the sun bore down as the day progressed, that sense of guilt was not long-lasting.

We found the trail to be the most crowded we had yet experienced, and for the first few miles, we were consistently walking among other pilgrims. As the day continued, the path became less congested, and the result was a fairly mundane day of hiking, with several sharp inclines and downhills but nothing particularly extraordinary.

Sometimes when we needed a boost in the middle of a long day, the Camino had a way of providing it, as with the unexpected food truck the previous day. On this day, in the middle of a long, rather boring stretch of trail, we heard music in the distance. When we rounded a corner, we found a lady sitting in a chair, playing an accordion. I'm sure there is a formal name for the tune, but what she was playing I recognized as the song from the Frito's Corn Chips commercials of my youth, otherwise known as the "Frito Bandito" song. ("Ay, ay, yay, yay, I am the Frito Bandito...") Bev dropped some coins in her accordion case. The next day, as we were walking through a vineyard, we started hearing some beautiful music from an acoustic guitar, with the melody amplified by a speaker hidden somewhere on a nearby hill. It was truly beautiful, a needed diversion, and Bev again made an artistic contribution. Each time, we approached the musician hot, tired, and a little surly. After briefly listening to the amusing and then the beautiful music, we left hot and tired, but smiling. The Camino had provided the little nudge we needed.

IN TIME, WE MADE it to Viana, an ancient hilltop village of 4,000. It's a neat and vibrant small city, with the Camino passing straight through the center of town. We arrived at around lunchtime and the business district was busy, making it difficult to find a place to sit down while one of us went to purchase some food. I went to a little storefront café and purchased two large slices of ham and potato casserole with a can of Coca-Cola for me and iced tea for Bev. I returned with these items to the outdoor table where Bev was sitting with our packs. As we started to eat, a man from a nearby restaurant walked up to us and started gesticulating in Spanish that (we assumed) we needed to move from that table that belonged or was assigned to his restaurant. He kept saying the same thing over and over, and we didn't understand his message better the eighth or ninth time than we did the first. If it hadn't been so aggravating, it would have been comical, reminiscent of the moronic teacher whose method of re-explaining a complex concept is to say the same thing slower and louder.

I'm certainly one to follow rules, and I understood and accepted that this gentleman needed to protect what were his tables for his customers. But he was acting like a jerk. We took our food to another table near the restaurant where we had purchased it. To this day, our memories of the otherwise wonderful village of Viana have been jaundiced by this unpleasant encounter, one of the very few we experienced in our month-and-a-half in Spain.

After we departed Viana, I thought a great deal about our interaction with this Spanish gentleman. When people are visiting a country and don't understand the language and aren't familiar with the local customs, they aren't stupid and they certainly aren't bad as a result; they just need a little assistance, and grace. It was a poignant lesson Bev and I would certainly take with us when we returned to the United States.

Seven long and hot miles after leaving Viana, we crossed a bridge over the putrid, green-looking Río Ebro and entered the downtown section of Logroño, a fairly large city of 155,000. On this Friday afternoon, this vibrant city, described as a "pleasant blend of medieval and modern," was bustling. Our hotel for the evening, the Los Bracos Inn, is older but upscale in what seemed to be the hip part of the city.

After showering, we ventured down the street from the hotel to a bar where we had a beer (me) and a glass of Rioja wine (Bev). The latter seemed fitting, given that Logroño is the capital of the Rioja province of Spain. On our way back to the hotel, we were on the lookout for a restaurant that would be open at an early hour. We were unsuccessful and eventually ate at another bar where we had several tapas items. It made for an inexpensive, but not particularly healthy, dinner.

After dinner, on a beautiful early autumn evening with the streets of Logroño filled with families preparing to begin their weekend, we went to a little plaza area where we each had a large frozen yogurt sundae. We were consuming huge numbers of calories each day, but were burning even more.

As we walked back to our hotel, we saw the two ladies we had met on the first day, our "Camino Angels," who were seated at an outdoor table finishing their dinner. They were staying in Logroño for another day before being shuttled the following day to continue their Camino on another route. As such, we knew this was the last time we would see these two nice people. We exchanged contact information, took photos, and said our farewells. I told them they would always have a special place in our hearts for guiding us into our first destination town.

As WE SETTLED INTO our hotel for the evening, one week had passed since we had departed St. Jean Pied de Port (it seemed longer), and we were five days of hiking from our first planned rest day in Burgos.

After the uncertainty of even being able to begin our Camino, and then the challenges of the first few days, the daily grind of walking across Spain was setting in. We were workmanlike in our approach as we settled into our routine and put miles behind us as we completed each hike. With each day, we were becoming more confident in dealing with the cultural and language differences we brought to this amazing country. And despite our original doubts about our ability to handle all these challenges, we were functioning surprisingly well. We were becoming pilgrims.

Life Lesson # 3

"The World is Not as Large as it May Seem."

"Our similarities bring us to a common ground; our differences allow us to be fascinated by each other."

Tom Robbins

"Sesenta y seis, sesenta y seis."

We had been a little unnerved at first, though we shouldn't have been. We were headed to the small city of Estella on a sunny afternoon, winding our way through a patchwork of vineyards on a day that seemed to get longer and hotter. It was the fifth day of our Camino journey, and though we were becoming more accustomed to our surroundings, we were still more cautious than we would become in the weeks to come.

The sight of the older Spanish gentleman sporting an almost iridescent jersey of CA Osasuna, the professional soccer club in nearby Pamplona, caught our attention; that he was walking toward us, against the stream of pilgrims trying to get to Santiago de Compostela, seemed odd and curious.

His English proficiency not much better than ours was in Spanish, through words and gestures, he inquired about whether we were okay. (Perhaps we looked like the heat was getting to us more than we had realized.) He was an amiable gentleman, and I gave him a thumbs-up sign to indicate we were fine. After letting him know that our Spanish proficiency was very limited, he told us he spoke several languages, but that English was not one of them.

He then asked us where we were from. Displaying my limited Spanish, I said, "Estados Unidos," to which he gave us an expression suggesting he would welcome more information. When one of us said, "Chicago," the conversation suddenly got interesting. The gentleman's eyes brightened, and his short, squatty body seemed to get taller. "Sesenta y seis, sesenta y seis," he kept repeating until we understood what he was saying. On a sun-drenched afternoon in the middle of a Rioja vineyard in northern Spain, this man dressed in a colorful soccer jersey had made the connection between us and Route 66, the "Mother Road" that begins in Chicago and runs all the way to California. Through our limited knowledge of each other's language, we learned that this man had traveled to the United States and ridden on a Harley-Davidson motorcycle from somewhere in Arizona to Santa Monica, California, where Route 66 ends. He told us, through gestures, simple Spanish, and broken English, that he was planning to return to the United States to ride the remainder of the road, starting in Chicago, where it officially begins. This older Spaniard spoke with such pride and seemed so happy to have made a trail connection with a couple of (sort of) Chicagoans. As he was searching on his phone for photos of the Harley he rode, and as the afternoon kept getting hotter, we said our farewells and headed down the trail. It had been a neat moment.

As we had prepared for our extended time in Spain, perhaps my greatest concern was how we would deal with our lack of proficiency in the Spanish language. Despite two years of Spanish in high school and several months of study before beginning our Camino, I could not follow, much less conduct, a normal-paced conversation in the language. I was concerned about how we could function during our six weeks in a foreign country in which we could barely read directional signs. While Bev had even less background in Spanish than I did, she also had less concern about any language challenges we might face.

I think back to my childhood days in "Sunday School" when we learned about the Tower of Babel. In the story, in response to efforts to build a tower to heaven in the sky, the Bible suggests God caused different groups to speak different languages so they couldn't work cooperatively to build the heavenly tower. Underlying this Biblical fable is the notion that without a common language, people can't work together.

But in our extended time in Spain, we simply didn't find that to be the case. Sure, there were times when a common language would have made our lives easier. But with kindness and a little creativity, we found we could function quite well. Perhaps the best example of this was our almost daily ritual of ordering a beer at the end of each hike.

Sometimes, even before locating our room in the inn in which we were staying, we went in search of a bar where we could get a cold beer. Once we found one with an open table, I generally went up to the bartender, smiled and made eye contact, held up two fingers, and said, "Cerveza?" In almost every instance, the bartender smiled back and placed his hands in front of his chest, one a short distance above the other. Then, with a quizzical look, he moved his hands farther apart to ask me if we wanted small beers or larger ones. I responded with a corresponding hand sign (typically farther apart). He then pulled out two glasses and poured the requested size of what was, in most such establishments, the only beer on tap. When the full glasses were placed on the counter, I held up my credit card. The bartender brought over a little device onto which I tapped my card. I then nodded, said "Gracias," and took the two glasses of beer back to our table where Bev and I celebrated the end of another long day. An exchange almost exactly like this one occurred at least thirty times on this trip, and most times, the important transaction was completed with just two stated words. While we rarely shared a language, we did share a desire to get something done... and some common kindness, as most of the Spaniards we encountered did their best to make us feel welcome in their country.

The beautiful humanity we witnessed across this great nation would be welcome in any society.

We saw parents and their children sitting and playing together in large open squares in Burgos, León, and the other larger cities, demonstrating family ties at least as strong as what we might witness back in the United States. We walked by large groups of locals sitting in outdoor cafés, often engaged in intense but cordial discussions. It reminded us of retirees meeting for coffee in neighborhood diners near our home, wise men and women working to solve the problems of the world (or at least lament the shortcomings of those in a position to do so). We encountered a few workers who seemed to dislike their jobs, but so many others who took obvious pride in the service they were providing. Most days, we witnessed examples of the rich history of the Spanish culture and the pride that was felt toward their nation and especially their autonomous region.

We may not have shared a language with many of the countless Spaniards we encountered, but we shared a sense of humanity and decency. When we compared ourselves to these fine people, we saw far more similarities than differences.

Which brings us back to the Harley-riding, soccer jersey-clad older man in the vineyard outside of Estella. Just like we completed our trek on the Camino de Santiago, we hope he can someday complete his ride on Route 66. Because regardless of culture, or nationality, or language, we all have dreams we want to fulfill.

Chapter Four

Immersing Ourselves in the Spanish Culture

Nájera to Burgos

We woke up eager to leave Logroño.

Bev and I had nothing against this growing and bustling university town. But of all the large cities we visited during our Camino, Logroño was the one with which we never felt a genuine connection. It was perhaps because we were there for just one night and could explore little of the city's history. But after a week of traipsing through the calm Spanish countryside, we found Logroño to be very hectic. And, oddly, a little intimidating.

After a wonderful breakfast buffet at the Los Bracos Inn, with scrambled eggs, bacon, sausages, and all the other items we had been enjoying, we were ready to tackle the long, eighteen-mile route to Nájera. Or at least most of it.

We had hiked almost eighteen miles each of the first two days, but the temperatures had been much cooler and there had been abundant shade or clouds (or downpours of rain) each day. As we prepared to leave Logroño, the forecast was for a high near ninety degrees with intense sunshine. According to our guidebook, there would be little shade on this long route. Particularly at our age, it again made little sense to walk eighteen miles in those conditions simply because that was what the route suggested. It's not uncommon for pilgrims to hike until they are tired and then try to get a taxi to shuttle them to their next hotel. We opted to cut a portion of some of the longer and hotter routes from the start.

As we checked out of the hotel, we asked the clerk to call for a taxi. It arrived quickly, and we were soon on our way to Navarette, the first town on the route. From this point, we ended up walking around eleven of the eighteen miles, less than we might have preferred, but it made the day much more manageable for the two of us. We had decided that as long as this intense heat continued, we would continue utilizing that strategy as needed, and we didn't believe it diminished our Camino in any way.

WITH OUR EARLY START and shortened route, we made it to Nájera much earlier in the day, around 12:30 p.m. In need of some healthier food after our bar food tapas of the previous evening, we stopped at a restaurant just off the trail and had a very nice lunch of baked cod in a red sauce with large salads, bread, and beers. It was an excellent meal that met our needs perfectly.

Nájera is an ancient town of 8,500 perched on the banks of the Río Nájerilla. Our hotel for the evening was the Hotel Duques De Nájera, which had been restored from an old 17th-century building. It was the first inn we stayed in on this trip that we were eager to leave the next morning. Our room had an air conditioning unit, but as we had found in other Spanish hotels, it provided little cool air. We tried to open the window of our second-floor room, but it was jammed and would only open a couple of inches. Then later, we were afraid to open the window at all, fearful the entire unit would fall out of the opening. It made for a warm and stuffy evening.

In our ongoing quest to find a restaurant that offered early dinner service, we found one that opened at 6:00 p.m.; we returned just a little after it opened. We sat on a large, paved terrace alongside the river, and several pilgrims had come to take advantage of the rare early opening time. There were perhaps ten or twelve tables spread out over the large patio, and just one server was taking care of this large number of hungry customers. There was little doubt he had too many tables to reasonably cover, and it was soon apparent that exemplary customer service wasn't his strong suit. As we watched him gruffly interact with others in an otherwise beautiful setting, the scene was reminiscent of the "Soup Nazi" in the *Seinfeld* episodes, but without the really good food. His angry antics elicited different responses from those around us. Some were irritably offended while others found his antics to be comical. Bev and I just wanted to eat our burgers, pay, and get back to our hotel. After a lengthy wait, we did just that.

When we returned to our hotel, the room was still hot. To create just a little ventilation, we opened the window as much as we could without it falling on top of us. Then around 9:00 p.m., we realized that just under our second-floor window was what we suspected was an outdoor bar. There was thankfully (for us, at least) no loud music, but it sounded like a large crowd was having a boisterous good time. We ended up closing the window when it came time to get some sleep. The room was stiflingly hot, but we slept better than we might have anticipated.

IN A VARIETY OF ways, our stay in Nájera had been memorable for the wrong reasons. The next morning, we ate breakfast and then left as quickly as we could. As we tried to leave, the route took some odd turns and became challenging to follow. As we climbed a hill on what we hoped was the correct path, I said to Bev, "It's like this shitty little town doesn't want to let us go." But go we did, gladly.

What followed, ironically, was one of the best days of hiking we experienced during our Camino. On our thirteen-mile route to Santo Domingo de la Calzada, after a steep climb of a couple of miles out of Nájera, we followed a long stretch of gently rolling hills on asphalt and then dirt and gravel. With no loose rocks or "dragon's teeth," it made for a very enjoyable walk.

Around five miles into the route, we met a young (at least young to us—they were likely in their early forties) married couple from Great Britain. While Bev walked with the wife for a few miles, I talked with her husband, a London police officer who had been banking vacation time for several years to take seven weeks to walk the Camino Francés. It was fascinating to hear him talk about his job and the challenges of law enforcement during the pandemic, a time when no one was typically out and about unless they were doing something nefarious. He shared stories about working at the 2012 London Olympics and the coronation of King Charles earlier in 2023. It was a fascinating conversation, and the miles went by quickly.

Bev would later share that the wife, a delightful young woman, was a breast cancer survivor who was walking in part to raise money for research to hopefully someday eradicate that disease. We would see this couple off and on for the remainder of our Camino. But on this day, we were particularly blessed to spend a few hours with two very nice people from another culture.

WE EVENTUALLY STOPPED TO eat a snack and said our farewells to this interesting young couple before continuing our walk into Santo Domingo de la Calzada. Of the locations we had visited thus far on our trek across northern Spain, this historic city was the one most heavily steeped in Camino history. The namesake of this town of 6,600, Dominic de la Calzada (Santo Domingo), was known for his work in improving the route for pilgrims, building hospitals, roads, and bridges along what is now known as the Camino Francés.

Our lodging for the evening was in the Hotel El Molino De Floren, an inn that had been built in an ancient building that formerly served as a water mill for this ancient town. While not a luxurious hotel, it was a definite step up from where we had stayed the previous evening. It had no air conditioning, but the windows opened wide (and didn't seem ready to fall out).

On a very hot and sunny Sunday afternoon, we went exploring this fascinating village and toured the Cathedral de Santiago de la Calzada. While we would visit cathedrals in larger cities that were more massive and more ornate, the cathedral in Santo Domingo was still impressive, particularly for a town of this size.

One of the most iconic legends of the Camino de Santiago, the "Miracle of the Rooster and the Hen," is associated with this town and its cathedral. According to this legendary tale, in the early days of the Camino, a devout German family stopped to stay at an inn in Santo Domingo as they traveled to Santiago de Compostela. The family included a handsome young son who captured the attention of the innkeeper's daughter. When the young man rejected the advances of this young woman, she became very upset. In retaliation, she placed in the young pilgrim's bag a silver cup from the inn. Upon telling her story, the young man's bag was searched, and he was arrested for theft and sentenced to death.

The boy's family continued to Santiago to complete their Camino and to pray for their son. On their return, they stopped in Santo Domingo to give their final farewells to their child, who they assumed, by now, had been executed. They found him still hanging from the gallows. As they stood in shock, they heard their son's voice suggest that his life had been saved through the intervention of St. Dominic, who was aware of his innocence. Realizing their son was still alive, they rushed to the home of the sheriff to ask him to take down their son from the gallows. The sheriff was eating a chicken dinner when the parents arrived, and, upset at having his meal interrupted, told the frantic parents that their son was as alive as the roasted rooster and hen he was about to have for dinner. With that pronouncement, the two chickens sprouted feathers and began walking and cackling across the table. Stunned and convinced of the innocence of the young man, the sheriff immediately went to take him down from the gallows, pardon him, and allow him to return to Germany.

As I read about the "Miracle of the Rooster and the Hen" on a display board inside the cathedral, I found it to be an amusing story, perhaps a rare example of the sense of humor of the Roman Catholic Church. But then we noticed that, in the back of the cathedral in Santo Domingo, there is a small chicken coop containing a hen and a rooster, both "descendants" of the original pair from the days of St. Dominic. I quickly realized that, to some, even the most comical of miracles is not a joke.

AFTER OUR QUICK TOUR of Santo Domingo, we returned to our hotel, where we experienced the two highlights of our stay in this village. First, we gathered up our dirty clothes (virtually everything except what we were wearing), put them in a plastic bag, and for ten euros, had them washed and dried. Bev particularly found laundry service to be the source of great joy on the Camino. Besides appreciating anything that made her happy, I enjoyed not having wet clothes hanging all over our small hotel room.

Then at 7:00 p.m., we went downstairs to the little dining area where we enjoyed a three-course pilgrim's meal. We both started with fresh tomato slices drizzled in olive oil, then Bev had tuna-stuffed cannelloni and I had slices of grilled pork, and we finished with slices of cheesecake, all with a bottle of vino tinto for sixteen euros for each of us. It was a wonderful meal at any price and the cap on what had been a very good day.

As we prepared to leave the Hotel El Molino De Floren the next morning, we handed our key to the innkeeper, the same gentleman who had checked us in the previous afternoon, who had served us our dinner, and who had made our café con leches that morning. He was a tall, middle-aged man with glasses and unruly hair who exuded a sense of calmness to those around him. As we prepared to leave, in a deep, raspy Spanish voice, this kind man wished us "Buen Camino" and shook each of our hands. He likely goes through this ritual at least fifty times each week, but we appreciated what seemed like a genuine expression of goodwill. It was a prime example of the type of hospitality we had hoped to experience as we trekked across northern Spain.

WE LEFT SANTO DOMINGO at 7:45 a.m., an early start designed to avoid some of the heat that was forecast for later in the day. As we approached mid-September, we noticed a subtle climatic change, with cooler mornings followed by afternoons that were sunny and warm but not as blisteringly hot as we had earlier experienced.

It was another good day of walking as we traversed the fourteen-mile route to the small town of Belorado. The trail was primarily a smooth natural surface of rock and dirt, and though there were a handful of steep inclines and descents, we mainly faced gently rolling hills. On our way, we passed from La Rioja to Castilla y León, the largest autonomous region in Spain. The transition was subtle, but after passing through countless Rioja vineyards for the past week, we found ourselves walking through enormous fields of sunflowers, acres of these huge daisy-like plants, all seeming to face the same direction.

Though we walked on natural surfaces, most of the trail was alongside or near highways. For much of the previous few days, we had hiked through the countryside, our solitude interrupted only by the occasional tractor, herds of cattle, or other pilgrims. Now, walking along a busy modern highway, the roar of large trucks was jolting.

Still, we appreciated the beautiful simplicity of what we were doing, joining thousands of peregrinos each day in walking westward along one of the most historic pilgrimage routes in human history. All of us on that trail, the few we knew and the many others we would never meet, shared the goal of reaching Santiago de Compostela, the burial site of the Apostle James. While Bev and I didn't share the religious motivation of many of our fellow hikers, we had a deep reverence for the countless pilgrims who have followed this path for centuries. On a typical day, we saw, passed, were passed by, or otherwise interacted with perhaps a hundred other hikers. Every one of those pilgrims had a unique story and a different motivation for completing this pilgrimage, but all shared the same ultimate destination. Collectively, this westward movement made for an amazing force, and being a part of it was both empowering and humbling.

A FEW MILES FROM Belorado, we stopped at a bar for a quick lunch of salami and cheese sandwiches on freshly baked bread with large bottles of Coca-Cola. The server asked if we wanted glasses with ice and lemon, and with that question, he became our best friend that day. That cold, sweet drink and those hearty sandwiches gave us the boost we needed to get to our hotel.

We made it to Belorado, a town of 2,000 on the Río Tirón. We stayed that night in the Hotel Jacobeo, a building constructed in 1850 that had been converted into what was advertised as being "completely restored and transformed into a coquettish two-star hotel." With a tagline like that, we weren't sure what to expect. But our small, second-floor room had two large windows with shutters that opened to a little false balcony. Not sure about "coquettish," but our room was clean, functional, and a little charming.

After dropping our backpacks and suitcases in our room and before even showering, we went to the bar on the first floor of the hotel for a beer and then in search of a farmácia. The beer was good and cold, but the pharmacy was closed and wouldn't reopen until 5:00 p.m. as staff members were on their siesta.

The notion of the Spanish and their "siestas," or afternoon breaks, has in the United States become a source of comic relief. But we found that the concept is taken seriously in Spain, a "non-negotiable" in a society that seems much slower-paced and less stressed than in the United States. Though there were certainly exceptions, the Spanish people seemed more community-minded, more social, and just happier. While one can't infer a causal relationship between daily siestas and greater happiness, there are obvious lessons available for our frantic society.

In our quest to find early dinner service, Bev found on the internet a nice restaurant that, according to its website, opened at 7:00 p.m. When we arrived just after the advertised opening time, some other pilgrims we knew told us the restaurant actually opened at 8:00 p.m. We walked to a pizza restaurant and found it opened at the same time. In serious need of calories, on our way back to the hotel, we stopped at a bar and had various tapas items and a glass of wine. For tapas from a bar, this wasn't bad fare, skewers of grilled shrimp in a garlic sauce, skewers of mushrooms on toast, and some sort of breaded fish, all heated in a microwave. It wasn't a great deal of food, but tastier than some tapas we had been consuming. Still, we had a serious need for some vegetables and other healthier foods.

THIS NIGHT IN BELORADO brought some clarity to a couple of issues we had been facing, both related to food. Throughout most of my adult life, I have been heavier than I would prefer. While training for a marathon twenty-five years earlier, while biking across Missouri and hiking across the Grand Canyon, and at the start of our cross-country bicycle trip, I had never dipped below 200 pounds, considerable weight on my 5'10" frame. I had worked on this issue during the pandemic, and as we left the United States for our Camino trip, my weight had stabilized at around 187. Bev, on the other hand, was much closer to her ideal weight.

From the first day of our Camino, I had eaten a large breakfast each morning, often consumed some sort of pastry with a café con leche on the trail, had whatever lunch we could find each midday, and had a beer at the end of most days and wine with dinner. But those dinners were too often sparser than we wanted, and a few tapas items weren't providing the calories I needed.

Each day, we were averaging a thirteen- to fourteen-mile hike over varied terrain with twenty-pound packs on our backs. Particularly given my weight and body type, I was burning thousands of calories each day. As we approached the end of our second week on the trail, I sensed I was shedding weight much more rapidly than I had expected. This was something I would have welcomed at virtually any other time in my life. But we still had a month of long hikes ahead of us, and the daily cannibalization of my body, which included the burning of fat stores *and* muscle, was not sustainable. I needed more calories each day. Though not nearly at the same pace as I was, Bev was also losing weight. If we were going to make it to Santiago, we would need to find those additional calories wherever and in whatever form they were available.

Complicating our calorie deficit was the second issue, our ongoing challenge of finding a restaurant that served dinner at what we considered a reasonable time. Every day as we walked into a new town, we began searching for a restaurant where we might eat a decent dinner before 8:00 p.m.; as often as not, we were unsuccessful in that quest. Particularly during the first few weeks of our Camino, we found this to be very frustrating.

With countless hours of time for contemplation on the trail, I gave this issue considerable thought. I came to realize that the core issue was not the timing of dinner service in Spanish restaurants. Rather, the real problem was us trying to follow our customs and habits in a foreign country, and it simply wasn't working. If we wanted a good evening meal, we could have simply waited until 8:00 or 8:30 and the options would have been virtually unlimited. For a variety of reasons, that didn't work for us, but it evidently works well for the Spanish people, which is what is most important. We were visitors to this amazing country, and we needed to find ways to adapt to the culture so our dietary needs would be better met.

The largest meal of the day for many Spaniards is often at midday, and the time for what we call lunch extends to 3:00 or 4:00 p.m. When we arrived in a city or village early in the afternoon, we considered eating a large late lunch and then a smaller dinner. To keep walking while avoiding unhealthy weight loss, we needed calories and sleep, with dinner time related to each. We would find ways of addressing both needs.

The fifteen-mile route from Belorado to the tiny village of San Juan de Ortega was classified by our travel company as "moderate to strenuous," which we found to be an accurate description. It was a long but good day as we walked on smooth, natural path trails. It had rained the night before and it would rain after we arrived in San Juan de Ortega, but the trail was smooth and firm all day. We were approaching the two-week point of our Camino, and after the deluge of the first day, we had experienced only a few raindrops. We hoped our luck would continue.

Shortly after we left Belorado, we started to climb at a barely perceptible pitch for the first six miles. Then, as we were leaving the little village of Villafranca, we started climbing steep inclines that continued for the next three miles to the top of Alto Mojapán. We descended a half mile, then climbed a companion mountain, the Alto Pedraja.

In between, we stopped and ate an apple at a nondescript little picnic area next to one of the most somber sites on the Camino Francés. At this location, at the start of the Spanish Civil War in 1936, over 300 people were executed and buried in shallow graves, one of many violent episodes that characterized this brutal conflict. We subconsciously felt an odd darkness as we sat at a picnic table and then looked at the simple marker commemorating the site. We were compelled to quickly move on down the trail; most pilgrims likely passed this spot without even realizing the significance of the location.

Around 1:30 p.m., we arrived at San Juan de Ortega, a tiny village with just a few buildings but a huge Catholic church. We were skeptical about the offerings available in this little twenty-inhabitant burg named after a disciple of Santo Domingo. What followed was one of the most pleasant stays of our Camino. Our reservation was at the Centro de Turismo Rural La Henera, a ten-unit hotel that overlooked the trail. When we arrived at the inn, a sign on the door indicated that "reception" (i.e., check-in) was at the Bar Marcelo, which was at the other end of the village, but still perhaps only 100 yards away; this is a small village.

We walked to the bar where we found the young English couple from a few days earlier seated at a table. They invited us to join them, and we had a very enjoyable lunch, sharing stories from the trail and discussing plans for the next few days. With our intention of making this our large meal of the day, I had a jamón (Spanish ham) and cheese omelet and salad, and Bev a platter of grilled pork and salad, all with a large beer. It was a good and hearty lunch, and we enjoyed reconnecting with this nice young couple. In time, they had to move on to the next village where they were staying that night.

We checked into the inn and walked back to our room. It was a large, second-floor room with a small balcony that overlooked the trail and large church. We opened the large windows and immediately felt the cool breeze rustling through the curtains. After some of the warm rooms we had stayed in that week, this was a welcome change. And then it started to rain, which added to the ambiance of this quaint, tiny village. It was surreal as we stood at the window and watched as dedicated pilgrims plodded down the trail during this brief shower. We were happy, and grateful.

For dinner, we returned to the Bar Marcelo, and each had a large salad with tuna and a glass of vino tinto. As we ambled back to our room, enjoying the cool night and receding sunlight, we reflected on what had been such a good day on the Camino.

GOOD TIMES ON A hiking trip like this one can be short-lived, and the following day was one of the most challenging we faced as we walked across Spain.

With a tough day ahead of us, our plan this Wednesday morning was to get an early start on our sixteen-mile trek to the large city of Burgos, the site of our first planned rest day. (The route ended up closer to seventeen miles, and probably posed more mental challenges than physical ones.) The same friendly folks who ran the Bar Marcelo were also proprietors of the inn in which we were staying. As breakfast was included in our travel package, after we finished dinner, we were given a large bag with a lot of food for the next morning. For each of us, there was a ham sandwich, two kinds of pastries, a bottle of orange juice, a bottle of water, an apple, and a banana.

The next morning, as we were preparing to leave the inn, we consumed everything in the bag, saving the fruit for later. We needed fuel for a challenging hike, plus it was all quite tasty.

We departed just as it was turning light, a little sad to leave the tiny hamlet of San Juan de Ortega. Within the next six hours, we transitioned from quiet and idyllic to loud, busy, and urban, and the change was a bit of a shock.

But first, we had a couple of long, very rocky hills to climb and descend, and those posed some challenges given the loose terrain. But, of course, we made it up and down. Then, as we were walking on the natural path trail alongside a rural road, with no one in sight (at least that I was aware of), I heard Bev behind me say, "Buen Camino." I thought she was being extra nice to me, or simply trying to break the monotony of a long morning. So, in response, I said something along the lines of, "Well, 'Buen Camino' back at you!" Then, I looked to my right and saw a young woman passing, startling me. Of course, she said to me, "Buen Camino" in what sounded like a distinctly American accent. Especially when I thought someone was from the United States, I often asked them where they were from, anticipating they would say something like "Colorado" or "Minneapolis." This young woman's response was simply, "France." So much for my knowledge of accents. She quickly strode on, probably glad to distance herself from this eccentric old American.

We stopped at a café along the way and had an excellent ham and cheese sandwich and a can of Coca-Cola. After climbing through forested hills and then alongside a highway, we were soon on the outskirts of Burgos, a large metropolitan area of 180,000 that was also geographically expansive; our hotel was on the other side of the city, so we still had a long way to walk. And it was getting hot. What a difference a day can make.

As we approached the edge of Burgos, we had a decision to make. Our guidebook included a passing reference to a "delightful riverfront path" into the city that followed the Río Arlanzón. Though this alternative route offered shade, tranquility, and beauty, it was not well marked and, as a result, offered a greater possibility of venturing off-route in this large, spread-out city. Concerned we might get lost, we opted to follow the more traditional path into the city, the route that was included on our GPS maps.

We wish we had not.

The route took us around the Burgos airport, a barren and wind-blown area, and then for miles through a never-ending industrial area. We were walking on concrete or hard tile surfaces alongside large and loud trucks, and we crossed streets and highways, trusting that motorists would obey stop signs and traffic lights. Unlike in the countryside where you could walk almost mindlessly and the miles seemed to pass quickly, on this brutal afternoon, we kept moving quickly, but the progress seemed so slow. During good days on isolated parts of the trail, with occasional shade sheltering us from the harshness of the sun and no noises beyond our shoes shuffling on the ground, we felt almost revitalized by the Camino. But on this day, as our feet pounded on the pavement and we warily maneuvered across commercial driveways and streets, hoping an aberrant truck driver wouldn't run us over, we could feel the energy drain from us.

In time, we transitioned from an industrial district to a densely populated commercial area. But as our hotel was on the far side of the city, we still had three miles of walking on concrete to get there. Finally, we made it to the hotel, our legs tired and our feet sore. It had been an unexpectedly tough day. And after spending days walking through rural areas, the hustle and bustle of this loud and vibrant city was like a slap in the face.

OUR HOTEL FOR THE next three nights was the Hotel Rice Bulevar, a nice and modern hotel in a residential part of the city. The next day was our first scheduled rest day, which we really needed after our challenging walk into the city. Then the day after that, we were scheduled to hike to Hornillos del Camino, another tiny hamlet, and then be taxied back to Burgos. Though we considered these shuttles to be just another potential complication, it was nice not to have to pack and unpack and lug our suitcases for an extra day.

Tired and hungry but not wanting to go searching for a full-service restaurant with early dinner service, we found a bar just down the street from our hotel that offered, you guessed it, tapas items. But unlike much of the other bar tapas we had been having, we ordered our selection off a menu, so it was cooked fresh rather than being reheated in a microwave. It was the best tapas we had since leaving Barcelona. As we were standing at the bar showing our ignorance of the Spanish language and culture as we had pondered what to order, a young man seated nearby and drinking a cup of coffee asked if we needed help. We didn't even need to respond. He described the various items on the menu and made suggestions about what we might like, a very kind gesture that we appreciated. We each had a variety of small items, including a deep-fried crab cake, a mayo-based salad of some sort with shrimp, a small roll with thinly sliced salmon, and a small burger of ground beef that had been mixed with different spices and ingredients, all with some very good red wine. By this point on our Camino, we were kind of over tapas for a while, but this was tasty.

Afterward, we went in search of ice cream and found a gelato shop just off the city square near the Burgos Cathedral. We each ordered two scoops and ate our cold treat on a bench on the edge of the huge open square. On a Wednesday night, it was a joy to sit and watch hundreds of Burgos residents, young and old, families and couples, and groups of friends, enjoy this beautiful September evening. One of the most indelible impressions of the Spanish people we took from our Camino, the sense of family and community that seemed to permeate the culture, was reinforced as we sat on that nondescript bench. As we watched the simple spectacle of people enjoying and appreciating each other's company, aided by the two scoops of gelato, we felt just a little revitalized. We were tired, but it had been a nice evening.

THE NEXT MORNING, AFTER a later and more leisurely breakfast, we gathered all our dirty clothes, put them in a couple of plastic bags, and went in search of a lavandería, or laundromat. Bev and I had not relied on coin-operated washers and dryers since early in our marriage, over forty years earlier. Our vision of a laundromat from the United States was one with rows of machines and ample areas to sort and fold clothes. In the cities of Spain, our lavandería experience was quite different.

We found one a few blocks from our hotel, a small storefront with three washers and three dryers, most of which were already in use on this Thursday morning. Still, we got everything clean, dry, folded, and back in our hotel room in less than an hour. In our regular, non-Camino lives, though admittedly we had to do our laundry at home, we had come to largely take clean clothes for granted. When you are living a relatively spartan life, you develop a much greater appreciation for the simple things in life (like wearing a shirt that doesn't smell).

Our main chore for this rest day completed, we went to tour the Burgos Cathedral, or as it is officially known, the *Cathedral of St. Mary of Burgos*. It's a massive structure with huge spires rising from the enormous Gothic edifice that was constructed in phases beginning in the thirteenth century. When we entered the sanctuary, we were struck by the vastness of the space and by the ornate carvings in marble, stone, and wood. So much of the interior was flaked in gold. Not unlike what we had observed in the cathedrals of Barcelona and Santo Domingo, this was almost over the top in terms of splendor, ornateness, and lavishness.

After touring the cathedral, we opted to have our largest meal of the day around the lunch hour. Around 1:00 p.m., we stopped at a restaurant across from the main entrance to the cathedral and secured an outdoor table under an awning to protect us from the midday sun. We each had a glass of vino tinto, large bowls of Catalan soup, a broth-based soup with ham, garlic, and pieces of a doughy substance; it was excellent. Bev then had a sautéed piece of fish with a salad and I had pollo asada, a chicken leg quarter marinated with different spices then grilled and served with French fries (which we are finding to be very popular on the Camino). It was a nice meal, and very filling.

As we sat under that restaurant awning waiting for our food, we talked about how, at times, we needed to remind ourselves of what we were doing. Though at that point we had been in Spain for two-and-a-half weeks and our Camino was around one-third completed, our surround-ings sometimes still seemed almost dream-like. In a bit of awe, we noted we were seated at an outdoor café across from the cathedral in Burgos, Spain, people-watching and sipping wine. What an amazing blessing!

On our way back to the hotel, we found an ATM where we withdrew some euros and stopped at a grocery store where we bought some snacks for the coming days on the trail. Then I was able to address a simple issue I had been pondering but had not yet solved. What little hair I still have on my head, I try to keep very short. (With long hair at this point in my life, I might resemble Doc Brown from the *Back to the Future* movies.) I hadn't visited a barber shop in ten or fifteen years. (Paying someone to cut my hair would be like hiring a farmer to harvest a couple of tomato plants on your back porch.) I had thought about bringing my rechargeable clippers, but for whatever reason, I had not done so. I didn't want to introduce myself to the Spanish barber shop culture if it could be avoided, so I needed to find some hair clippers. As we walked back to our hotel, we passed a small store that exuded the charm of an establishment that had a little bit of everything. As I looked around, I found a set of electric clippers that would serve me well. When I went to pay, the older lady at the check-out stand asked me, in a mix of Spanish and English, if I wanted warranty verification. I wasn't exactly sure what she was saying when another older lady took over, opening the box, taking out the warranty brochure and writing the purchase date on it, and attaching the receipt. These clippers weren't expensive, and I knew that if they didn't work, I wasn't going to trudge back to that store to return them. So, I began to inform this lady that we didn't need her to go to all that trouble when Bev lightly touched my arm. We were in Spain, she was non-verbally suggesting to me, and if warranties are important in this country, I needed to just roll with it. Point well taken. The clippers worked just fine, and this lady could rest more easily knowing that I was covered if they had not.

THAT NIGHT, IN SEARCH of a lighter but healthier evening meal, we found our way to, believe it or not, a storefront Taco Bell just off the main city square. We each had a burrito bowl, which appeared to be the most nutritious item on the menu, and a can of local beer. Then, given my continued mission to counter my rapid weight loss (or at least that was what I told myself), I also had an ice cream sundae. We hadn't traveled to Spain to eat at a fast-food restaurant popular in the United States, but it fit our needs nicely.

As we walked back to the hotel, Bev and I talked about the beauty of this wonderful city, with its tree-lined walkways and striking architecture. And on this Thursday evening, just as they had been the night before, the good people of Burgos were out in force, drinking in outdoor cafés, walking around with their families, and just enjoying another gorgeous evening.

During our cross-country bicycle ride six years earlier, Bev and I adopted the practice of using rest days to assess and discuss how we were doing. We did this again as we walked along the beautiful walkways of Burgos. We agreed we were doing well, a little banged up and sore, but otherwise hanging in there. After the hectic and horrendous first day, there had been doubts about whether we could make it all the way to Santiago, as well as some questions about whether we even wanted to do so. Now, two weeks in, we were confident we could be successful and, though we had adopted the notion that we didn't *have* to do anything, we were now sure we wanted to see this journey to its conclusion. One of my greatest concerns before we even departed for Spain involved being able to function without sufficient mastery of the Spanish language. After two-and-a-half weeks in the country, while our Spanish wasn't much improved, we both agreed we were functioning just fine. And though walking an average of fourteen miles each day was challenging, and though conditions often made the hikes even tougher, we were finding enjoyment and satisfaction each day.

But the next day, we were scheduled to begin a several-day crossing of a plateau area called the Meseta, an undeveloped "wilderness" that has, over time, taken on mystical qualities in Camino lore. After the busyness of this beautiful and vibrant, but very loud and busy, city, we anticipated another jolting change.

Our day of rest behind us, we were ready to get moving again.

LIFE LESSON # 4

"TRYING TO LIVE YOUR 'REGULAR LIFE' IN A FOREIGN CULTURE IS A RECIPE FOR FRUSTRATION."

"If you reject the food, ignore the customs, fear the religion, and avoid the people, you might better stay home."

James A. Michener

WE WERE HUNGRY AND a little frustrated, again.

We were a week into our Camino, and on this night, we were enjoying the hustle and bustle of the city of Logroño. We were getting into the groove of our daily routine and were increasingly enjoying the local culture and the Spanish people. But one issue continued to frustrate us, a challenge we had faced since our first night in St. Jean Pied de Port.

If only we could find a serviceable restaurant that offered dinner service at what we considered a decent hour.

We had read about the wonderful cuisine in this part of Spain, particularly the bountiful pilgrim's meals that offered three courses and a bottle of wine at a reasonable price. When we scoured the neighborhood around our upscale Logroño hotel, we found several enticing restaurants, many offering the aforementioned pilgrim's meals. But every one of these establishments opened for dinner at 8:00 or 8:30 p.m.

Back home in our "regular" lives, dinner time most evenings was around 6:00 p.m., and we were comfortable with maintaining that schedule in Spain. Of greater importance, with an average of fourteen to fifteen miles of hiking each day, by 9:00 p.m. each night we were tired, and we seldom stayed up past 10:00. Having dinner at 8:00 or 8:30, getting back to our room at 9:00 or 9:30 and going straight to bed seemed uninviting and counterproductive to our digestive systems.

No, we wanted to eat dinner at 6:00 or 7:00 and struggled to understand why restaurants weren't serving dinner at that time. Particularly during the first couple of weeks of our Camino, we resorted to having dinner in bars, eating microwaved bar food masquerading as "tapas" that was barely filling and seldom very good. We were trying to follow our regular schedule in this foreign land, and the results were unappealing.

Similarly, early in our time on the trail, we often walked into our destination town or city in the mid-afternoon in need of special bandages or some other product from a pharmacy. Invariably, we found those establishments closed, the workers having gone home for their siesta, or afternoon break. They would return and reopen in a couple of hours. This, too, had been frustrating in the beginning, as pharmacies in the United States seemed to always be open, ready to cater to your needs at virtually any hour. In time, we just took for granted that most pharmacies and other stores would be closed during mid-afternoon hours and made a mental note to take care of that business in the early evening.

After a couple of weeks, we realized we were trying to live our Midwestern, older American lifestyle in the middle of Spain, and it wasn't working. Nor should it. The Spanish way of life seemed to work just fine for those who lived here, and we were mere visitors.

As an illustrative example, if you visit the non-touristy parts of large American cities, you're likely to see people with their heads down, rushing to get to their destination, often oblivious to their surroundings and feeling the pressure to work harder and accomplish more. Conversely, we found the Spanish culture to be far more relaxed, less hectic, and the people seemingly happier. To the American way of life, taking a couple of hours in the middle of the afternoon to decompress and get some rest and then return to finish your day would be viewed as a waste of time and a blow to productivity. But would it be, especially if workers were more contented and less burned out as a result? Perhaps we could learn some lessons from this less hectic approach to life.

Similarly, Spaniards started and ended their days later, following a schedule far different from that of the typical American. As such, serving dinner at 6:00 p.m., which we found to be very rare, made little sense except when it was provided to meet the needs of Camino pilgrims.

If we wanted water with a meal, as is offered at virtually every American restaurant, we had to purchase a bottle. We were seldom provided a glass of ice with a can of soda, but when we were, we came to view such a mundane practice as a luxury. And at the end of every meal, it was a struggle to get the server to bring our check, a far different practice than at restaurants in the United States where moving you along means more customers (and more tips). We took this reticence to ask for payment as an implicit suggestion to "take your time." There were countless ways in which our experience on the Camino differed from what we were accustomed to back home.

But we were in Spain! We were the visitors, and we were the ones injecting ourselves into their culture. It took us a while, but we soon realized the silliness of being frustrated with practices in this country that differed from those more familiar to us. If maintaining the same routine, diet, customs, etc., was important to us, as James Michener suggested, we probably should have just stayed home.

For the remainder of our Camino, we seldom found a restaurant that served dinner that perfectly fit our schedule. But we adapted, and needless to say, we didn't starve. If we arrived at our destination before 3:00 p.m. or so, we found many restaurants were still serving lunch with a menu similar to what they would again serve later that evening. As a result, we often had our large meal of the day as a late lunch. And we found that a 7:00 p.m. dinner time was very workable for us when available. And if an available restaurant was a special one, we ate as late as 8:30 on a few occasions, and these were some of the most memorable meals we experienced.

We found that attempting to live our "regular lives" while visiting a foreign land not only resulted in great frustration, as we experienced in the early part of our time in Spain. It also prevented us from experiencing the uniqueness and vitality offered by this vibrant culture. When we relaxed, adapted, and went with the Spanish "flow," our experience was much richer and our time much more enjoyable.

Chapter Five

Entering the "Mystical Meseta"

Hornillos del Camino to Carrión de los Condes

Based on what we had read and heard, we were leery about entering "the Meseta," the iconic plateau-like region between the large cities of Burgos and León. We shouldn't have been.

In our research before traveling to Spain, we had read accounts of countless pilgrims who bypassed this section of the Camino Francés, simply taking a bus from Burgos to León. The Meseta was described as hot, barren, undeveloped, monotonous, and downright boring. Some authors called it the "mind section" of the Camino, the part that played head games with hikers as they traversed this 100+ mile section of the trail.

Conversely, in the guidebook we were using, author John Brierley, the late sage of the Camino de Santiago, wrote of the route out of Burgos, "Today we leave behind the built environment and enter the relative wilderness of the sublime *Meseta*." After experiencing the bustling culture of Burgos, a "sublime wilderness" seemed almost attractive.

Because of these diverse viewpoints, as we prepared to climb onto the Meseta, we weren't sure what to expect.

What we found was a region that was relatively undeveloped, with long, barren sections and a hot and dry climate, though temperatures were not as elevated as we had experienced earlier on the trail. And we didn't feel like the experience on the plateau "played with our mind," at least no more than did other parts of the Camino. It was challenging, at times boring, and, in some respects, fascinating.

RESTED FROM OUR DAY exploring this vibrant city, we left Burgos at 7:45 a.m., an early start for us as we wanted to beat any heat and harsh sunshine that might arrive in the afternoon. Our route for the day was thirteen miles to Hornillos del Camino, where we would be picked up and shuttled back to the Hotel Rice Bulevar. It was cool and breezy as we departed, and the sun never broke through the clouds all day as temperatures struggled to reach the mid-seventies. It made for a great day of hiking, and with just a few long inclines and downhills, the miles passed fairly quickly as we made our way through the suburbs of Burgos and into the rural area that led to the Meseta.

The sun had not fully risen as we left the hotel, and with the cloud cover, it was still a little dark. At an hour when, back in our pre-retirement days, we would have been gearing up for a long workday, the city seemed to be just waking up. We learned that the typical workday in Spain is from around 9:00 a.m. to 3:00 p.m. and then from around 5:00 to 8:00 p.m. The common dinner time is around 9:00 to 10:00 p.m. (hence our challenge in finding early meal service), and a typical adult bedtime is 12:00 midnight to 1:00 a.m. We found this to be so unlike in the United States.

It was a relatively easy day of hiking, largely level for the first eight miles, followed by a gradual, steady climb for a few miles, and then a sharp downhill into Hornillos. We stopped for a snack in the village of Tardajos and had café con leches and shared a slice of potato casserole and some sort of baked dish with tuna. The snack was more filling than tasty, but the coffees were excellent.

After an uphill section around halfway through the route, we entered what our guidebook calls "the relative wildness of the mystical Meseta." We didn't even realize we had entered that region until we reviewed our materials later. Such is our focus, perhaps too sharp in retrospect, on simply getting to the destination for the day. Over the next week, as we made our way to León, we would come to marvel at the unadorned simplicity of this flat hilltop region.

We made it to the tiny village of Hornillos del Camino, population seventy, at around 1:00 p.m. As the tour company could not secure lodging in this little Camino crossroads, we were to be picked up at 3:00 p.m. and shuttled back to the Hotel Rice Bulevar in Burgos. Hornillos is a nondescript and rather bleak outpost, but we found a table in a nice little restaurant where we had our large meal of the day. It was good to relax and take in the Camino vibe of the pilgrims packed into the compact dining room. We each had large beers and a large salad (again with pasta and tuna), then I had a bowl of white beans with clams simmered in a white wine sauce, and Bev had what could only be described as a Spanish version of Spaghetti Bolognese. These were dishes we had never tried before, and they were excellent.

Feeling very full after such a delightful meal, we walked out of the restaurant at around 2:15 p.m. to find it raining. As we were always concerned about being stranded in these little villages (I guess we trusted the Camino more than we trusted the travel company), Bev called to confirm our pickup. As if on cue, a taxi driven by a very personable young man from Burgos arrived to pick us up.

It was odd and a bit surreal to travel back over the terrain we had hiked earlier in the day, a thirty-minute drive alongside a route that had just taken us five-and-a-half hours to walk. The driver spoke serviceable English and explained to us various points of interest along the way. Oddly enough, we likely noticed more of the countryside on this drive than we had while walking two to three miles per hour.

As we were arriving back at the Hotel Rice Bulevar, the young driver indicated he was scheduled to pick us up the next morning at 9:00 a.m. to be shuttled back to Hornillos del Camino to resume our hike. When we asked if he could pick us up an hour earlier, he said he could certainly do that, but that he was concerned that the hotel breakfast didn't open until 8:00 a.m. After parking in front of the hotel, this outgoing Spaniard got out of his taxi, walked into the hotel, and asked the front desk clerk when breakfast would be available the following morning. He wanted to make sure we would be fully fueled when he drove us back to the trail. Breakfast would open at 7:30 a.m., as we had thought, but we were touched by his concern.

As he grabbed our backpacks and hiking poles out of the trunk of his taxi, I handed the driver some euros and thanked him for taking such good care of us. It was an awkward moment, as he kind of looked at me oddly as I was offering what I thought was a modest tip, but one that had been earned by this caring young man. He eventually accepted it.

Especially after leaving Barcelona, which had a more American feel regarding the issue, we tipped very little. Our research suggested that tipping in Spain is very rare and should be reserved for times of particularly stellar service (such as, I thought, this one).

Throughout most of my adult life, I was a steady, fifteen percent tipper, which was always considered an appropriate amount of gratuity for good service. Since the pandemic shut everything down and industries struggled to regain their footing, and as individuals working in the service industry literally kept us alive with their efforts, I had (I think) become a much more prolific tipper, helping ensure that American workers could make a more adequate living.

In Spain, as we were reminded by the skeptical look on the taxi driver's face, tipping is just not very common, as servers, drivers, and other service workers receive a much more livable wage. Lesson learned, and we rarely left a gratuity for the remainder of the trip. We maintained, however, a subtle, subconscious feeling of guilt on those many occasions when the service was particularly stellar.

It had been a relatively easy day, but we were still tired. Our large meal of the day behind us, after getting cleaned up and needing a light supper, we walked back to the same Taco Bell and had a similar meal to what we had eaten the previous night. Monotonous, yes, especially to Bev, but healthier and more flavorful than the microwaved tapas we would have otherwise likely found on a Friday evening in this bustling city.

BY THE NEXT MORNING, though we found it to be a wonderful city, we were ready to leave Burgos behind us. After enjoying a large breakfast promptly at 7:30 a.m., we found our happy taxi driver waiting for us right outside the hotel a little before 8:00 a.m. It felt odd to be driven back to Hornillos, where we had ended our hike the day before, but we were finding these shuttles to be minor and usually insignificant complications. The drive passed quickly, with our driver again sharing information about the area we had passed through the day before.

It was another fairly easy day, a twelve-and-a-half-mile route with a climb back onto the Meseta, a few rolling hills through a virtually shadeless stretch of trail, and then a long, gradual downhill to Castrojeriz, an ancient hilltop town that for centuries served as an important crossroads for peregrinos.

Bev Walking into Castrojerez

In time, we made it to La Posada de Castrojerez, our hotel for the evening. Located just off the Camino and converted from a sixteenth-century mansion, we found La Posada to be an interesting and comfortable twenty-one-room property. Though the inn had a front desk, we were prompted to check in at a restaurant across the street. Though polite and professional, the lady at the restaurant who gave us our room key seemed to speak no English, which, given our limited Spanish, could have posed an insurmountable challenge. But, of course, all three of us were able to communicate adequately.

With our room not yet available, we went in search of a restaurant for a beer and a light lunch. We ended up at a bar where we each had a slice of Spanish omelet, the casserole made with potatoes, eggs, onion, and in this rendition, jamón and cheese, served with bread. We had enjoyed this tapas staple several times, but this was the first time we had been served this item at room temperature. We were a little surprised when we watched the server place the slices on plates without heating them, though we learned this was not uncommon in Spanish bars. Sitting at an outdoor table at this bar in Castrojerez, drinking a frosty mug of local beer, we found the cold slices of Spanish omelet to be surprisingly tasty.

When we had checked into the hotel, the lady had informed us that dinner would be served in a dining room around the corner from the inn beginning at 7:00 p.m. We arrived at around 7:01, excited about having a full dinner at an early hour. We were seated at a large table in the traditionally decorated dining room where we enjoyed a wonderful, three-course pilgrim's meal. From the rustic old beams across the top of the ceiling to the stone walls to the worn tiles on the floor, the room reeked of history.

Bev ordered the gazpacho, a cold soup made of blended vegetables that is common in Spain, baked chicken with fries, and rice pudding. I had a large salad with pasta and tuna, grilled pork loin with fries and very ripe sliced tomatoes, and a large ice cream sundae. With a bottle of Spanish red wine, the total cost per person was fifteen euros, or around $16.00. It was a delightful meal in a warm and comfortable setting, the type of dining experience we had hoped for on the Camino.

EACH DAY, WE ENCOUNTERED many pilgrims on the trail, typically sharing "Buen Camino" greetings. Whenever I sensed a hiker was from the

United States (based on their accent, which occasionally, as I have suggested, allowed for haphazard accuracy), I often asked where they were from. In the days before arriving at and after leaving Burgos, some of these encounters were a little odd, admittedly coincidental, and a bit weird. As we were working our way through a rocky patch of trail between San Juan De Ortega and Burgos, we happened on a married couple from Sacramento. The husband was outgoing and boisterous, and the wife was much more subdued. After telling them we were from Chicago, I mentioned we had a sister-in-law who lived in Sacramento. The gentleman asked for her name. Sacramento has a population of well over half a million, so the odds of these two older Californians knowing her were very remote. I told him her name, and though our sister-in-law has some notoriety in the California state capital, they didn't know her. I suggested that, on a visit many years ago, we had visited the San Francisco 49ers training camp in Rocklin, a suburb of Sacramento. At this point, the husband and wife got into a tiff about when this could have been and when the 49ers stopped having training camp there. Not wanting to be a bystander in what was becoming a marital dispute, we quickly said our goodbyes and moved on. Luckily, we didn't encounter these folks again for the remainder of our Camino.

Then, as we were hiking into Castrojerez, we came across an older gentleman who stood out because of his long, flowing white hair and matching long beard, and a huge backpack that he couldn't seem to get centered on his back. He had passed us as we had stood on the side of the trail eating a snack. I said hello to him and noted his American accent from his response as he continued down the trail. Perhaps an hour later, as we passed him, I asked him where he was from. He said, "Chicago. Well, really, north of Chicago." As we live north and west of Chicago, I turned around and went back to ask him specifically where he was from. He said, "Gurnee" (another suburb located a half-hour north of where we live). I responded that we lived in Arlington Heights, to which he said, "No shit!" Over the next few miles, as we walked together, we learned of his story. His wife had recently passed away, and he was walking the Camino in part as a response to losing her. He suggested he had hiked the Appalachian Trail, the Grand Canyon, and in other notable locales.

He was a fascinating guy. He had somehow misplaced his cell phone and was crossing the Camino with no means of reserving lodging, seeking help, or letting his family know how he was doing. But he was completely unconcerned, confident that everything would work out. I admired his carefree attitude and positive outlook, particularly given the recent loss of his wife. Over the next couple of days, we saw him a few times walking with an American woman we had also met earlier, likely older than him, and also traveling alone. After that, we never saw either of them again, but we're confident they made it to Santiago de Compostela.

And then, as we were finishing our wonderful pilgrim's meal in Castrojerez, at a nearby table, we heard multiple mentions of "Kansas City." Before moving to the Chicago area in 2022, we lived for decades in a northern suburb of Kansas City, Missouri, not far from the small town in which I grew up. For many years, I served as the superintendent of the mid-sized school district in this community. As we were leaving the dining room, we stopped at the large table and asked the boisterous group of peregrinos if we had heard the mention of Kansas City. An older couple brightened up and said they were from a larger suburb just south of where we had lived. I shared that we had recently moved from the Kansas City area after living there for many years. In passing, I mentioned that fourteen years earlier, I had retired as superintendent of the school district in that community. With a look of astonishment, the lady told us that their grandchildren were students in this school district.

To place the level of strangeness of this encounter in perspective, we were all seated in a small dining room in Castrojerez, Spain (population 500). We had lived in a small community (population 10,000), and I had been associated with a medium-sized school district. We overheard the mention of Kansas City and stopped at the table to inquire about these folks, something we would not typically do. We were all a little dumbfounded, and the coincidence of this encounter was astounding. But as we were finding, that is how the Camino can work its magic.

After some easier days, we faced a much more challenging hike on the sixteen-mile route from Castrojerez to Frómista. The accurate forecast for the day was for cool temperatures and overcast skies with a good chance of rain.

Castrojerez sits atop a hill offering impressive vistas of the terrain onto which we would travel, and those views were daunting. After a pronounced downhill hike into the valley of the Río Odrilla, which we crossed early on the route, we could see the trail up ahead. It was a long, steep climb onto Alto de Mostelares, the entry to this section of the Meseta. From our perspective in the valley, the trek up that long hill seemed never-ending. And it was long (though not as long as it looked from a distance, perhaps a mile-and-a-half) and very steep, with inclines approaching 10%. As we descended into the valley, Bev and I both saw this challenging climb approaching us, though we didn't discuss it until we reached the top. When we reached the base of the incline, we simply got out our hiking poles and powered to the top. Though certainly challenging, it was not as difficult as we might have anticipated.

When we reached the top, the views were incredible. We looked back down the trail into the valley and toward where we began the climb, and the perspective of where we had started and where we ended was impressive. We have hiked on mountains in Colorado, on mountainous sections of the Appalachian Trail, and into and out of the Grand Canyon. But rarely have we had such an unencumbered view of the route we had taken. It was amazing to look back down at where we had started and gauge the steepness of the climb. It was a neat moment.

We hiked along the Meseta for several miles and then began a long, steep descent into the valley of another river, the Río Pisuerga. On the way down, we crossed paths with a recently retired couple from Alaska, two very nice and interesting people. Bev and I are likely winding down from these long, multi-week excursions, but these two younger folks were just getting started and their perspective was refreshing. We talked about travel and grandchildren and, as the wife is a working author, our respective thoughts on the writing and publishing process. We saw this couple many times before and after we arrived in Santiago, and we always enjoyed hearing their views on the Camino issues of the day.

In time, we said our farewells to our new friends from Alaska and continued our hike into Frómista. The rest of the day was uneventful until, as we were approaching a little village where we planned to get some lunch, it started to rain. With the lessons learned on our first day on the Camino, we quickly put on our ponchos, which covered both us and our packs. It was day sixteen of our journey, and after the deluge we encountered on the first-day hike from St. Jean to Roncesvalles, we had encountered no more than a few raindrops; we had been fortunate. On this day, it never rained hard but continued for several miles.

We made it to a very nice albergue in the little village of Boadilla del Camino, where we had delicious cheese omelet and tomato sandwiches on homemade rolls with cans of Coca-Cola. It was a wonderful lunch in a very nice setting, just the boost we needed to get to Frómista.

The dining area of the albergue was crowded, with pilgrims who were staying there for the night or who, like us, were seeking a nice lunch, and some who were simply waiting for the rain to stop. As we sat there after finishing our sandwiches, we talked with a young man from Dallas whom we had met on the second day. Hiking with his wife, he had a distinctive appearance that made him easy to spot, unruly black hair and always wearing a long-sleeved white shirt and black shorts. And he seemed to be everywhere. We had talked briefly two weeks earlier, sharing little more than our places of residence. Since that day, every time he saw me, he yelled, "Hey, Chicago!" I always responded with a little less exuberant, "Hey, Dallas."

He and his wife were seated at the next table with a large group of hikers. I always wore a dark green, wide-brimmed Tilley hat, but I had taken it off when we sat down at our table. As we were finishing our lunch, I looked over and said, "Hey, Dallas." He looked at me with a befuddled expression before responding, "Hey, Chicago. I didn't recognize you without your hat." As he had apparently never seen my largely bald head, I said, "So, you like my haircut?" We ended up having a pleasant conversation about professional football, me a Kansas City Chiefs fan and "Dallas" a Cowboys fan. For months after returning from Spain, I still smiled when I remembered hearing, "Hey, Chicago!" yelled from some random restaurant patio as we walked by.

As we left the albergue, the sky was still overcast and dreary, but the rain had stopped. Then, a mile or so down the trail, the precipitation started again, and we scurried to put our ponchos back on. But within five minutes, the rain stopped, and the sun was shining for the first time that day.

For the last couple of miles into Frómista, the trail ran parallel to the Canal de Castilla, an ancient, man-made, narrow waterway that had been constructed for irrigation and transportation purposes and to power old corn mills. Now, the canal is used for the irrigation of neighboring fields and occasional excursion barges. With the sun adding to the now humid conditions, the trees that lined the canal provided needed shade, and the water added to the ambiance of the hike.

Soon, we were walking through downtown Frómista, which, given the town's population of 850, didn't take long. We found our inn for the evening, the Hotel San Martín, which was described by our tour company as a "friendly hotel." Not sure about that, but we found it to be a quintessential Spanish inn on the Camino, with a handful of basic rooms over a bar and restaurant.

AFTER WE TOOK OUR backpacks to our room, even before getting cleaned up, we went down to the bar for a beer. With the suddenly abundant sunshine, the afternoon had warmed up nicely. The bar had a patio area with awnings and umbrellas, so we went outside to enjoy the fresh air and ambiance on this Sunday afternoon in Frómista.

There is a strange phenomenon on the Camino, different flocks of people inadvertently working their way together across northern Spain. As a result, we saw many of the same people day after day, those who had started on the same day we did and were following the same itinerary we were. And for those using the same travel company we did, we often stayed in the same hotels.

A prime example of pilgrims following the same itinerary as us was an older German couple we saw every day. They were sitting outside the bar drinking a beer, and as we had not shared a conversation, we asked if we could join them. It was very nice to get to know these two fascinating people to whom we had previously said little more than "Buen Camino."

Though you would never know it by the speed with which they hiked, we suspected they were around ten years older than Bev and me. The husband spoke a little English (and, of course, we spoke no German), and we learned about their very interesting backgrounds. Both grew up and lived in what, until the fall of the Berlin Wall, was East Germany, a totalitarian, Communist state controlled by the Soviet Union. Though I was curious to hear stories about what it was like living in such a controlled political state, it seemed inappropriate to focus on that aspect of their past. Both are retired structural engineers who are clearly proud of their careers. They talked about the various hiking trips they have taken to destinations around the world. The wife's eyes lit up when her husband told us their daughter would join them in León to hike the last third of the Camino.

We found the Camino to be a true, multicultural experience, and it was wonderful to share stories with these very nice folks from a country that had at one time been an avowed enemy of the United States. But on the Camino de Santiago, we all shared a common goal and a common destination.

FORMERLY A VITAL CROSSROADS on the Camino Francés, Frómista over the centuries has lost both population and significance. Just down the street from our hotel is the most noteworthy attraction in this village, the Iglesia de San Martín, or the Church of Saint Martin, considered one of the best examples in Spain of churches built in the Romanesque style.

Constructed in the eleventh century, the church is beautiful, with turrets and other rounded sections highlighting each corner. Though not huge like some of the cathedrals we had visited, the church still seemed almost out of place in this small town.

For dinner that evening, we arrived at the hotel restaurant just as it opened at 7:00 p.m. We enjoyed another delightful pilgrim's meal. Both of us started with a large salad, then Bev had the pan-seared trout, and I had the grilled chicken with a special sauce and fries, and both ended with some ice cream. All with a bottle of Ríoja red wine, it made for another wonderful meal.

Perhaps in part because of the challenging climb at the start of the day's hike, we were particularly tired and each of us commented about having sore legs. Perhaps it's also because we've been completing long hikes almost every day and we're approaching the halfway point of our Camino.

The next day, our seventeenth since leaving St. Jean Pied de Port, offered the easiest day of hiking we had experienced as we traveled a largely flat thirteen miles from Frómista to Carrión de los Condes. With a shorter route, we left later than usual, around 8:15, and we found chilly and blustery conditions, with temperatures in the fifties and a persistent wind. Bev and I wore jackets most of the day, and I had to use the drawstrings on my hat to keep it from flying away. Still, it was a nice day of walking as we traveled alongside roads for several miles before moving onto a gravel path that followed the Río Ucieza, a nondescript but occasionally scenic little river. There were no significant sights to see for the first eight or nine miles, so we were able to average around three miles an hour, which is very good for us given stopping and starting, carrying daypacks, etc. There were no albergues for that first stretch, so we ate bananas and peanut butter sandwiches Bev had made that morning. They were tasty and served us well.

In time, we made it to the little village of Villalcázar de Sirga, where we stopped at a nice bar with a shaded patio and shared an order of seafood paella. We talked briefly with the couple from Alaska and with the trio of ladies from Wisconsin. And, of course, we shared greetings with "Dallas," who seemed to be everywhere.

For most of the day, we had been walking on a flat trail alongside a highway. But after Villalcázar, we turned onto a natural path with a slight but steady incline that followed a straight line into Carrión de los Condes, our destination for the evening. Starting several miles outside of town, we could see the buildings of this small city in the distance, though our progress in getting there seemed excruciatingly slow.

Carrión de los Condes had the feel of a robust medieval city on the Camino Francés, though its current population of 2,200 was continuing to decline from its peak of 10,000. Our lodging for the evening was located on the other side of town, and we passed countless bars, albergues, and retail shops that seemed to cater to the needs of pilgrims. But though the route on that Monday had been a shorter one, we were still tired and looking forward to getting to our hotel.

EXCEPT FOR THE HOTELS in the larger cities of Pamplona and Burgos, we always approached our lodging in each town with a bit of trepidation. We hoped, and based on experience were starting to trust, that they would be clean and serviceable, but expected little more. When we had read in our materials that in Carrión de los Condes we would stay in what was formerly a working monastery that had been converted into a luxury hotel, we were brimming with curiosity. Our experience far exceeded our expectations.

After crossing the Río Carrión, we saw to our left the imposing edifice of the Real Monasterio San Zoilo, an ancient building that had served as a Benedictine monastery between the tenth and nineteenth centuries. It was massive and had an ancient feel as we passed through a garden area to get to the main entrance of the hotel. Though now a private lodging establishment, the property had retained much of its historical charm and significance. It was stunningly beautiful and provided a most unique and memorable lodging experience.

When we walked into the reception area, we could hear Gregorian chanting in the background. Though the soothing rhythmic sounds were recorded, it was as if a group of monks was chanting in an adjacent room. After checking in and receiving our key, we quickly toured the area around the reception area; this was truly a magnificent and historic property.

Our second-floor room was large and modern, a welcome change from the cramped accommodations we had been experiencing the past several nights. It had large windows with shutters that opened onto a beautiful courtyard, openings that, like in every other inn we had stayed in since arriving in Spain, had no screens. The restaurant in the hotel was somewhat famous and opened for dinner service at 8:00 p.m. Wanting the full experience in this wonderful hotel, we made a reservation. With such a late dining time, we decided to have a late lunch. We went to the bar and had beers and shared a personal-sized pizza with Spanish ham, cheese, and mushrooms. It was a tasty treat in a neat setting.

As the dinner hour approached, we dressed in the nicest clothing we had brought and went in search of this noteworthy restaurant. Located in an out-of-the-way location, the restaurant is called Las Vigas, or The Beams. We understood the name the instant we walked through the door because, throughout the large dining area, huge, rough-cut wood beams dominated the décor. And many of these beams were fairly low to the floor. I'm no giant, but as we were escorted to our table, I had to duck multiple times to avoid banging my head on one of these prominent structural supports. We are confident these beams were part of the original construction when the monastery was built centuries ago.

And the food was as amazing as the surroundings. With some of the house vino blanco, we started by sharing a salad made with fresh, ripe tomatoes diced and drizzled with olive oil and balsamic vinegar. Then, we enjoyed a dish that was famous in this region of Spain, grilled squid. We both ordered this house specialty, and it was served with some sort of green sauce, which we used only sparingly. From the first bite of the grilled squid, we could taste the wonderful, intense flavor. At times in the past, we have tried regional fare that simply, in our view, didn't live up to the hype; the grilled squid at Las Vigas in Carrión de los Condes, however, was as flavorful as we had anticipated. We ended the evening by sharing a piece of cheesecake served with a scoop of what was called "cookies ice cream." The setting and the wonderful meal with such unique cuisine made this one of the most memorable meals Bev and I have ever enjoyed.

With a shorter day ahead of us, we slept a little later the next morning. As we prepared to leave the room, Bev commented that she had not wanted to get out of bed, feeling the warmth and security emanating from this former monastery. I agreed, and we both hated to leave. But our Camino beckoned us, and after a nice breakfast, we toured the beautiful cathedral that had been attached to the monastery. It was impressive and ancient enough that archeological digs were continuing in parts of the building.

We were five days and sixty miles from León, the next large city and the location of our last rest day. We had found our stride, gaining enjoyment from each hike, and finding the challenges of the "mysterious Meseta" to be more hype than real.

With the halfway point of our Camino approaching, we were increasingly confident we could actually pull this off and make it to Santiago de Compostela.

"OCCASIONAL MONOTONY IS NOT NECESSARILY A BAD THING."

"The monotony and solitude of a quiet life stimulates the creative mind."

Albert Einstein

WE HAD ENTERED THE "sublime Meseta," and we weren't sure what to expect.

Known as the "mind" or "contemplative" section of the Camino Francés, the hundred miles or so between Burgos and León are famously flat, relatively barren, largely undeveloped, and considered boring. Because of this negative reputation, some who traverse the Camino Francés simply bypass this section, taking a train or bus from one city to the next. We never considered such a drastic measure, missing over one-fifth of the Camino route. But as we climbed up and onto the plateau we would cross for several days, my attitude was an odd mix of nervousness and intrigue. We were two weeks into our trek across Spain, so I wasn't concerned about our physical capacity to complete this section. But I wondered how I would handle the barrenness, the monotony.

A few months before leaving for Spain, I had read the book, *Walking with Sam: A Father, a Son, and Five Hundred Miles Across Spain* by Andrew McCarthy. McCarthy is best known as the "Brat Pack" actor who starred in movies like *St. Elmo's Fire* and *Pretty in Pink*. Following a complicated and troubled period of his life a quarter century earlier, he had walked the Camino Francés and found the experience to be life-altering. As his son, Sam, was approaching adulthood, McCarthy wanted him to have a similar experience. The book details their Camino adventure.

McCarthy discusses in great detail the challenges, primarily mental, he encountered the first time he traversed the Meseta. At one point in his earlier trek across this barren section, he had experienced a seemingly un-provoked meltdown, dropping to his knees as he sobbed uncontrollably. In his writing, one can sense the trepidation he felt as he and his son approached this challenging part of the trail. With this in the back of my mind, I wondered, "How bad could this part of the Camino actually be?"

As it turns out, not that bad. And in some odd ways, kind of pleasant.

We had just finished a rest day in Burgos, a city of 170,000 we had entered on a long, stressful, and exhausting slog through an expansive industrial area. Though it was a nice enough city, we found Burgos to be far less charming and beautiful than the other larger cities we passed through on the Camino Francés. Particularly from our hotel on the outskirts of the downtown area, we found Burgos to be bustling and loud.

So, our entrance into the undeveloped and unstimulating region known as the Meseta was almost welcomed. It was good to get back into the quiet, into an area largely unaffected by industrialization, a section that offered fewer encounters with other people but a lot of time with our own thoughts. In time, as we passed through towns like Castrojeriz, Frómista, Carrión de los Condes, and Sahagún, I forgot we were even passing through a "dreaded" section. And when, after eight days crossing the barren plateau, we arrived in León, we were ready to take in all that vibrant city had to offer.

Stated simply, negative experiences help us better appreciate the positive ones. If every day was a major holiday, those special occasions would have far less meaning and significance. If each day we saw a beautiful rainbow on the horizon, we would eventually stop taking notice. And from someone living in a northern climate, if every day was warm and sunny, such beautiful weather would become largely taken for granted. Especially when you have just experienced a harsh winter, those beautiful days are something to be cherished.

The monotony of the Meseta gave us time to think and to better process what we were attempting to accomplish. The flat barrenness of the plateau positioned us to better appreciate the majesty of the mountainous region around O Cebreiro and Rabinal Del Camino we would later experience. The quiet of this section helped us to welcome the vibrant atmosphere of León and Santiago de Compostela.

So it is with life in general. Past illnesses and injuries help us to not take for granted the good health we are now experiencing. Time away from family makes us appreciate the times when we can be together. And our mundane, regular lives better position us to enjoy vacations and other special occasions. The monotony helps us to better appreciate the excitement.

The Meseta was just another section of our 500-mile-long journey across northern Spain. Had we bypassed this section by riding a bus or train from Burgos to León, our Camino journey would have been incomplete in more ways than we could have imagined.

CHAPTER SIX

JUST PUTTING MILES BEHIND US

Calzadilla de la Cueza to León

THERE IS AN ALMOST inevitable part of any long journey, the dreaded middle. And as we left the monastery in Carrión de los Condes, we were right in the midst of the middle of our Camino.

Eighteen days had passed since we departed St. Jean Pied de Port, and the newness and luster of our journey had largely faded. But we still had more days of hiking ahead of us than behind us, and though we were confident we would reach our destination, it was still too far away to visualize. Add in the monotony of the Meseta, the crossing of which we had not yet completed, and the doldrums were starting to seep in.

We were, in essence, getting up each day and simply putting miles behind us. And that, from our perspective, was not only inevitable, but okay. We had experienced the same feelings six years earlier as we worked our way across the southern United States on our cross-country bicycle ride.

Every day in our "regular" lives didn't elicit fireworks and rainbows; that's what made them special when they occurred. And so it was with our trek across northern Spain.

ALL OF THIS LIKELY added to our reticence about leaving the warm and luxurious confines of the Hotel Real Monasterio San Zoilo. But with a twelve-and-a-half-mile route to the little hamlet of Calzadilla De La Cueza ahead of us, we eventually departed a little later than our typical start time. The route ended up being less than eleven miles, almost all of it on virtually flat natural trails. Most of the day, we walked through what our guidebook called "a flat and somewhat featureless landscape with little or no shade." It was a particularly barren section of trail, with no towns, cafes, water spigots, or bathrooms for the first ten miles of the day.

Unbeknownst to most, the gravel on much of the trail we followed to Calzadilla had been laid over an old paved Roman road, the Via Aquitania, which was constructed almost two millennia ago. Other than some ornate, centuries-old concrete walls that occasionally lined the trail, there were no signs that we were walking on a historically significant ancient thorough-fare. Like so much of the Camino, our time on this old Roman road was rather humbling, yet another indication of our relative insignificance in the annals of the history of this trail.

Though there were no villages or facilities between Carrión de los Condes and Calzadilla De La Cueza, there was a food truck near the halfway point of the route. Its placement was yet another example of the Camino meeting our needs. It was also another subtle sign of the commercialization that has occurred along the Camino Francés. For centuries, peregrinos hiking between these two towns had to pack extra water and any food they needed. Now, with the popularity of the Camino fueling the expansion of related enterprises, a mobile café was available to meet our culinary needs. And from all indications, business was brisk. We each had a very good café con leche and a piece of chocolate coffee cake. Clearly, the entrepreneurial spirit was alive and well on the Camino.

As we approached Santiago, the trail would get exponentially more crowded. But in this middle section of the Camino Francés, the number of pilgrims was surprisingly sparse. On a typical day in this part of our Camino, unless passing or being passed by others, or if we were walking with others, there was seldom anyone within 50 to 100 yards of us. But, except for hilly or curvy sections of the trail, it was rare to be able to look all around us and not see someone ahead of or behind us. Over the 500 miles of the Camino Francés, we were just two of the tens of thousands of pilgrims making their way westward. It was kind of like being on a huge cruise ship with 5,000 travelers and 2,000 crew members but seldom feeling cramped or crowded.

We were struck by the number of individuals walking by themselves. Some, no doubt, were traveling with a group but simply walking alone at the time. But we sensed that many were making their way across Spain by themselves. Bev and I were especially impressed by the number of young women (say, twenty to thirty years old) who were seemingly traveling alone.

After arriving in Calzedilla de la Cueza, we dropped off our packs at the inn where we were staying and walked back to get lunch at an albergue near the entrance to the tiny village. The true albergues, which are like Camino hostels that offer large group sleeping rooms, are magnets for young peregrinos. As we ate our lunch on a terrace outside the albergue, several young people were gathered in an impromptu circle passing around a guitar and singing songs, a few of which some of the young musicians suggested they had composed. It was neat to watch, reminiscent of a scene from an American commune from the 1960s. There was no competition and little apparent ego, just a group of young people enjoying each other's company and talents.

In essence, most young people traveling alone appeared to find their "tribe;" they were walking alone but as part of a large group. Still, young people, especially young women, traveling alone on the Camino Francés was impressive and something I could never have imagined doing at that age.

As we were serenaded by this impromptu band of musicians, we enjoyed a very nice lunch on the shaded terrace of this albergue. We each had a large beer and a salad (in typical Spanish tradition with tuna, corn, white asparagus, lettuce, and tomato wedges), and shared an order of calamari. In many Midwestern restaurants, an order of calamari would include small rings of squid, breaded and deep-fried; often, restaurants will include (I might say sneak in) deep-fried vegetables like red peppers. This calamari was deep-fried, but came in large, long chunks that resembled chicken strips, only much tastier. It was an excellent lunch.

We stayed that night in the Hostal Camino Real in a small and very basic, but functional, room. It differed greatly from our room in the former monastery the previous night, but it met our needs. Calzadilla de la Cueza is a tiny village that, were it not for the Camino Francés, might have little reason to exist. It had the feel of a depressed little burg, with broken-down cars and wandering chickens outnumbering the permanent residents.

Though decidedly comfortable, we were still living a spartan existence. And in those settings, you find your joy and excitement where you can. For us, and especially for Bev, a highlight of our stay here was having our clothes washed. For twelve euros, all the clothes we could fit into a large plastic bag were washed, dried, folded, and delivered to our room. Luxury is a relative term, especially on the Camino.

Even though we had left Carrión de los Condes later than usual, with an unexpectedly short eleven-mile route, we arrived at our destination early in the afternoon. The challenge of ending a short day in a tiny village, especially when the wi-fi was weak and the cell phone data reception was little better, was that there wasn't much to do during the four to five hours between lunch and dinner. This challenge was magnified when the hotel room was small. But, of course, we were able to fill our time just fine, reading, planning for the next few days, and watching programs we had previously downloaded.

The inn had a large dining room, and we were seated and ready for dinner at 7:00 p.m. We had a pilgrim's meal, a three-course dinner with wine, and it was excellent. Bev and I both had fish soup (kind of like chicken noodle soup, but with fish instead of chicken), then Bev had the Spanish version of Chicken Cordon Bleu, and I had thin-sliced beef filet, both with the ever-present French fries. Then Bev had a cream dessert of some sort with strawberry sauce and I had an ice cream sundae. It was a lot of food, but we scarfed it down.

One of the many allures of the Camino de Santiago is the constant opportunity to meet interesting people, particularly those from different cultures. At dinner, we sat at a large table of eight pilgrims. Included was the married couple from Ohio we saw most days at breakfast and then at the end of the day; they were following the same itinerary, but hiked with a sense of urgency we didn't share. Next to us was a retired military couple currently living in Texas. But most interesting were the two Italian men sitting next to us at the end of this large table. One spoke no English, but the other was very fluent. They were lifelong friends who lived in different towns outside of Venice. The English speaker was an oncologist, and he spoke eloquently about his profession, the Italian medical system, the shortage of doctors in Italy, and how the Italian retirement system was going to require him to work much longer than he had expected. It was fascinating to hear this unique and intimate perspective on the healthcare system of another country. He spoke at length about the prevalence of smoking in Italy and lamented that his grown children had taken up such a damaging habit. He was complimentary of public relations efforts in the United States that have dramatically reduced the smoking rate.

Because he and his friend had limited vacation time to complete their Camino, the doctor told us they were averaging thirty-two kilometers each day, nearly twenty miles. (Wow!) The doctor had a rugged handsomeness and looked to be in his early forties; he told us he was fifty-eight. It was one of the most interesting conversations of our Camino.

WITH MORE CHALLENGING TERRAIN and a longer, fourteen-mile route to Sahagún, we left Calzadilla at 7:45 a.m., before the sun had risen; our early start provided one of the most stunning images of our trip across Spain. Just a mile or so into the route, as we were climbing out of town, Bev told me to look behind us. Over the distant hills, the sun was just popping into view. And whether it was that beautiful, or we were just a little tired, we were awestruck by that image of the intense orange orb slightly obscured by some wispy clouds in the foreground.

It was a long and tedious day, with no particularly steep hills but a constant gentle incline for much of the route. With little memorable terrain of note, it was a quintessential day of putting miles behind us.

During our three weeks on the trail, we had become spoiled by the amazing coffee we had enjoyed, often several times each day. The rich, intense coffee combined with the steamed milk offered amazing flavors that we remember to this day. But that morning at breakfast, the gentleman serving us poured our coffee from a large pot. It had been a little nasty, the very rare subpar coffee we experienced in Spain. So, when we came to Ledigos, the first village we encountered that day, we stopped for an excellent café con leche.

On our way out of this small village, we struggled to find the trail. There was a large tourist bus parked alongside the road, and when we turned onto a road and stopped to consult the maps on our phones, (looking, no doubt, like the befuddled pilgrims we were), the bus driver honked his horn at us and pointed in a manner that suggested the Camino was in the direction we were headed. The GPS app provided by our travel company, which had served us well from the start, suggested we were walking away from the trail. We were in a conundrum.

About this time, the couple from Texas we had met at dinner the previous evening arrived on the scene. The wife suggested they didn't know where they were going. Predictably, the husband disagreed, suggesting that "Camino Ninja," the app they were using, advised that the trail was in the direction the bus driver had suggested. (Rather than "El Paso," where they were living in Texas, this gentleman was henceforth known to me as the "Camino Ninja.") Just wanting to get moving, we continued in the direction the bus driver (and the "Camino Ninja") suggested, and we made it to Sahagún with no further hiccups. We would later realize that this was the first of two times that day that multiple Camino routes were available.

Other than our brief trail uncertainty in Ledigos, it was a nondescript, rather boring day on a gravel trail that ran parallel to a major highway. We stopped for lunch at a bar in a nameless little village. When we asked the bartender if bocadillos were available, he responded in rough English that anything we asked for, they could make. We asked for ham and cheese with tomatoes, along with a can of Coca-Cola and a bottle of water. The sandwiches were tasty, but when I went to pay, the bill seemed pricey. It was one of the very rare times on the Camino we felt like we might have been taken advantage of as peregrinos.

As we approached Sahagún, we crossed a medieval stone bridge spanning a tranquil little river. Though I didn't think of it at the time, as I look back on ancient bridges like this one, I ponder how many pilgrims have crossed this span in the centuries since it was constructed. We also didn't realize the significance of the two large statues on either side of the trail just past the bridge. As we later learned, these two statues represent the mid-point of the full Camino Francés, the 500-mile route from St. Jean Pied de Port to Santiago de Compostela.

Without even realizing it, we were halfway finished with our Camino.

We were soon in the industrial section of Sahagún, passing light commercial buildings and other businesses. As we approached the downtown area, we passed a wall on which had been painted an elaborate, detailed mural welcoming pilgrims to this small city. The mural depicts with amazing accuracy the four main characters from the movie "The Way." It serves as a testament to the profound impact this poignant movie has had in luring countless pilgrims, like us, to the Camino de Santiago.

Sahagún is an ancient and historic small city with around 2,500 permanent inhabitants, though on any night from spring through fall, the population swells with hundreds of peregrinos. With a shuttle scheduled to transport us back at the end of the next day's hike, our lodging for the next two nights would be the Hostal La Cordoniz in yet another small, nondescript room. As the inn was on the other side of town, we walked through much of this very old and historic Camino crossroads city to get there.

When we checked in, the gentleman at the front desk told us in rapid-fire Spanish that the hotel restaurant started serving dinner at 8:30 p.m., too late for us. But as we were drinking a beer, we noticed that, at 2:00 p.m., the restaurant was open. So, in the middle of the afternoon, we had our large meal of the day, the three-course menu del día. Bev had a green bean dish and I had a salad and then we both had the "fish of the day," which on this day was salmon with fries. For dessert, Bev had a bowl of some sort of lemon cream concoction, and I had a really tasty piece of cake. All with a bottle of vino blanco, it was a lot of food, but we didn't need to worry about another meal for the rest of the day.

With some time to kill, and though we were tired and a little run down, we explored some of this unique city and then found a shaded bench where I read some emails and Bev listened to a book. On our way back to the hotel, we stopped at a farmácia for some bandages.

WE HAD EXPECTED THE next day's eleven-mile route to the small town of El Burgo Ranero to be a relatively easy hike. But as the forecast had predicted, when we got out of bed and looked out our small window, the rain was pouring. We were scheduled to be picked up in El Burgo Ranero at 3:00 p.m. and shuttled back to the inn in Sahagún. We had originally thought the 3:00 p.m. pickup time might be a little late for such a short route and assumed we would call the travel company to request the time be moved up at least an hour. But as we assessed the wet, cold, and windy conditions, and knew the weather forecast suggested the rain would end by midday, we opted to wait and leave Sahagún at around 10:00 a.m.

So, we donned our rain gear, which for each of us included a raincoat, poncho, long pants, and, for me, a goofy-looking plastic cover for my Tilley hat that kept flipping up the front brim. It made me look like one of those hillbilly comedians in Branson, albeit with no teeth missing. We took off for El Burgo Ranero in what was never a heavy downpour, just a pesky, steady rain that was just enough to aggravate and slow us down.

Then, around noon, the wind started blowing, hard and directly into our faces. Luckily, the rain had largely stopped, but the twenty mph winds, with occasional harder gusts, were enough to impede our progress. Our expected easy and flat eleven-mile hike had become much more challenging.

Between the rain and the winds, we weren't very interested in the surrounding scenery. This was good because there wasn't much to see, just a gravel path running alongside a seldom-used highway. Around the halfway point of the day, we stopped at a very nice, modern albergue in Bercianos del Real Camino and had omelet sandwiches on huge homemade rolls. They were excellent, the atmosphere was inviting, and we hated to leave. But we still had several windy miles to get to El Burgo Ranero, and we were getting tired.

We arrived at around 2:30 p.m. at the bar where we would meet our taxi driver at 3:00. With some time to wait, we went inside and had a large beer. As we had since the early days of our Camino, when we ordered a draft beer in a Spanish bar, we simply accepted whatever was available, which was typically either Estrella Galicia or Estrella Dramm. These were good, basic beers, and we never had to pick from a menu of fifteen or twenty draft beers to make our selection, as is common in the United States. We simply said "cervezas," held up two fingers, and watched as the server poured our beers. In some respects, greater satisfaction came from the simplicity of the offerings. After a day of fighting rain and then winds, sitting at a little table in that tiny bar, we found great satisfaction in those large beers.

Afterward, we found a bench near the meeting point where we waited for the taxi to arrive. It arrived at 3:15 p.m.; that same driver would pick us up in Sahagún and ferry us back to this same spot at 9:00 a.m. the next morning.

When we got back to our room in the Hostal La Cordoniz, even before getting cleaned up, Bev and I both just lay on our respective twin beds for a good hour. It had been an unexpectedly challenging day, a tough hike on what we had anticipated would be an easy route. It had been almost three weeks since we had departed from St. Jean Pied de Port, walking almost every day anywhere from eleven to eighteen miles, and fatigue had been building up in each of us. We were two days from León, the location of our last rest day, and we were ready to give our legs a brief break.

By the time we arrived back in Sahagún, most of the restaurants, including the one in our hotel, were closed. The guidebook we were using included a recommended itinerary that did not include an overnight stay in this town, which might explain why there weren't many people on the streets, unlike in most of the other towns and villages in which we had stayed. We walked to a small albergue near our hotel where we each had a bowl of pasta Bolognese, which was surprisingly good, and a glass of vino tinto.

On the way back to our hotel, we stopped at a little market to buy fruit and snacks, but it was closed. Sahagún had a rundown feel, a formerly prominent Camino crossroads now experiencing a state of decline. We found a little bar where I got an ice cream bar, a "Drumstick." I love these little ice cream sundaes on a cone, though I seldom allow myself to have them in my regular, non-Camino life. But as I ate it as we walked back to the hotel, with cooler temperatures and the wind still blowing, it was almost uncomfortable. We suspected we weren't yet finished with warm temperatures, but on this September 22nd, it was apparent that the seasonal weather was changing.

After a lighter-than-usual breakfast provided by the hotel, we were picked up at 9:00 a.m. by the same taxi driver as the previous afternoon, an older Spanish gentleman who exuded a no-nonsense persona. Our destination for the day was Mansilla de las Mulas (name derived from "hand on the saddle of the mules"), a bustling Camino crossroads village of 1,900. From there, we would be picked up by yet another taxi and shuttled to a hotel in León that would gloriously be our home for the next three nights. But first, we had to get back to El Burgo Ranero.

Though there were no hiccups with them the entire trip, we sometimes found these shuttles to be rather stressful. Some of the simplicity and allure of the Camino involves, in part, walking from one village to the next, eating, sleeping, and then getting up and walking to the next village. With transfers, which were necessitated by a lack of available lodging in a particular locale, we had to get to the designated meeting point by the predetermined time. It was not uncommon to arrive before the meeting time and have to wait an hour or two in a tiny village with little available to do. Always in the back of our minds was a concern that the shuttle wouldn't show up and we would be stuck in some tiny burg with nowhere to stay. These are, no doubt, "first world" problems, and we could always contact our travel company if issues arose (or taxis didn't arrive). But the concept of "shuttles" always created just a little undue stress.

The thirteen-mile route from El Burgo Ranero to Mansilla de las Mulas was uneventful. With the Meseta largely behind us and the outskirts of León a day away, we walked on a dedicated gravel path that again followed a sparsely used highway. Except for a short incline, most of the trail on this day was gently downhill. While it was cool most of the day, the path was shaded in many parts by trees that had been planted along the trail and were just approaching maturity. Because El Burgo Ranero is not a typical starting point for peregrinos, we saw relatively few people throughout the day. Of our nearly five weeks of hiking, this was the day we felt most alone, as we walked miles without seeing another pilgrim. It was a little eerie.

Bev is not a trained horticulturist, but her ability to grow plants would suggest otherwise. Especially in this section of the Camino, we saw a variety of different flowers and other plants. (It would be more accurate to suggest that Bev saw them; I more likely just walked by them without noticing.) She has an app on her phone that provides the name of a plant based on its photo. Frequently during our Camino, and especially on this day, I turned around to find Bev squatting down, taking a photo of some small, obscure plant she had spotted along the side of the trail. It was yet another way she thrived on being in nature.

With a smooth, level trail and few other pilgrims with whom to interact, a hike like this one can become tedious, not particularly challenging, but one that simply has to be completed. Bev sometimes listened to audiobooks on her headphones as we walked. I occasionally got a song in my head and started singing it (only when no one else was around, and then, barely loud enough for Bev to hear me). And occasionally, I said something completely stupid to break the monotony. As an example, as we were descending into Mansilla de las Mulas, we could see what we thought was the skyline of León in the distance. I said with an air of anticipated hilarity, "You know, if the city of León had a baseball team, maybe they could be called the 'León Redbones,'" and proceeded to offer a chorus of "Ain't Misbehavin'" in my best Leon Redbone voice. I don't know that Bev was particularly amused, and it was probably yet another example of a time when she simply tolerated me. But it provided me with a couple of minutes of needed diversion.

We stopped for coffee and a pastry at an albergue three miles outside of Mansilla de las Mulas. It was around 12:30 p.m., and we had requested that our pickup time be moved from a very late 4:00 p.m. to an hour earlier. But we had not heard back from the travel company whether they had made that change. (They had.) Regardless, we intended to use our time in Mansilla to have our large meal of the day.

We reached our taxi meeting stop, the Alberguería Del Camino in the center of this surprisingly large town, a little before 2:00 p.m. Just as we found the entrance, we saw the couple from Ohio, who told us they were staying in that albergue. (They said it was kind of "dumpy.") It did look a little depressed, so, with even lower expectations, we went to the albergue's restaurant and asked for a table. We were taken to a courtyard that was shielded from the sun and wind. And it was absolutely beautiful, with a floor made of large, rustic tiles and walls lined with hanging plants. The shade was provided by awnings and umbrellas and, in the center of the courtyard, the overhanging limbs of an old tree that had been planted outside the building. It was a neat setting.

We had the menu del día, the three-course pilgrim's meal. Bev started with a salad (with tuna, as usual), and I had a tasty vegetable stew. Then we both had the grilled hake, a type of fish that is very popular in Spain, and it was excellent. Instead of the ubiquitous French fries, the fish came with sliced tomatoes, meaning we were finally getting a good dose of fresh vegetables, which we had found to be surprisingly scarce in Spain. We each finished with a chocolate mousse served over a crumbled cookie. All with a bottle of vino blanco, it was an unexpectedly very enjoyable meal. And just as we were getting ready to pay, our taxi driver walked into the restaurant.

Our taxi driver was a smiling, affable-looking young man who seemingly spoke no English. But he got us to our hotel in León quickly and with no undue excitement. Since leaving Burgos over a week earlier and entering the Meseta, we had been hiking through a largely barren and undeveloped region of Spain, and for the past several days, we had walked largely in isolation. We had been staying in a string of functional but rather bleak inns in small villages where the inherent charm of the locale could provide only a limited amount of entertainment.

So, when the driver pulled up to the Hotel Silken Luis de León, it was as if we had been transported to another time and place. And we kind of had been. It is a huge, modern, and wonderful hotel in the heart of the city, in one of the swankier parts of León.

After checking in and locating our suitcases, we took an elevator to our seventh-floor room, our home for the next three nights. The room was large, well-equipped, and modern, and offered impressive vistas of the city. Over the decades of our marriage, Bev and I have stayed in countless rooms of this quality or better, almost to the point that we had begun to take such luxuries for granted. But as we surveyed this beautiful room and looked out our windows at this amazing city, we were swept up in a wave of gratitude; we felt so fortunate to be there.

Our itinerary called for us to be picked up at 8:30 a.m. on Saturday and shuttled back to Mansilla de las Mulas so we could walk back to our hotel in León. We were using a guidebook written by John Brierley, a revered expert on the Camino de Santiago who had passed away in the months before we traveled to Spain. In the section regarding the route into León, he suggested pilgrims might consider taking a bus from Mansilla to León to avoid the route that passes through busy industrial areas (kind of like the route we followed into Burgos). Anticipating the reaction from some of his readers, he suggested some pilgrims might consider using a mode of transportation other than walking to be a form of "heresy." (Not us; for Bev and me, that ship had already sailed.) He then offered that those peregrinos who commendably want to walk every step of their trip to Santiago should ask themselves about their purpose in doing the Camino. It's a worthy and, to many pilgrims, surprisingly complex question.

For Bev and me, as we pondered the notion of taking a taxi from Mansilla de las Mulas to León, and then a taxi from León back to Mansilla de las Mulas just so we could walk back to León, doing this made no sense. (Had we stayed in Mansilla the previous night, we might very well have hiked the eleven miles into León.) So, we canceled our shuttle and, as a result, had two full days to explore this beautiful city and enjoy the Hotel Silken Luis de León. Besides seeing what this amazing city had to offer, we would use the time to rest up, resupply, get some warmer clothing we thought we would need as we headed back into mountainous terrain, and get ready for the last fourteen days of hiking that would take us to Santiago de Compostela, And our feelings of gratitude just kept flowing.

After getting cleaned up and settled, we went out to briefly explore what we decided was the most beautiful city we visited in Spain. We ended up outside a huge, modern, and attractive six-story building located across the street from our hotel. We saw a stream of people entering and exiting from the corner entrance, and though we didn't know if it was a store or a theater or something else, we joined the throngs of Spaniards and entered to learn about the source of all this excitement. What we found in El Corte Inglés, as it is called, was one of the nicest, most well-staffed, and well-stocked department stores we had ever visited. With six attractively appointed floors, each with a different category of merchandise, it was reminiscent of the Macy's on State Street in Chicago or at Herald Square in New York City, just newer and nicer.

Looking for warmer clothing items, we made our way to the top floor, which was entirely devoted to "Sports." We looked around, but tired and a little hungry, we decided we would come back the next day to make our purchases. Also on the sixth floor was the cafeteria, an informal, sit-down dining area. Needing something for dinner after having had our large meal of the day in Mansilla de las Mulas, we each ordered the hamburguesa de pollo, or chicken burger, and fries. It was very good but much more food than we needed.

Very full, we walked the short distance back to our hotel, thrilled to have some extended time in this beautiful locale.

ON OUR FIRST DAY in León, we slept much later than usual, fatigue having accumulated over the past three weeks. After a very nice breakfast buffet, we set out to explore the very vibrant and beautiful city of León. And the city of 130,000 was hopping on this warm and sunny Saturday morning. On our way to the Catedral de León in the center of the city, we walked through a large outdoor market that had been set up in the city square. Produce, fabrics, and different types of clothing could be purchased from the many vendors. There were hundreds (perhaps thousands) of people milling about, and the atmosphere was electric. We didn't make any purchases, but it was fascinating to observe.

Breakfast at the hotel had been great, but the café con leche from a coffee machine had been mediocre. So, as we headed to the cathedral, we stopped at a small café called a "chocolateria" to get a café con leche. We knew this establishment specialized in chocolate drinks, but we assumed we could order regular coffee drinks as well. The server came to our little table and, before we could peruse the menu, started asking for our order. He started listing items in rapid-fire Spanish with an air that suggested this was what most customers ordered. With barely a notion of what we were ordering, we simply nodded our heads at what the server had suggested. Then he said, "Churros?" And we said, "Si." What he brought us were two cups of "drinking chocolate," which were like cups of really good chocolate that had been melted down to liquid form. He also brought four churros, the long, thin, sugar-coated pastries we dipped into the chocolate. Though not what we had intended and far more sweets than we needed, particularly at 10:00 a.m., it was a wonderful and memorable treat.

As we continued toward the cathedral, we passed through a series of very impressive stone walls that had been built to protect the city center. With some built as early as the first century, these were some of the best-restored Roman walls in the world. Around much of the central district had been built two sets of walls, the main protective wall spanning fifteen to twenty feet high and a shorter wall built ten feet in front of the taller one. Much of the shorter wall was topped with triangular stone structures designed to provide soldiers on the frontlines with protection from attacking forces. To even approach the taller wall, attacking soldiers had to first scale the shorter outer wall, which would be manned by forces defending the city. As we walked along the paved space between the two walls, it was easy to imagine, during a time of primitive weaponry, how formidable these walls would be. Their magnificence was surpassed only by how they had been preserved.

Soon, we were standing in front of the massive and impressive main cathedral in León, known officially as the Santa Maria de Regla de León Catedral. It is an immense structure that was constructed beginning in the thirteenth century and is considered one of the greatest architectural works of the Gothic style. It was buzzing with tourists as we entered, and we found it to be as magnificent as the cathedrals we had toured in Barcelona and Burgos. Particularly because most of the signage in these iconic cathedrals is in Spanish, I found it challenging to historically and architecturally differentiate one from the others. As we walked through the Catedral de León, though, we were struck by the thousands of stained-glass panels that dominated the huge main sanctuary. I am certainly not an expert on stained glass and am not even much of a fan of the art form. But given the intense colors of these panels as the morning sun shone through the stained glass, the sheer number of these beautiful panels was beyond impressive.

As we were leaving the cathedral, as if on cue, we heard, "Hey, Chicago" from our friend from Dallas. He and his wife were leaving León the next day, a day ahead of our schedule. Though we didn't realize it at the time, that was the last time we would hear that greeting from this affable young man.

We visited another smaller, more intimate chapel, which we soon realized was the "working" version of the huge, iconic cathedral we had just exited. We stopped at the Casa Botines, a large building designed by Antoni Gaudí that was completed in 1892. Though not nearly as weird and whimsical as some of the Gaudí-designed buildings we had seen in Barcelona, its architecture made it stand out in the skyline of León. More striking than the building that Saturday afternoon was what was taking place in the large plaza in front of it. Several people holding signs and placards were demonstrating for the protection of women. One woman was speaking into a microphone, and though we couldn't understand everything she was fervently expressing, it was clear from what we could decipher as well as the signs and placards behind her, that the group was advocating for the elimination of prostitution, pornography, sex trafficking, and other practices considered harmful to women. Everyone was passionate but calm. The small number of spectators listened briefly and then moved on, but the group was clearly getting its point across.

As we finished our exploration of the central part of León, we rode the Tren Turístico León, the "Tourist Train." It was a goofy-looking tram driven by a "conductor" in a vehicle designed to look like a locomotive. We used the provided headphones to listen to the English version of the description of the various buildings we passed by, though the static and crowd noise prevented us from gathering much information. Still, the train drove by iconic buildings we would not have otherwise seen.

By now, it was around 1:30 p.m., and we began looking for a restaurant at which we could have our large meal of the day. The area within a few blocks of the cathedral was teeming with people and the restaurants seemed overflowing with diners. And after several days of walking largely in isolation in the Spanish countryside, these swarms of people were making us a little nervous.

We started heading back to our hotel, and after walking perhaps a half mile from the cathedral, the sidewalks were much less hectic. We came to a restaurant that looked interesting and, at least from the outside, not very busy. So, we went inside to look at the menu. As soon as we walked in the door, we were asked if we had a reservation; the restaurant was packed. Of course, we had no reservation, so we were told we could select one of several empty tables on the patio between the restaurant and the street. It was a beautiful, sunny afternoon, so we took a table under an awning and started perusing the menu for Pegus, which featured pasta and meat dishes. We shared a Caprese salad with really ripe tomatoes and fresh mozzarella; it was wonderful. Bev ordered ravioli with cheese, spinach, and ham, and I selected a pasta dish with a creamy red sauce and chunks of beef and pork. It wasn't a pilgrim's meal in the heart of this bustling city, but it was exceptional.

As we made our way back to the hotel, we knew that at some point during our stay in León, we would need to do laundry. Our original intention had been to get up early the next day and find a lavandaría before the residents of the city started going about their day on a Sunday morning. But as we walked by a couple of small laundromats in the late afternoon, during siesta time, we noticed they weren't busy at all. So, we hustled back to the hotel, gathered our dirty clothes into plastic bags, and hurried back to do our laundry. Little "luxuries" took on special meaning for us on the Camino, and having clean clothes was particularly satisfying.

Still full from our large meal of the day and overflowing with clean clothes, we made our way back to the hotel, where we lounged around for an hour or so. We had noted that El Corte Inglés, the huge department store across from the hotel, was closed on Sundays. We were tired from our day of exploring León (the rest day notion hadn't quite kicked in yet, and we had likely walked nearly as far as we would have had we hiked in from Mansilla de las Mulas), but we knew we needed to get these purchases completed. Having scoped out this massive store the previous evening, we made quick work as we purchased gloves for each of us, a scrunchie kind of item to keep Bev's ears warm, a long-sleeved top for me, and two ponchos. Before we left Chicago, on a whim, we had purchased ponchos at Target. By the time we arrived in León, they had come in handy a couple of times, but they were what you might expect for ponchos purchased on a whim at Target. These new ponchos, however, were the real deal, larger, thicker, and longer, sufficient to cover both our bodies and our packs. Ponchos aren't particularly exciting... until it rains. Fortunately for us, during the two weeks we hiked from León to Santiago de Compostela, we never took these new and improved ponchos out of our daypacks.

El Corte Inglés seemed to represent yet another difference between Spanish culture and what we experience in the United States. If, for example, you were to walk into a large American department store like Macy's or Dillard's and then turn around in a complete circle, you might see anywhere from zero to maybe two employees available to assist you. If you did the same in the middle of one of the floors of this huge Spanish department store, you might spot ten employees, all ready and willing to help you in any way they could. It spoke to the service mentality we witnessed throughout Spain, and it made for an enjoyable shopping experience. It had been a wonderful, memorable day in León.

AFTER ONE OF THE longest nights of sleep we had enjoyed in some time, we had another leisurely breakfast in the hotel dining room. It was enjoyable to take our time, drink multiple cups of café con leche from the coffee machine, and discuss how we were doing. It was our twenty-third day on the Camino, and we had gotten into a groove, a routine of trying to enjoy ourselves as we progressed from one village to the next. While it had been stressful when we arrived in Spain as we struggled with the language and customs, we were now much more comfortable dealing with those issues (though our language fluency and understanding of customs weren't much better than when we had entered the country).

The experience of walking the Camino de Santiago had, thus far, exceeded our expectations, and we still had two weeks of hiking ahead of us.

Around 11:00 a.m., we walked the mile-and-a-half to the MUSAC, or Museum of Contemporary Art. Like most of the contemporary art museums we have visited, the MUSAC was quirky, edgy, and interesting.

We walked back to the hotel along a riverfront promenade, sharing the path with the many León folks who were out for a Sunday afternoon stroll. Bev and I both commented about how stunningly beautiful this city is, with wide walkways lined with flowers and other lush vegetation. The history of this wonderful city could be seen everywhere, but the way planners blended the past with modern beauty was so impressive.

We found a restaurant for a late lunch that we hoped would be our large meal of the day. It was an Italian restaurant where we found a table outside under a large umbrella to shield us from the midday sun. With a couple of beers, we shared a large salad and a pizza with Spanish ham and mozzarella. It was a serviceable meal in a very pleasant setting.

WE WERE FOURTEEN DAYS and 205 miles from Santiago, and we were now confident we could complete our Camino. But our last rest day was now behind us and we would have no breaks until we reached our destination. The week before we had arrived in León had been relatively easy, with shorter routes on smooth, mainly flat trails. But in the next two weeks, we would face another set of mountains and some very long days. Bev and I both felt as ready as we could be to make the last push to the end of our Camino.

Unknown to us as we prepared to leave León, we would face unforeseen challenges, some physical, others psychological, and still others logistical.

A common saying on the Way of St. James is "The Camino provides what you need." Evidently, sometimes it provides you with what you may not want.

"WHEN YOU'RE LIVING A SPARTAN LIFE, THE LITTLE PLEASURES TAKE ON ADDED MEANING."

"The art of being happy lies in the power of extracting happiness from common things."
Henry Ward Beecher

IT WAS A JOY to snap the photo, to capture a happy moment in the middle of a tough stretch of our Camino. We had completed several days of long, grinding hikes that had drained us both physically and mentally. We needed a light moment.

When we checked into our inn for the evening, Bev had asked the innkeeper if laundry service was available. The affable lady behind the desk said in her heavily accented but spot-on English, "Of course," and proceeded to tell us what we needed to do and how much the service would cost. We paid her the nominal charge and then gathered up our dirty clothes and took them to the same woman. A couple of hours later, when we returned from dinner, we entered our room to find our clean garments, folded and piled neatly on our bed.

Most evenings, Bev hand-washed, wrung out, and hung up to dry some of our more essential clothing, hoping that they would be ready for use by the next morning. But not on this night! To show her delight, Bev walked to the side of the bed, lay her head on top of the pile, and gently caressed our newly clean clothes. The photo of that moment is one of the most memorable that I took during our time in Spain.

For who could have imagined we would be so moved by the sight of clean clothing?

Bev Caressing Clean Laundry

Of course, Bev was being playful for the camera, but only to a point. We were at a stage in our journey where we welcomed any lighthearted moments, any reasons to smile. But we were also at a point where we found more satisfaction and joy in little occurrences, many of which we took for granted back home in our non-Camino lives. And on this evening in a nondescript little inn in a small Spanish town that otherwise provided few memories, freshly folded laundry did the trick.

We were living such a simple existence, our days focused on walking from one inn to the next. We weren't worried much about our appearance, about what brand of clothing we were wearing, about hairstyles and make-up, or calorie counts. If anything, we were eating to avoid losing weight. Though we had occasional conversations with others on the trail about our backgrounds, hometowns, and occupations, we were all just pilgrims sharing the same journey. And it was all so liberating.

With our lack of concern for what some might call the more superficial issues of life, we seemed to focus on the little things. As just a few examples, after enduring a brief downpour of rain, we relished the glorious sunshine that resulted from the parting of the clouds. In the middle of long stretches of unremarkable trail on the Camino, we rejoiced at the appearance of an unexpected truck offering coffee and treats that could replenish our spirits and our bodies. In our regular lives, our primary coffee-related challenge involves whether to brew a cup of regular or decaf, or which of the countless coffee shops located less than five minutes away we might visit. Somehow, an unexpected café au lait in the middle of nowhere made such a common item seem like a special treat.

After days of walking through secluded forests and staying in isolated little hamlets, we welcomed the amenities we experienced in cities like Burgos and León, little conveniences we seldom even thought about back home. Then, after a couple of days of the cacophony of these urban centers, we similarly welcomed a return to the quiet of the isolated trail.

Given the hectic nature of our daily lives, we seldom take the opportunity to marvel at the beauty of nature that exists around us. Walking up a long hill outside the tiny village of Calzadilla de la Cueza in the early morning hours, we turned around to witness a stunning sight as the sun rose above the eastern horizon. As we walked along the eerily quiet, history-soaked streets of Astorga, Bev stopped me, pointed upward, and said, "Look." I did just that and was rewarded with a most beautiful sight, billowy clouds and sky turned red and blue as the rising sun struggled to shine through.

After days of long hikes, my feet started to show wear and tear that was only partially eased by alternating between the two pairs of hiking shoes I had brought to Spain. As a precaution, I began carrying hiking sandals in my backpack, a pair of orange-strapped Chaco sandals that provided support without the confining aspects of a full shoe. On days when my feet were giving me problems, I often changed into the sandals for the remainder of the route. The relief was instantaneous, and I was grateful I could complete the hike without soreness. A lack of foot pain had become a luxury, and I was oh, so grateful.

This seems almost too mundane to be of any importance, but that is the point. Being devoid of foot discomfort became a source of joy. And it was stereotypical to an extreme, an old man walking around with sandals and socks, something I would never do in any other setting. But I didn't care as I put aside my pretensions so I could finish a long hike in relative comfort.

We were living a spartan life that, despite being in an unfamiliar foreign country in which we weren't conversant in the language, was surprisingly uncomplicated. Devoid of much of the static and clutter that characterized our regular lives, even in retirement, we could focus on the simple joys we had so often taken for granted.

After we completed our Camino and returned home, we soon reverted to our regular, more rushed, and more complicated lifestyle. Perhaps we would have been better served had we maintained our simpler Camino approach to life just a bit longer. But because of this amazing experience, to this day, I believe I still have just a bit more appreciation for the mundane luxuries in life. And now and then, I yearn for the simplicity of life on the Camino de Santiago, for the joy of the "little things" we had experienced.

CHAPTER SEVEN

LONG DAYS AND CAMINO ICONS

Villar de Mazarife to Molinaseca

IT IS SUGGESTED THAT the halfway point of a 26.2-mile running marathon is the twenty-mile mark, the spot where ten kilometers remain. The runner has completed over three-fourths of the race, but the most challenging part is still on the horizon. As we left León, our trek along the Camino Francés was much like that. Our last rest day was behind us, we still had two weeks of hiking to get to Santiago de Compostela, and some of the toughest terrain and hardest climbs were in our future. There were abundant challenges ahead of us, mental in addition to the physical. By now, we had been in Spain for nearly a month and we were trying to milk as much out of this amazing experience as possible. But we increasingly missed home, missed our family, and missed our routines. Despite the rest days, we were physically and mentally drained and torn between wanting this journey to continue and being ready for it to end. And the most challenging one-third of our Camino was staring us in the face.

WE RELUCTANTLY LEFT THE Hotel Silken Luis de León at 8:00 a.m., an early hour for most Spaniards, and we witnessed this beautiful city come to life on a Monday morning. While we had been ready to put Burgos, the location of our previous rest day, behind us, we were hesitant to leave this wonderful setting. We had found León to exude a warm charm, a gorgeous metropolis that offered a unique blend of history, nature, and modern progress. But we had a thirteen-mile route to the outpost town of Villar de Mazarife ahead of us, and with a forecast of rising temperatures and sunny skies, we wanted to put as many miles behind us as we could before those conditions became oppressive.

There is a couple from Ohio we have seen almost daily since leaving St. Jean Pied de Port. As they hiked at a quicker pace than we did, we typically saw them at breakfast and then at the end of the day. In the second week, the husband developed severe shin splints, a potentially debilitating condition in which pain along the front of the leg becomes excruciating.

For three weeks, he could not walk more than a few steps without the pain making it impossible to continue. He had tried every conceivable remedy, from ice to anti-inflammatory pain medications to rest, yet had found nothing that would alleviate his pain to a point where he could continue walking. As a result, each morning, he watched as his wife began the route alone or with Camino acquaintances. He then took a bus or taxi to wherever they stayed that evening. It was so frustrating for him, as he had come to Spain to hike the Camino Francés rather than experience it from a bus seat or the back of a taxi.

Because the route out of León was complicated (our hotel was off route, so we had to hike some distance to simply get back to the trail), the wife from Ohio asked us at breakfast if she could walk with us as we departed the city. (She was evidently unaware of our suspect navigational abilities, as evidenced by our getting lost, twice, as we crossed the Pyrenees on the first day.) Two other women, friends from Pennsylvania whom we had seen many times in the previous several days but had not yet gotten to know, also walked with us for the first five miles until we reached the suburbs of the city. We enjoyed getting to know these ladies as we put León behind us.

In the suburb of La Virgen del Camino, we stopped for coffee and pastries and said our farewells to our hiking mates. Despite the forecast, it was still cool as we sat outside and enjoyed our warm drink, and we kind of hated to leave. But we still had eight miles of hiking to get to Villar de Mazarife, where we would be picked up and shuttled to our inn for the evening.

We arrived in Mazarife at 1:30 p.m., an hour and a half before our shuttle was scheduled to arrive. We would find it to be an odd little village of 400, a rather dead town that bore some resemblance to one of those desert outposts in an Indiana Jones movie. The major difference was that this town seemed like a ghost town, as there was no one out and about. Our meeting point for the shuttle, the Albergue Tio Pepe, had a sign on its front door indicating, for some reason, it was closed for the day. Still in search of a restaurant where we hoped to have our large meal of the day, we ran into the lady from Ohio. She suggested she had gone into a bar, seemingly the only place open in this town, and the one young lady who was the only server was "one of the rudest people" she had ever dealt with. With an hour and a half to kill and wanting a beer and something to eat, we decided we had to give the bar a try. Bev went up to the bar, which was crowded with what looked like local men. The young server never acknowledged her, ignoring Bev as she catered to the needs of her regular customers. Bev suggested I try to get the server's attention, but by this point, we were done with this young lady and her bar. We found a tiny market and purchased a bag of potato chips and cans of cold iced tea. We found a bench in the shade where we enjoyed our "lunch" and waited for our shuttle to arrive.

In time, the friendly, older German couple arrived to wait for the same shuttle. While in León, their daughter had joined them and would hike the rest of the way to Santiago. We found her to be a delightful young woman who brightened any room she entered. She speaks very good English, having completed a student exchange program in, of all places, Cedar Rapids, Iowa. We sensed the delight her mother and father felt from having their daughter with them as they completed this momentous journey. As we all sat waiting in the shade, another pilgrim, a lady from Australia who appeared to be close to our age, arrived to be shuttled to the same hotel at which we were staying. A little after 3:00 p.m., two compact cars arrived to take the six of us to our hotel for the evening. Bev and I, and our new friend from Down Under, crammed ourselves and our packs into one of the tiny vehicles.

We were driven back toward León to our inn for the evening, the Domus Oncinae, a surprisingly nice property located right on the trail that we had passed earlier in the day. The property had been constructed in the 1700s in a tiny village that dated back to the second century, but the building had been completely restored into a unique and very modern inn. It was one of the nicer hotels we stayed at on our Camino.

After checking in and taking our packs and suitcases to our spacious room, we headed to the tiny hotel bar for a beer. We ended up sharing a table with our new Aussie friend, who, Bev and I agreed, could be categorized as a "piece of work." We heard detailed accounts of the substandard lodging she had experienced on the Camino, of the poorly prepared meals she had endured, and of the many aches and pains she had developed on the trail. In time, we found her ongoing banter to be a form of comic relief, and it ended up being good to get to know someone from another culture.

Dinner in the hotel restaurant was scheduled for 8:30 p.m., painfully late for us, but it was the only restaurant in this tiny village. So, when the doors opened, we were there waiting with the nice German couple and their daughter. Having eaten little since breakfast in León, we were past ready for a good dinner. And this wonderful meal did not disappoint, the menu del día served with a very tasty bottle of Rosado wine. To start, we had croquettes, little fried pastries filled with meat and cheese, and a Caprese salad with fresh mozzarella and very ripe tomatoes. For the main course, Bev had grilled pork, and I had braised beef ribs, all with homemade chips and roasted jalapeno. For dessert, I had a piece of cheesecake. It was a very memorable, but late, meal. We returned to our room at 9:30 p.m., satisfied but almost too full to sleep.

Our route the next day from Villar de Mazarife to Astorga was very long, over nineteen miles. But our scheduled pickup time at the Domus Oncinae was for 9:00 a.m., which would put us at the beginning of the route at around 9:30. To tackle a nineteen-mile hike, especially with a forecast of sunny skies and high temperatures in the eighties, we should have departed from Mazarife two hours earlier. As there were at least four other pilgrims departing at the same time, we didn't feel we could ask for the shuttle time to be moved to an earlier hour.

So, the day before, after we studied the route and schedule, we scheduled a taxi to pick us up in Villar de Mazarife and transport us to the first little village on the route, reducing the length of the hike by around five miles. It still ended up being an almost fourteen-mile hike, but under the circumstances, we had no regrets about our decision. It made sense for us and, as the saying goes, we were walking our own Camino.

The day was still challenging, with fourteen miles of long climbs with some steep downhill sections. Late in the morning, we crossed a long, magnificent, multi-arched, and ancient stone bridge over the Río Órbigo into the ancient village of Hospital de Órbigo, a famous locale in Camino lore. Further down the trail, we stopped at an albergue in a little town with a name we never knew. In this little bar run by a loud and vivacious young woman, we ordered the "lomo y queso bocadillo" with water and a can of Coca-Cola. We weren't entirely sure what we had ordered, but when the young server brought our order to our table, we were delighted to find huge, freshly baked bread rolls with a slice of grilled pork loin and some melted white cheese. These sandwiches were wonderful and provided tasty, needed fuel for our long trek to Astorga.

The rest of the day was a long, rather warm slog into this ancient, historic city. At times, it felt like we would never get there. One of the most challenging aspects of the hike was dealing with pesky flies (the infamous "Spanish flies"), swarms of them that persistently pestered us in the still conditions for what seemed like miles. They were nerve-wracking, and there was nothing we could do about them until, finally, a breeze would blow and the flies could not fly against the wind.

After climbing to the little village of San Justo de la Vega, we could look down on the skyline of Astorga, our destination for the evening. We descended a long downhill section of the trail that had been paved with small, smooth stones. The trail leveled out near an ornate water spigot adorned with an iconic statue of a pilgrim drinking water from a gourd.

BY NOW, THE AFTERNOON was getting warmer and, for some reason, my legs and feet felt extra tired. As we made our way toward the city center of Astorga, the trail came to an odd, multi-level structure of ramps. The purpose of this monstrosity was at first unclear, but we climbed one long ramp, then turned around and climbed another, then a third and a fourth. The path leveled out, and we realized this massive structure was designed to cross one set of railroad tracks. We descended an identical set of ramps to return to ground level. In the United States, these ramps would meet building standards related to the Americans with Disabilities Act; this was one of the very few examples on the Camino Francés where accessibility issues seemed to be much of a consideration.

Astorga is an ancient fortress city originally built on top of a hill, and as we approached the historic city center, we were looking upward at buildings that had been constructed on the hill. At each little town in which we were staying, to locate our inn for the evening, Bev used the map application on her iPhone to get directions. On this day, the app sent us on an elongated route that ended up requiring the scaling of multiple flights of stairs. I was dragging, and climbing these countless stairs no doubt seemed far more excruciating than it was.

Once we reached the section of Astorga within the ancient city walls, we quickly found our hotel for the evening. The Hotel Exe Astur Plaza is described as "a charming hotel in the historic district of Astorga," and it was exactly that. With just forty rooms, this quaint inn had been beautifully restored into a modern establishment. It is located directly on one of the most prominent city squares in Astorga, the Plaza Mayor, and the front entrance of the hotel opened to a huge open space that was partially filled with tables and umbrellas for the customers of the many bars and restaurants in the area. After a long day, it was a treat to have ready access to such an inviting atmosphere. The crowd on the patio in front of the hotel was like a reunion of many of the peregrinos with whom we had been walking for the past few weeks, good people sitting around tables drinking well-earned cold beers.

Hotel Exe Astur Plaza in Astorga

After checking into the hotel and taking our luggage to our very nice room, we went down to the hotel bar and sat outside as we enjoyed our own large, frosty mugs of beer. Later, I soaked in a hot bath, and those two actions together seemed to miraculously revive me. Astorga is a noteworthy Camino crossroads town of around 11,000 permanent residents, with many historic sites and attractions. It was late in the day when we arrived, so we had little time (or energy) to take in what this wonderful little city had to offer.

The hotel restaurant opened at 8:00 p.m., workable for us if necessary, but later than we preferred. We toured the area around the square looking for a place that offered early dinner service. Around the corner from our hotel, we found an Irish bar that didn't seem to offer much traditional Irish food but was ready to provide a meal at 6:30 p.m. when we arrived. With a décor that was more rustic than Gaelic, the bar was hopping with patrons who seemed to have been enjoying themselves for some time. With glasses of vino blanco, we each had a large bowl of soup (creamy vegetable for Bev and creamy seafood for me), followed by different pasta dishes. Again, not typical Irish cuisine, but it was a filling, adequate, and early dinner.

THE NEXT MORNING, AFTER a nice breakfast buffet, we left the Hotel Exe Astur Plaza at 8:00 a.m., anticipating a tough twelve-and-a-half-mile route to the tiny village of Rabanal del Camino that would be dominated by long, constant climbs as we returned to the mountains. The day would prove to be a pleasant surprise.

But first, we had to find our way out of Astorga. It was just after sunrise when we left the hotel. As we walked down the narrow streets, Bev turned around abruptly and urged me to look at the sky. It was a cloudy morning, and the sun filtering through those fluffy clouds created a brilliant red, orange, and blue sky, a blending of colors that would be difficult to describe. It was a stunningly beautiful start to our day.

As we continued our exit from the city center of Astorga, we passed some of the iconic historic sites we had not seen the day before. We walked by the stunning Episcopal Palace that had been designed by Antoni Gaudí. Though not as whimsical and weird as Sagrada Família or Casa Mila in Barcelona, the early morning lighting accentuated the curved walls and castle-like motif of this Gaudí masterpiece. Next to it was the Catedral de Santa Maria, the most prominent Roman Catholic cathedral in the city. Though an impressive example of Gothic architecture, the large edifice was still dwarfed by what we had visited in the larger cities of Spain. As we exited the main section of Astorga, we passed by the defensive wall the Romans had built centuries earlier to protect the city from attack. We were ready to move on at this early hour, but we lamented that we had been unable to tour these relics from centuries earlier.

In time, though, we were out of the city and walking on sidewalks through the Astorga suburbs. The elevation profile for the route suggested that almost all day would be spent climbing. While we walked uphill most of the day, the incline was at times so subtle we barely realized we were climbing. Inclines are inclines, however, and even subtle climbing is extra tiring. But our hike to Rabanal del Camino was pleasant, nothing like the long, uphill trek we had anticipated.

We stopped for coffee and pastries around four miles into the route. And then, just past the halfway point, we ate some peanut butter sandwiches Bev had made a day or two earlier. They were a little stale, but still nourishing. Otherwise, it was a rather nondescript day of hiking as we gradually made our way into a mountainous area. The next day, we would reach the highest point on the Camino Francés.

We arrived in the quaint little village of Rabanal del Camino, population fifty, in the early afternoon. Our hotel for the evening, the Posada el Tesin, is located directly on the trail at the entrance to the village. Ours was a neat room with a balcony overlooking the patio of the hotel's bar, where most of the residents of this tiny burg come to eat and drink. After checking in and lugging our suitcases to our second-floor room, we enjoyed a cold beer in the shade of an umbrella on that same patio. It was a memorable setting.

After showering and lying around the room for a while, we went to explore this little village; it didn't take long. We found a little market in search of a jar of peanut butter (a rarity in Spain), but didn't find any. At around 5:30 p.m., we returned to the hotel bar and enjoyed a three-course pilgrim's meal. We each had a bowl of vegetable soup for starters, followed by fried calamari and a small salad, and an ice cream drumstick for dessert, all with a bottle of white wine. The meal was unspectacular, but at thirteen and a half euros, it was a great value. And at 5:30 p.m., no less.

There is a small monastery in Rabinal del Camino, the Monasterio Benedictino San Salvador Monte Irago. Each evening at 7:00 p.m., the monks and local parishioners offer a vespers service "in the Gregorian tradition." We had been warned that the small chapel in which this service was conducted often reached capacity, so we arrived early. As we entered the dimly lit space, we were struck by our surroundings. The long and narrow chapel looked more like a bomb shelter than a place of worship, with parts of the ancient walls appearing to be crumbling. But places of worship are what you make of them, and this one reeked of history and Benedictine tradition.

We were handed an order of worship when we entered, a lengthy document written in multiple languages, including English. Once the service began, though, we stopped trying to follow along in our native language and simply immersed ourselves in the beautiful ceremony. Except for some short readings in Spanish, German, and English, the entire service was conducted in Latin, and virtually everything was chanted. We didn't grasp a great deal of what was being said, but the service was warm and welcoming, and fascinating to experience.

We had been spiritually uplifted in an odd sort of way, and as we walked in the cool night air through this sleepy little village, we felt just a little more upbeat. We were eleven days and 163 miles from Santiago de Compostela, and we could visualize the end of our Camino. But in the meantime, we faced the highest and longest routes of our journey. We were increasingly ready to get back home, but we also realized that, like what we had experienced in that crumbling little chapel that evening, there were aspects of this adventure that were going to be difficult to leave behind.

WE DEPARTED RABINAL DEL Camino just after sunrise, and the little village was eerily peaceful on this dark and chilly morning. With our early departure, we faced a very long and tough sixteen-mile route to the suburban village of Molinaseca. We spent most of the morning climbing to perhaps the most iconic spot on the Camino Francés and then on to the highest point on the route. As we climbed, the incline was seldom steep but unrelenting for eight or nine miles.

A highlight of any pilgrimage on the Camino Francés is visiting an obscure pile of rocks with a long wooden pole sticking out of it, with an iron cross at its top. Legend has it that the cross was placed there at the behest of Charlemagne, but that may be just a part of Camino lore. The cross at the top of this otherwise nondescript pole is a replica of the original, which is on display in the Museo de Los Caminos in Astorga. Camino tradition suggests that each pilgrim who passes the Cruz de Ferro ("Iron Cross") is to bring a rock with them either from their home or that they have picked up along the Camino. It is then placed on the pile of rocks with a dedication to someone and/or ridding oneself of a burden brought with them to Spain. As the Camino sage, John Brierley, writes in the guidebook we were using, "Take time to reconnect with the purpose of your journey before adding your stone or other token of love and blessing to the great pile that witnesses our collective journeying." Beautifully stated, and yet more evidence that the placement of a stone at the base of the Cruz de Ferro has become a sacred ritual.

Cruz de Ferro

As we were continuing to climb, around four miles outside of Rabinal, we looked up to find a crowd of people making their way up this mound of rocks. The rock pile, pole, and cross were not impressive, but the ritual was surprisingly spiritual and a little emotional as Bev and I each took our turn placing our small rock (which we had brought from Illinois) on the pile and processing our thoughts.

The Cruz de Ferro has long been considered a sacred site on the Camino Francés, and pilgrims have traditionally been required to earn the right to place a rock on the pile by hiking up the mountain to get there. The arduous journey added to the significance of the ritual. But after we climbed the rubble and placed our rocks, and as we prepared to continue down the trail, we noticed that several buses of tourists had arrived. As we passed by, we were struck by the loud conversations as they filed off their buses to take in this sacred rite. It was unclear to what degree these individuals understood (or appreciated) the significance of this pile of rocks, wooden pole, and cross. But clearly, the Cruz de Ferro had become a tourist attraction, something to be driven to, looked at, and then left behind as the crowd moved on to see the next item on their checklist.

From the high point of the Cruz de Ferro, we started descending for several miles until we again began climbing, ending at the Alto Altar Mayor, which at 1,515 meters is ten meters higher than the Cruz de Ferro and is the highest point on the Camino Francés. From there, it was a steep downhill into Molinaseca, our destination for the evening. Those seven downhill miles were among the roughest and most challenging of our entire Camino.

After the chill of our early morning start and our climb into the mountains, the sun was glowing and the temperature was rising as we completed our steep descent. The trail was occasionally covered by large rock piles, some rocks were loose and slick, and there were patches of slate that reminded us of a milder version of the "dragon's teeth" section out of Roncesvalles. We were headed downhill and wanted to get to Molinaseca and out of the sun, but we simply could not go very fast. It was a long, frustrating, and exhausting day.

After what seemed like a hike that would never end, we finally made it to the village of Molinaseca on the outskirts of the larger city of Ponferrada. When we arrived at our inn for the evening, there was a notice on the door, written in Spanish and English, indicating that we should ring the bell for the hostess who was assisting a guest at another property she managed. We rang the bell, and the lady on the other end told us in rough English that she would walk down from the other property, which was around five minutes away.

We took off our packs and found some shade to shield us from the mid-afternoon sun. As we waited, a stately older American gentleman walked up to us. He said, "You've chosen wisely," and proceeded to tell us that the young lady we were awaiting was the "best hostess in the village." He briefly shared his story of how he had walked the Camino, how it had changed him, how he had returned to the United States and sold his business, and then returned to Spain, eventually settling in Molinaseca. In a calm, deep voice, this fascinating gentleman suggested we likely wouldn't know how our Camino experience had changed us until we returned home. He gave us a business card that included his website address, where he had posted reflective questions to consider about our experience. His story was fascinating, and we wished we had more time to talk with him.

As he turned to leave us, Bev asked a simple question that had been weighing on us all day. "Where can we buy a new suitcase?"

THAT MORNING AS WE were preparing to leave the tiny village of Rabanal del Camino, as I walked out of the bathroom ready to lug our suitcases down the stairs to where they would be picked up, I saw that Bev had a crestfallen look on her face. "The zipper on my suitcase broke," she told me with a touch of panic in her voice. Those are words you don't want to hear on any trip, particularly when you are in the middle of nowhere, on foot in a foreign country where you don't speak the language. We quickly strategized about how to proceed. Both of us had been using a roll of funky-looking, rainbow-colored duct tape to protect blister-prone parts of our feet. We decided we would use the last of that duct tape to secure the suitcase together and hoped the tape would be strong enough to get it to the next inn. To address all eventualities, we stopped at the little market as we left Rabanal and purchased two rolls of duct tape, likely the only such tape available in the village, but we knew duct tape was not a long-term solution. We needed a new suitcase but had no idea where we could get one.

Enter the stately older American gentleman in Molinaseca.

I suspect that over the years, he has been asked countless Camino-related questions, but this was likely a new one. He smiled and offered a detailed plan for getting a new suitcase. With his thorough directions in mind, after checking into our inn at 4:00 p.m., we scheduled a cab to pick us up at 5:00 p.m. for the fifteen-minute ride to the El Rosal Mall in Ponferrada.

Our cab driver was Luis, a very nice, jovial man who spoke virtually no English. But he carried on a conversation with us through the voice command function of the Google Translate app on his phone. He would say something in Spanish and then show us the English translation. Then we would respond, and he would read the Spanish translation. It was cumbersome, but we had a delightful conversation with this genial and helpful Spaniard. When he dropped us off at the entrance to the mall, we asked if we could schedule a return pickup for 6:30 p.m., and he said he would be there. (He was.)

THE EL ROSAL MALL is enormous, and one of the cleanest, nicest, and largest shopping malls we have ever visited, with three floors of virtually every type of store, restaurant, and entertainment venue imaginable. Having no idea where to go, and with the Spanish language signage providing little assistance, we walked down one of the many corridors hoping to find a "luggage store." Instead, we came to an enormous store called Carrefour, kind of like a European version of Walmart, only larger and with higher-quality merchandise. The store offered an extensive selection of brand-name luggage, but we still had over an hour before Luis would return to pick us up. We left the store and found an open bar, not so simple during siesta time, and had a beer. We returned to Carrefour and picked up a few needed items before selecting a new suitcase for Bev, a nice American Tourister model. Bev and I exited Carrefour with me maneuvering our new luggage on its rollers. We have often been amused by foreign tourists lugging around new luggage they had purchased at an American outlet mall. On this evening in Ponferrada, Spain, as we rolled our new suitcase to the entrance where we would meet Luis, we epitomized what had so often been a source of amusement for us.

As we approached the line of taxis outside the mall, Luis honked his horn to let us know which cab was his. He smiled as we entered the back seat of his vehicle with our purchases. We were back at the Hostel El Horno by 7:00 p.m., physically and emotionally exhausted from a hard and stressful day. But we had a suitcase we could reliably close.

We walked the short distance to a restaurant behind our inn where, on a gorgeous late September evening, we sat on a riverside patio and had the menu del día. All with a bottle of local white wine, Bev started with grilled prawns and I had a salad, then we both had the grilled sea bass, and we each finished with flan for dessert. While it was a decent meal, sitting on that patio watching the Río Maruelo flow by after the challenging day we had experienced made it even more special.

We didn't linger, though, because we had business to take care of. Bev had to transfer all her belongings from her old, damaged suitcase to her new one. Of greatest importance, we needed a good night of sleep because the next day we would face the longest route of our Camino.

IN THE PRE-DAWN HOURS the next morning, we walked to another property where the same innkeeper who had checked us in served us a very nice and filling breakfast. Bev and I sat and talked with an interesting lady from Canada, perhaps fifteen years younger than us. We found her to be impressive, a newly single woman regrouping after her recent divorce and using her newfound freedom to walk the Camino by herself. We would encounter her several times as we made our way to Santiago. Also sitting at our table was a lady from Brazil whose ongoing requests of the innkeeper suggested she was a bit of a diva. It was her birthday, after all, but we surmised she might have over-celebrated the night before because, other than her terse requests for this menu item or that, she had little to say.

We left Molinaseca just before 8:00 a.m., a twenty-mile route ahead of us, the longest hike of our Camino. Beyond that were more climbs, more mountains, and in the week-and-a-half of hiking that remained, some self-inflicted challenges we could not have anticipated.

"THE CAMINO PROVIDES US WITH WHAT WE NEED, SOMETIMES EVEN BEFORE WE KNOW WE NEED IT."

"In every walk with nature, one receives far more than he seeks."
John Muir

"WE ARE SO SCREWED," I thought to myself before diving headlong into problem-solving mode. We were preparing to leave the tiny hamlet of Rabinal Del Camino following a very nice and memorable stay there. It was about to get even more memorable. As I came out of the bathroom, Bev calmly, but with a touch of franticness in her voice, told me the zipper on her suitcase had broken. We were in Spain in a tiny mountainous village, we were still barely conversant in the local language, we had a transport company on the way to pick up our luggage, and we had a tough fifteen-mile hike ahead of us to get to our next village. While neither of us panicked, we had no idea where we were going to get a new suitcase.

What followed was one of the toughest days we experienced on the Camino, a long climb to the Cruz de Ferro followed by a precarious, rocky descent that seemed never-ending. We were standing outside our inn in Molinaseca waiting for the innkeeper to walk from another property to check us in. An emotional start had contributed to making the day even more challenging, and we still had no idea how we were going to replace Bev's uncloseable luggage.

As we stood in a little sliver of shade protecting us from the afternoon sun, and with our minds still racing, we were startled to hear a deep, resonant voice say, "You've chosen wisely." It wasn't James Earl Jones quality, but this distinctly American voice had some gravitas and authority. We turned to find a tall, stately looking older man with a physical presence that matched his voice. After sharing his admiration for the innkeeper we were waiting on, he told us his story about how his Camino experience of many years earlier had led him to sell his business in the United States and resettle in Spain, making his home in the village where we were staying. He suggested we probably wouldn't know how our Camino experience had changed us until after we had returned home.

His presence was a gift, a calming influence on our racing minds. But then Bev addressed the issue we had struggled with all day. She said, "Just one question—where can we buy a new suitcase?" Probably more accustomed to addressing inquiries of a more existential and metaphysical nature, this fine gentleman didn't hesitate and began offering detailed instructions about what to do and where to go. An hour later, an amiable taxi driver dropped us off at the beautiful El Rosal Mall in nearby Ponferrada, where we enjoyed a beer and experienced a part of Spanish commercial culture we would not have otherwise observed. Oh, and we purchased a new suitcase from the huge selection offered by an enormous department store. As we walked out of the mall with our purchase and were greeted by the same taxi driver, we weren't just relieved... we were happy.

I don't know that I'm glad we experienced the panic of a broken suitcase in an isolated part of a foreign country. But that equipment malfunction led to one of the most memorable and oddly gratifying experiences of our Camino. And as we were struggling to figure out how to address this problem, a stately older American gentleman showed up to give us direction.

The Camino provides for your needs.

I can recall countless examples of this during our journey across Spain, some seemingly insignificant and a few almost life-saving. Like the two college roommates who unwittingly led our ill, water-logged, and hypothermic bodies down the mountain into Roncesvalles on the first day. Of less magnitude but still timely were other amenities that seemed to just pop up when they were needed. Like the cheery lady with the accordion serenading us with the "Frito Bandido" song when we needed a pick-me-up. Or the young college student in a bar in Burgos who guided us in selecting tapas items when we were particularly hungry. Or the man in the unexpected coffee wagon who offered us a boost when our energy levels were waning. There were many more examples of our needs being met, often without us even realizing the benefit we had received.

I have often found that to be true in my regular, non-Camino life. There have been so many occasions when, in the middle of especially difficult times, something would happen that lessened the sense of gloom I was feeling. It could be an unexpected check providing payment for something I had largely forgotten, that addressed some cash flow issues we were facing. Or a career-related phone call that came at just the right moment as I was dealing with challenges in whatever position I held at that time.

And sometimes I received what I needed even before I realized I needed it.

Such as a conversation Bev and I had with my father just days before he died.

My dad was not what society considered well-educated, at least in the traditional sense. Having grown up during the Depression in a family focused simply on trying to earn a living, higher education was never even a consideration for him and his siblings. But he was very intelligent in his own practical way, and he was a deeper thinker than I realized during most of our almost fifty years together. And though he developed a love of gospel music late in his life, he never struck me as being very spiritual.

But as Bev and I sat with him in his hospital room just before he began a brief stint in hospice care, Dad started talking about family, and love, and his belief in an afterlife. He shared his pride in his family, what my brother and I had accomplished in life, and the joy he had felt in watching his two grandchildren grow into adulthood. Though he never used these words, it was as if he was suggesting that he had had a good, blessed life and that he would go out a fortunate man.

Before he left the hospital to return home, where he would pass quietly just a few days later, he made sure he told each of his doctors how much he appreciated what they had done for him. Once his intense pain was brought under control, he was calm and amazingly relaxed. Though he didn't necessarily want his life to end, he was ready.

When he passed in the early morning hours a few days later, my dad did so peacefully. And though we didn't want to see him go, we were all peaceful, too, in part because of his attitude and approach to the end of his life. As I processed all of this later, I came to realize that my dad had taught us how to die with dignity, a powerful lesson I didn't even know I needed that was delivered to me by a good, simple man whose thoughts ran far deeper than I had ever realized.

Similarly, we received unsolicited but powerful lessons on our Camino that were needed and important, though we wouldn't appreciate their value until later. They included lessons about the need for patience, and humility, and tolerance, and teamwork. There were lessons about the power of community, the value of nature and the environment, and the need for perseverance in the face of physical and mental challenges. As the sage older gentleman in Molinaseca had intimated, we didn't understand so much of this until we had returned home and had time to process our experience.

Our trek on the Camino Francés was hard and pushed us well out of our comfort zones. But we never really lacked for anything we needed. We left Spain weighing less than when we had arrived, but carrying the added weight of the wisdom we took home with us. The Camino had provided for our needs, and then some.

Chapter Eight

The Weariness of a Long Journey

Villafranca del Bierzo to Sarria

A long adventure like the one we were experiencing, an arduous hiking journey that would encompass nearly 500 miles, offers countless moments of excitement and joy. As we entered the last week-and-a-half of our Camino, we had experienced our share of those emotions. But such a challenging trip also entails the buildup of fatigue, which can crack open emotions that had similarly been building up under the surface. Those emotions can create a barrier, albeit a temporary one, between two individuals needing to work together to reach a challenging goal. As we approached the end of our trek across northern Spain, that is what, oh so briefly, happened to Bev and me.

We left Molinaseca a little after 8:00 a.m., the sky still a little dark, the sun obscured by clouds that would soon dissipate as the morning progressed. Under those sunny skies and with temperatures that would reach the mid-eighties, we began what would end up being a twenty-mile day, the longest of our Camino. After we made our way through the confined streets of the small village, we headed downward toward Ponferrada on a paved trail that ran parallel to a roadway. As we made our way into the valley of the Río Boeza, the route followed a steady but subtle decline.

It was a surreal morning as we caught glimpses of Ponferrada in the distance. There were low-hanging clouds, and the newly risen sun filtering through with rolling mountains in the background made for some of the more memorable images of our time in Spain.

A couple of miles into the route, we passed two pilgrims we had not seen since we had spoken with them in Burgos two weeks earlier. They were a couple from Seattle, several years older than us, and we were rather surprised to see them. They had been struggling when we first met them, and the husband had been dealing with some severe leg pain. But they had been undaunted and were still making steady progress along the Camino Francés. As we briefly talked with them about the challenges of their walk, Bev and I were struck by the perseverance of these two older pilgrims. It was a testament to their tenacity, but also further evidence of the power and pull of the Camino de Santiago. They would arrive in Santiago de Compostela on the same day we did.

After five miles of hiking, we crossed the Río Boeza and then climbed up to the city center of Ponferrada. Though we will always remember this city of 65,000 for the luggage-related adventure we experienced, it is one of the most historic locations on the Camino Francés. As we climbed up from the river valley, we passed by the beautiful Castillo de los Templarios, the ancient castle of the Knights Templar, the short-lived military order of the Catholic Church. Active between the twelfth and fourteenth centuries, the Knights were originally formed to protect church members completing pilgrimages to Jerusalem and Santiago de Compostela. The castle has been meticulously restored and we would have enjoyed touring such a vaunted site. But it was early in the day, and we still had nearly fourteen miles to get to Villafranca del Bierzo.

Ponferrada is yet another beautiful Spanish city, a mixture of historic and modern with a mountain range beckoning in the distance. The city was still sleepy as we passed through the downtown area, though we stopped and watched as a large group of police cadets paraded around one of the larger squares. We crossed the Río Sil, the larger of the two rivers flowing through Ponferrada. We stopped briefly on the bridge to take in the beauty of the tree-lined waterway, a waterfall creating a constant flow in the foreground.

As we headed out of the city center, our surroundings changed to residential neighborhoods lined with modern, multi-level apartment buildings with restaurants and small businesses on the ground floor. We stopped at a busy bar and had café con leches and glazed chocolate croissants. With many miles still ahead of us, we continued on and soon were walking through a suburban area that was almost rural. We walked for a brief time with the lady from Canada we had met that morning at breakfast. She shared a little more about her background and past professional life before she left us to hike at a quicker pace.

We stopped for a quick sandwich in the surprisingly busy little town of Camponaraya. On our way out of town, we walked by a roadside winery with an outdoor tasting area. It looked very enticing, and as we looked over, we saw our new friend from Canada waiting to be served her flight of wines. She waved at us and invited us to join her, and the sight of her relaxing in the shade of this winery patio was certainly alluring. But we still had eight miles to go to get to our destination for the night, so we politely demurred. We hoped she could get to her albergue that evening; if at that point, I had sat down to taste some wine on such a long and scorching afternoon, I'm not sure I would have been able to continue down the trail.

Still tired from the challenging hike of the previous day, it was a brutally long and tough afternoon. After leaving the small city of Cacabelos, the trail entered an especially hilly section that took us on a roller coaster ride of relentless uphills and downhills. We were in the Bierzo wine region, and we could see vast vineyards all around us. Unlike our time in the Rioja region, we never walked through any of these vineyards, but they provided a beautiful panorama on this hot and sunny day.

Finally, after over eight hours of walking, we made it to Villafranca del Bierzo, an interesting and very hilly village of which we saw very little. Our inn for the evening was located just a few steps off the trail. As we arrived, our GPS told us we were at the correct location, but we couldn't identify which of the many buildings around us was our destination. We eventually found the understated signage for the Hostal La Puerta Del Pérdon, a seven-room guesthouse that provided one of the more enjoyable stays of our Camino.

The host was one of the nicest, most personable individuals we met during our time in Spain. He would be our server at dinner that evening and at breakfast the next morning. With a very modest external appearance, the inn had been beautifully restored, and the innkeeper took great pride in the facility and the service that was provided. Our room was on the top floor, reachable only by multiple flights of stairs that were challenging to climb after such a long and difficult day. Luckily (very luckily, given our tired legs), our suitcases were waiting for us outside our room, so we didn't have to lug them to the top floor.

Especially when compared to some of the postage-stamp-sized guest rooms we had experienced in our month on our Camino, this room was enormous, with a sofa and living area separate from the bedroom. There were two televisions, which doubled the number of sets we wouldn't turn on. (In our month-and-a-half in Spain, we watched none of the TVs that were often in the rooms.) Clean and tastefully decorated, it was a very nice room.

Whenever we arrived in a new village, we often went exploring in search of a beer. But our inn was perched on the upside of a steep incline, and walking down into the main part of the village would have meant we had to climb back up the same incline to get back to our inn. After a hot and hilly twenty-mile day, a tour of Villafranca del Bierzo held no appeal for us. Across the street from the Hostal La Puerta Del Pérdon was a little bar with an outdoor patio where we leisurely drank a cold beer, recounting the challenges of that long hike and those we would face in the coming days. Afterward, we returned to our room to get cleaned up, wash out some clothes, and get ready for dinner at the hotel restaurant that would open at 7:30.

Our room had a small bookcase with a variety of books, some in English. One of those books was a "Guide to Spain" written by Rick Steves in 2012. I opened it to the section on the Camino Francés, and in discussing Villafranca, it was suggested that the best place "for weary pilgrims to stay" was the Hostal La Puerta Del Pérdon. This was high praise from the author many in the United States consider to be the master of European travel.

Along those same lines, we did not know the hotel's restaurant was a Michelin-starred establishment. Bev and I have dined at some wonderful restaurants over the years, but the number of such highly esteemed ones has been rather limited. So, when we arrived promptly at 7:30 when service began, we suspected we were in for a treat. The space was small and very unassuming but, as with many internationally acclaimed restaurants, the menu was both regional and eclectic. We ordered a bottle of the local house vino tinto, and then we both started with sliced tomatoes with mozzarella cheese, the house variation of a Caprese salad. Then, for the main course, we opted to eat like a local, ordering menu items we had to ask about. (Which, as I think about it, can be a risky strategy.) Bev ordered what were called the "stewed pork stompers," which were pig feet. Michelin star or not, they were fatty and rather gross. I was more fortunate, ordering the "Mozillas with Scallops," which were lamb sweetbreads in a cream sauce made with scallops. It wasn't a large plate of food, but the way the rich flavors blended so beautifully would be difficult to describe. Bev finished with a slice of cheesecake, without crust as is common in Spain, and I had the Oreo ice cream, which I suspect was homemade and was very smooth and rich. Overall, it was a very memorable meal.

As we were finishing our meal, the two ladies from Michigan we had first met in the early days of our journey, stopped by to say hello to us, the German family, and a lady from Texas we had not previously met. Now, just over a week from reaching Santiago de Compostela, one of the Michigan ladies commented about how it was going to be difficult to miss some of the many people they had met on this amazing journey; we couldn't have agreed more.

On our several adventure journeys, from running a marathon in Texas to biking across Missouri to hiking across the Grand Canyon and, most notably, biking across the southern United States, our superpower was our ability to work together. Cooperatively working together to reach a challenging goal, we sensed there was little Bev and I could not accomplish. In over forty years of marriage, there had inevitably been times when we found ourselves briefly at odds with one another. On those rare occasions when that occurred, accomplishing tough tasks seemed next to impossible. As we left Villafranca del Bierzo, such a conflict arose in the most untimely manner, and as a result, our Camino was clouded for the next few days.

There were multiple routes from Villafranca to Herrerías, our destination for the evening. Since leaving St. Jean Pied de Port twenty-nine days earlier, we had relied on a GPS-enabled mobile app provided by our travel company. It would suggest where we should go and, more importantly, indicate when we drifted off course. It had saved us on several occasions, most notably on our first day as we crossed the Pyrenees. On this day, the route suggested by the mobile app was much more scenic but would take us up, over, and down three small but still challenging mountains. We were still exhausted from our hilly twenty-mile hike of the previous day, so following the recommended mountain route was not something we wanted to tackle. The primary route described in our guidebook took us across the Río Burbia, then alongside the Río Valcarce and a busy highway to the little village of Trabadelo, where the two routes converged. Bev and I agreed we wanted to take the easier path, but as we studied our maps, it was unclear how to get there. We had discussed possible options the night before but had not agreed on how to proceed. We should have.

The map showing the less strenuous route out of town was confusing, and there were yellow arrows and Camino shells in abundance, signifying the various routes. I thought I could find our way to Herrerías, but I was tired and possibly not thinking clearly, so I couldn't guarantee that my pathfinding would lead us to our destination. Bev, who was equally tired, had a different view and kept saying, "We need to get to the highway," referring to a busy road our map suggested the trail would cross several times that day. As I looked at the map, I noted that each highway (there were two in this area) passed through a tunnel. We were at least a half mile away from the closest highway, and there was no guarantee there would be pedestrian access to the tunnels, so this did not seem to me to be a viable option for reaching the trail. As we stood on the bridge across the Río Burbia with no agreement on what to do, we just sort of looked around in silence. As I most often walked in front (typically after agreeing on the direction whenever the route was in doubt), and with no consensus on what we needed to do but with a sense that we needed to do something, I started walking on what I thought was the correct trail. It was at that point that exhaustion and personalities and egos all collided to create a rift between the two of us, a wedge that would continue for the next few days. Of course, we eventually worked through our issues and were soon back on the same page. Until then, though, by not working together, it made the challenging terrain into which we were heading even that much more difficult to traverse.

As HIKES GO, THIS was an easy thirteen miles, a natural path following a very subtle, almost unperceivable incline toward the mountains. We stopped in the little town of Trabadelo and had café con leches and slices of Spanish tortilla, the traditional potato casserole that was offered in virtually every bar we visited. By 1:30 p.m., we made it to the tiny (and I do mean tiny) village of Las Herrerías. This little hamlet of just thirty inhabitants got its name from the four blacksmith shops that were active in the community during more prosperous times. ("Herrerías" is Spanish for "blacksmith.") It consisted of a handful of old buildings that perched along a narrow ribbon of road that also served as the Camino route. In Camino lore, Las Herrerías is perhaps best known as the starting point of the steep climb to the mountaintop village of O Cebriero, which we would tackle the next day.

That night, we stayed in a surprisingly nice little eight-room inn called the Casa Do Ferreiro in a room that offered views of the mountains we would tackle the next day, with a huge pasture filled with large grazing cattle in the foreground. From our second-floor room, we could see where the Río Valcarce weaved its way through the valley. The one thing smaller than the tiny village of Herrerías was the size of our room. We struggled to find space for our suitcases and daypacks (and us), which made an afternoon at a location with little to do even more challenging.

We walked to a little bar down the road from our inn and had beers and huge bocadillos with Spanish jamón and cheese. They were tasty and filling. After a few hours in our tiny room made more challenging by the spotty wi-fi, at 7:00 p.m., we went down to the cozy little hotel restaurant where we enjoyed the menu del día. We both started with the salad (again with tuna, which we were enjoying). Bev then had the grilled chicken breast and I had grilled pork ribs, both flavorful but a little overcooked. We finished with cheesecake for Bev and an ice cream drumstick for me, all with a bottle of red wine from the Bierzo region we had walked through the previous week. It wasn't a great meal, but it was filling.

On this last night of September, at a higher elevation, it was a cool evening. But our little room offered no ventilation other than the window, so we kept it open all night. Many of the cattle in the herd grazing not thirty yards from our room were adorned with the ever-present cow bells. Each bell made a distinctive clanging noise every time the cow moved to a new grazing spot, every time they bent over to chomp on a clump of grass, almost every time they breathed. At times, the sounds of the clanging bells were almost deafening. It was amusing at first, but the novelty of the serenading cowbells soon wore off. We wondered if the noise would keep us awake at night, but luckily, cows aren't nocturnal and sleep at night like we do. We both slept surprisingly well.

SEVERAL MONTHS EARLIER, WHEN we first studied our trip itinerary, we noted that the route from Herrerías to the iconic mountaintop village of O Cebreiro was listed as just over five miles long, a virtual rest day. At the time, though, we didn't dig deep enough into the guidebook to learn that this short route was one long, challenging climb.

Because breakfast at the inn wasn't served until later than usual, we didn't leave Herrerías De Valcarce until after 9:00 a.m. Much of the route was a rough and narrow natural path on an almost continual incline. The pitch was never particularly steep, but it was unrelenting. Given the climb and terrain, it took us over three hours to complete the five-mile hike. It was tough going, but the views were spectacular. As we continued to climb, we looked down on hills and small mountains that, even on the first day of October, were still lush and green. The terrain made us think of Ireland. And sure enough, as we approached the outskirts of O Cebreiro, we passed a marker signifying our entrance into the autonomous region of Galicia, leaving Castilla y León behind.

Between St. Jean Pied de Port and Santiago de Compostela, we passed through countless small towns and villages, far more than we could differentiate, as one often looked the same as the next. None, however, was more unique or more Camino-focused than O Cebreiro (pronounced "oh thay bray **air** oh"). As we entered the tiny village on an ancient cobblestone street, we were struck by the hustle and bustle of this little burg of fifty permanent inhabitants. People were milling about, many who appeared to be peregrinos, but others who had been dropped off by the tour buses parked on the outskirts of the village.

Also striking was the architecture that was dominated by centuries-old buildings constructed of rough rock walls with slate or even thatch or grass roofs. Perhaps of greatest historical significance were the few surviving "pallozas," odd-looking oval buildings with thatched conical roofs largely made of straw. These large buildings were common in Galicia but are most closely linked to O Cebreiro. In their time, they housed large families and their animals. Only a few remain.

Our room for the evening was in the Casa Navarro, less an inn and more just three rooms located over a series of shops. When we arrived, we knew we were in the correct location, but we couldn't locate the office where we could check in. Finally, we found a bartender who spoke enough English to direct us to the shop where a clerk could show us to our room.

We were only a short distance into Galicia, and we had failed to equate "Galicia" with "Gaelic," and then "Gaelic" with "Irish." But when we stepped into the little gift shop where we could check into our room, it was as if we had been transported to Dublin or County Cork. In this little store overflowing with customers shopping for mementos of their Camino experience, Gaelic (or what we would call Irish) music was blaring from several speakers. We felt like we had been transported into yet another world, one far from the mountaintop ridge in Spain where this quaint little village was located. We stood in line while the gentleman, who appeared to be the manager or proprietor, assisted other customers. When we reached the front of the line, this nice man welcomed us and treated us like we were the only two people in the store.

After taking information from our passports and securing the key to our room (not complicated, given there were only three rooms), the shop/innkeeper directed us to our suitcases and then to our room. When we arrived, we discovered two critical attributes of where we would stay that evening. First, it was located above the gift shop where we had checked in, the one playing a never-ending loop of loud Gaelic music. Instead of the prospect of hearing cowbells all night, as in Herrerías De Valcarce the previous evening, we now heard a ceaseless soundtrack of Gaelic music. Luckily, the shop, and all of O Cebreiro for that matter, became quiet around 9:00 p.m.

Second, our room was small and a little weird, with a sloping ceiling to match the pitch of the roof. Both the sleeping area and the bathroom had little dormer-like shuttered windows. But of greater significance, at least to me, was the pitch of the ceiling. Except in certain parts of the room and bathroom, I had to stand stooped over to avoid banging my head on the ceiling. The entry door and the door to the bathroom were both cut at a sharp angle to match the pitch of the roof. It was like a setting from *The Hobbit* or the living quarters of a Keebler elf. I've never been injured by a hotel room, but if we had stayed much longer than one night,

I might have left with concussion-like symptoms from the countless times I thoughtlessly banged my head on the ceiling.

AFTER DROPPING OFF OUR suitcases and packs in our room, we went in search of a place for a mid-afternoon lunch. The little town was busy and most of the bars and restaurants were overflowing. With beers, we shared the "empanada platter" (which was not what we expected but still tasty) and a "Cebreiro Salad," the local version of a Caprese salad. Afterward, we went back to our room to get cleaned up. The room had an ancient bathtub, and when we fully turned on the faucet, only a trickle of hot water came out. So, it took some time for each of us to draw enough water to take a bath, but, of course, we were eventually able to get clean and ready for the evening.

We had amassed a lot of dirty clothes in need of actual laundering rather than hand washing, and with three rooms, we were confident the Casa Navarro didn't offer laundry service. We went in search of any available washing machines and dryers. There was no lavandería in this small village, but there was a modern and impressive albergue. Most of the albergues we had seen in our month on the trail had been created out of ancient buildings constructed for other purposes. The Xunta albergue on the far edge of the village had been constructed specifically to serve the needs of pilgrims. But it was as busy as the village was, and when we found the laundry room, as expected, all the washing machines were in use. Our dirty clothes would be hand-washed yet another day.

In the early evening, still feeling a little full from our late lunch, we returned to the same restaurant for a light dinner. The building had to have been centuries old, and the restaurant had a very rustic motif, almost as if little thought had been given to how it would be decorated. We each had a glass of a very good Bierzo red wine, followed by large mixed salads (again with tuna and corn). We then shared a chicken burger with fries. While it wasn't an especially memorable meal, it was filling.

Across the cobblestone courtyard from the Casa Navarro where we were staying is a humble little Catholic Church that serves this Camino-centric village. Santa Maria la Real (St. Mary the Royal) was built in the early ninth century to serve the pilgrims who climbed this steep pass on their way to Santiago. It is considered the oldest church on the Camino Francés, and the simple structure and the surprisingly spacious interior had a decidedly ancient feel.

It was in this humble sanctuary that Camino and Catholic lore suggest a miracle occurred a few centuries after the church was built. According to the story, on a blustery winter evening, a monk was preparing for the Eucharist, or Holy Communion, when a devout local farmer arrived for the scheduled mass. This monk was experiencing a lapse of faith, and he ridiculed the peasant for his devotion and for climbing the mountain in a blizzard simply to receive communion. The miracle occurred before the eyes of this doubting monk when the bread and wine were transformed into flesh and blood. The faith of the monk was restored, and the peasant was rewarded for his continued devotion. Reminiscent of the miracle of the chickens in Santo Domingo, the remains of the monk and peasant are buried in the church, and a blood-stained linen and the chalice and small plate used in the miraculous Mass are preserved elsewhere on the grounds.

After dinner, we made our way to the church where a young priest and a full sanctuary were partway through an evening mass that would be followed by a "pilgrim's blessing." The interior of the church was unassuming, built with large arches and walls of crude stone designed to protect worshipers from harsh winter conditions. Though over fifteen centuries old, the appearance of the structure suggested it could withstand another millennium. All the pews were full, so we stepped outside to enjoy the crisp, early October evening. When we returned, the priest had invited all pilgrims to come onto the raised platform. As several peregrinos stood around him, the personable young priest dressed in traditional robes shared a blessing and then asked individuals of different nationalities to complete the same reading in their native languages. The mass exuded a positive, welcoming message, wishing love, safety, happiness, and success for each pilgrim as they neared the completion of their journey. We were happy we had returned to experience such a unique service.

Pilgrim's Mass in O Cebreiro

The service put me in a self-reflective mood, and I looked back on the past week. It had been a tough, exhausting, and emotional past few days, but we were persevering. But uphill climbing days are inevitably, eventually, followed by easier, downhill days. We were a week out of Santiago de Compostela, and though there were still some small mountains in our future, the next couple of hikes would be far easier, at least physically.

AFTER A QUICK BREAKFAST in the little bar in the basement of the old building in which we were staying, we prepared to leave O Cebreiro just before 8:00 a.m. The sun had just risen and the views in the valley below us were absolutely beautiful. Ahead of us was a thirteen-mile route that began with some rolling hills before beginning a six-mile descent that was, for some stretches, very steep. As an indication of the steepness of the latter half of the route, the guidebook we were using warned, again, that more injuries were sustained on downhills than on uphills. As predicted, the last few miles put a great deal of strain on our already tired and sore legs. Our hiking poles were helpful, but we were very glad when, after an especially long downhill section that seemed to never end, we reached the little hamlet of Triacastela, our destination for the evening.

Triacastela (the "town with three castles," none of which are still standing) had a barren look and depressed feel as we passed through the little hamlet of 900 residents. Our inn for the evening, the Casa David, was located at the far end of the village, and we had low expectations of what would be a surprisingly nice establishment. We entered a small restaurant where we assumed we could get the key to our room. A brusque older woman was manning the restaurant and inn, and she checked us in with little conversation and even less eye contact.

The notion of "laundry service" was always enticing, especially for Bev, for whom clean clothes were particularly important and who did the bulk of the handwashing. At the Casa David, we got half of a laundry service. As the no-nonsense, drill sergeant lady sort of showed us to our room (she spoke about as much English as we did Spanish, so she did a considerable amount of grunting and pointing), Bev asked about said laundry service. Her response was hard to decipher, but she told us she could machine wash the clothes, but we would then need to hang them up to dry on the clotheslines that crisscrossed the adjacent "garden area" of the inn. So, an hour or so after getting settled into our room, we collected our clean but wet clothes and hung them up to dry. With the intense late afternoon sun and persistent southerly breeze, the garments were mostly dry in the time it took to walk down the street to a bar and drink a cold beer.

Later that evening, we returned to the same restaurant for the menu del día. With a bottle of red wine, we each started with mixed salads, then Bev had the salmon and I had the grilled pork. I finished with dessert, an ice cream sundae. As pilgrim's meals go, this one was quite good.

THE NEXT MORNING, WE enjoyed a little more substantial breakfast than we had been receiving, provided and served by the same no-nonsense lady who had checked us in and, we assumed, washed our clothes. As we crossed Spain, we found that to be very common, an entire inn and bar/restaurant run primarily by one individual. This older woman was not one with an outgoing personality, at least that we observed, but she ran a pretty good inn.

We left Triacastela for what would be a challenging twelve-mile route to the surprisingly robust little city of Sarria. There were two route options for the day, a longer but flatter course of almost sixteen miles or a shorter but hillier route. Because the travel company app would guide us on the shorter route (and it was a significant four miles shorter), we opted for that one.

Since we entered Galicia, we had noticed on the trail an abundance of manure, whether from cows or horses or some other beast. In some places, it was so prevalent that it was challenging to pick your way around the different piles. As we made our way to Sarria on a very narrow lane just outside an unnamed little hamlet, up ahead, we saw the trail blocked by a herd of cows. These were huge, lumbering animals being herded by an older man with a long stick, accompanied by a feisty dog. Neither the cows nor their tender seemed in any hurry to reach their destination. So, we thought we might have to stop on the trail, sort of like waiting for a crawling freight train to clear a roadway. But by the time we reached that point on the road, the farmer and his dog had herded the eight to ten cows through a small opening in the fence and into the pasture. It was as if these cows had been trained to pass through this tiny opening, lured by the prospect of greener and more abundant grass. But then we had to pass through the "aftermath" of the herd's passing.

It was a tough day, with a long four-mile climb out of Triacastela followed by a steep then gradual downhill into Sarria. The sky was cloudy and overcast most of the day, though it never rained on us. This was Day 32 of our Camino, and we were tired and emotionally spent after a challenging week. Any newness had long worn off, and with just five days of hiking after this one, the end was in sight.

In our other comparable experience to this one, our month-and-a-half bike ride across the United States, as we approached the end, we were similarly ready to be finished and looking forward to getting back home to our family and our regular life. But on that trip, we shared the experience with a group of riders to whom we had grown close, good people we knew we would miss. In that experience, there was a significant part of us that was not ready for the trip to end.

Not so with our Camino.

It had been an amazing experience, no doubt. And we met some wonderful people along the way. But we would leave Spain with some wonderful memories of these folks, though with no deep, lasting relationships to hold on to. Perhaps it was circumstantial, or that we were six years older than we had been during our biking trip. But by this point, just seventy miles from Santiago de Compostela, we were physically and mentally exhausted. We were going to finish what we started, and we suspected this journey had changed us in ways we might not realize for some time, as the wise old gentleman in Molinaseca had suggested. But we were ready to go home.

For a small city of 13,000 permanent residents, Sarria was bustling as we made our way along busy streets through the center of town. Our hotel for the evening, the Hotel Mar de Plata, is located on the edge of the downtown area and is some distance from the Camino. As we trudged along busy sidewalks for block after block, I got a bit frustrated because we had to walk so far off the route just to get to our hotel. When we arrived and checked in, we quickly realized that this inn was worth the extra effort.

The previous few nights, we had stayed in ancient inns with rooms barely large enough for two twin beds, not to mention the two of us and all our garb and equipment. We were excited when we arrived to find that the Hotel Mar de Plata was a much newer property, the first modern inn we had stayed in for some time. When we opened the door to our second-floor room, we were surprised to find two sleeping areas, one with two twin beds and another with a queen bed. For the first time in weeks, we had sufficient room for our suitcases. While having to walk nearly a mile off route had been unexpected, we were so grateful for the added space. And we were on the edge of town; when I looked out the window, I saw a cornfield behind the hotel.

After getting settled, we went downstairs to the hotel restaurant for lunch. With beers, we each had a nice mixed salad and large bowls of "Galician Broth," a concoction we had been wanting to try since entering this region. It was a very hearty, broth-based soup with white beans, potatoes, and kale. Our server was a pleasant woman with whom I tried to communicate, assuming she spoke minimal English, like most in this part of Spain. I was wrong, as I realized when she said with a confident but accommodating tone, "I speak English." We had some questions about the soup, about Sarria, about the climate, and other issues, and she was very helpful.

After a surprisingly filling lunch and getting cleaned up, we spent a few hours enjoying our spacious room. Around 6:00, we walked down the busy street looking for a restaurant that served dinner at such an early hour. Though there were countless establishments serving coffee and drinks, dinner options were sparse. We entered one restaurant to inquire about the availability of food, and a lady, the owner or a server, we weren't sure which, responded to our question with a look that suggested, "Well, of course we're serving dinner." We sat at an outdoor table on a slightly cool early October evening. The same lady came out with the restaurant's version of a menu, a list of items handwritten on a little notepad on which she would write our orders. It was a little hard to read, and we didn't recognize most of the Spanish terms anyway, and the lady didn't seem to speak much English, so we just took a stab at ordering. Bev ordered something that sounded like a pasta dish but ended up being a large plate of huge clams or mussels. They were tasty but served cold, which always gives us a little pause, especially in a foreign country where we were unfamiliar with the stringency of health standards. I had a huge plate of seafood paella, delicious, and we each had a glass of vino tinto. Afterward, we found a little bodega near the hotel and each had an ice cream sandwich.

FOR THE PAST SEVERAL days, we had noticed a subtle but steady increase in the number of pilgrims on the trail. Since starting over a month earlier, most days we had seen many of the same people over and over. Now, most of the peregrinos were new to us, likely because they were new to the Camino. We had been expecting such an increase in traffic on the trail.

For those wanting to complete the full Camino Francés, the starting point is St. Jean Pied de Port, where we began our journey. But for those with limited time or others who want to complete the shortest route to qualify for a Compostela, the certificate presented in Santiago de Compostela signifying a pilgrim has "completed the Camino," one must walk at least 100 kilometers, or around sixty-two miles. Located just over seventy miles from Santiago, Sarria is the logical starting point. As a result, many begin their Camino from this small city.

The next day, as we departed the Hotel de Plata, we expected the trail would be busier. Nothing prepared us, however, for the onslaught of humanity we encountered and the many ways those throngs of hikers would alter our Camino experience.

"A PILGRIMAGE DOESN'T HAVE TO BE 'RELIGIOUS' TO BE SPIRITUAL."

"The journey is the reward."

Steve Jobs

IT JUST WASN'T HAPPENING for me, again.

We were touring the stunning main cathedral in León, and it was impressive. The main sanctuary was enormous, ornate, and adorned with an array of some of the most beautiful stained-glass panels we had ever seen. We were enjoying a rest day in this beautiful city, and on this Saturday afternoon, the cathedral was teeming with visitors, the resulting noise unexpected in such a reverent space.

For some, the purpose of trekking across the Camino de Santiago is religious, completing an arduous journey to earn the right to pay homage to the remains of the Apostle James. For others, the Camino journey is about the adventure, the cultural experience, and reaching a long-held goal. Bev and I fit into the latter category, but we were open to any spiritual messages the Camino might provide. I, in particular, was hoping for such an experience.

In León, as I had in the huge cathedrals we had visited in Barcelona, Santo Domingo, and Burgos, I tried to find a quiet spot to sit and meditate on our Camino experience. There was no quiet area in the vast sanctuary, but we found a spot as secluded as any and sat in a pew for a few minutes. Using meditation techniques I had utilized for years, I tried to quiet my mind, focus on my breath, and melt into the moment.

We were surrounded by depictions of the crucified Christ and other medieval artwork with strong religious themes. But in a structure designed to foster faith, I was unmoved. The cathedral, the artwork, and the traditions and customs that dictated how each congregant should worship were all steeped in religion. And that meant little to me beyond respect for those for whom these symbols and customs were important and the historical significance that imbued each of them.

I probably shouldn't have been surprised by my response, or lack thereof. Though we continue to attend church and explore our spirituality in our own ways, Bev and I had put traditional, "organized religion" behind us decades ago. My faith is deeply personal and self-determined, and any relationship between me and a higher power or life force is direct and without the need for a "middle man," a role the clergy so often plays in many faith traditions. Though I long ago eschewed religious experiences in which I was told what to think or how to worship, I still have a deep and abiding respect and appreciation for those who genuinely believe in and follow such practices. I simply haven't followed them since my youth.

No, our Camino journey was not a religious pilgrimage. And these huge cathedrals we visited in the larger Spanish cities, stunningly impressive as they were, seemed over-the-top and either ego-driven or odd attempts to impress God. As I sat in that pew in León hoping to feel some sort of connection, it was no wonder the atmosphere didn't bring forth any sense of spirituality.

This is not to say those spiritual connections didn't occur elsewhere on our Camino, sometimes in unexpected settings. Such as walking through ripe Rioja vineyards on a warm September afternoon, the beauty of the rolling hills and the smell of the ready-for-harvest grapes reaffirming the magnificence of nature. Or walking along a ridgeline in the mountaintop

Gaelic hamlet of O Cebreiro, taking in the vista of the lush, green mountains in all directions. On this 500-mile walk, we felt more connected to the earth than we had in any other experience.

Still, we felt some of those spiritual connections in more traditional settings, like the small church in that same village where we sat in on the simple pilgrim's mass. We were moved not by the words of the priest, which we couldn't understand, but by the connectedness we felt with the small group of peregrinos in attendance. We knew virtually none of them, but we shared a common goal, and likely similar hopes for humanity. Then there was the tiny sanctuary in Rabinal del Camino, where we were mesmerized by the rhythmic power of a chanted vespers service. To us, sitting in that small, crumbling, and ancient chapel, we were moved not by the message but by the beautiful way it was delivered.

But without doubt, the most powerful spiritual moment we experienced during our Camino journey involved a mound of dirt, a pile of rocks, and a crude wooden pole with an iron cross affixed to its top. We were three-and-a-half weeks into our trek across Spain, and we were tired. The novelty of the experience had left us weeks earlier, we were ten days of challenging hikes from Santiago, and the stress of the journey was affecting us in ways both physical and mental. Adding to that stress and exhaustion, on that day, we were burdened with trying to figure out how to replace a broken suitcase.

After a nearly four-mile climb, we reached the Cruz de Ferro, nearly the highest spot on the Camino Francés. At one of the most iconic spots on the Way, Camino lore suggests that each pilgrim bring a rock of significance to be placed at the base of the wooden pole. (Bev and I each brought small rocks from our home in Illinois that we had carried with us across Spain.) In placing the stone at the base of this historic monument, the pilgrim is to let go of something that has been mentally burdening them and/or dedicate the offering to an individual who holds a special place in the pilgrim's heart.

We took turns placing our stones on the pile, an action that sounds mundane but is as meaningful as one makes it. As I took photos, Bev climbed the small mound and laid her rock at the base of the wooden post, taking time to ponder the significance of the ritual. After she walked back down to join me, I climbed up, took the common little rock I had brought from our patio, and placed it among the countless stones of all sizes and descriptions. As I did so, I focused on the "emotional burden" I wanted to leave at this iconic spot.

As I stood atop a mound of dirt and rocks, a physical feature that wouldn't warrant a second glance in any other circumstance, I was surrounded by several other pilgrims who were completing the ritual at the same time. As I gently laid my little stone in the location I had selected, I was swept up in the moment. While I didn't start sobbing, I got a little misty-eyed as I pondered where I was standing, what we had done so far, and the gratitude I felt for the opportunity to be there. We still had a grueling eleven miles ahead of us, so I didn't linger atop that mound.

Rob at the Cruz de Ferro

But I had been spiritually moved by that simple action and the thoughts that had accompanied it. Whether it came from some external force or, more likely, from the consciousness bubbling inside me, that brief ritual had affected me and continues to affect me to this day. I left the Cruz de Ferro a subtly different person than I had been when I had arrived there just a few minutes earlier.

As I thought about this moment in the days and weeks that followed, I came to understand an odd juxtaposition. The ornate cathedrals that had been constructed to glorify God, Christ, and other icons of faith had elicited from me no spiritual response. But a small mound of earth, a crude wooden pole, an iron cross, and a ritual involving a small rock from our patio had moved me spiritually and emotionally.

No, our Camino was not a religious exercise for Bev and me. But in my mind, religion and spirituality are not necessarily synonymous, with the former sometimes impeding the true development of the latter. Though far from religious, our Camino experience was a deeply spiritual one, perhaps even more so than we had realized at the time.

CHAPTER NINE

HORDES ON THE CAMINO

Portomarín to Santiago de Compostela

AFTER MORE THAN A month on the trail, we had come to cherish the sanctity and solitude of the Camino de Santiago. We had been among mostly like-minded pilgrims who had started their Camino in St. Jean Pied de Port and had, during their time on the Way, developed a deep respect for their fellow peregrinos and the journey they were sharing. And though we could typically spot other hikers either in front of or behind us, we could each be in our own little world, basking in whatever degree of isolation we desired.

Much of that changed in Sarria.

As WE HAD THE previous thirty-two days on the trail, we got ourselves dressed and ready for the day's hike and then went down for breakfast. Typically in the past, there had been just a few people eating in the restaurant or area designated for breakfast, and we often knew most of them. We would say "good morning" to acquaintances, but the dining rooms were largely quiet as most were studying route maps or contemplating the upcoming hike.

As we entered the restaurant at the Hotel Mar De Plata, the room was buzzing, and packed. We had to search for an open table, something that had been unheard of in even the smallest establishments. We were sporting the same shirts and pants we had been wearing off and on for the past month, and though they were clean, there was a dinginess born from days on the trail. But so many of those in the breakfast room that morning in Sarria were adorned in bright new hiking attire, sort of like wearing new clothes on the first day of the school year or the first day back after Christmas vacation.

And these new pilgrims were excited and exuberant, almost giddy. As Bev and I sat quietly eating our traditional Spanish breakfast and taking in the scene around us, I thought back to our breakfast in St. Jean Pied de Port as we contemplated our first day on the trail. Perhaps it was because we faced fifteen miles up and over the Pyrenees rather than that same distance over a far gentler uphill and downhill into Portomarin. Perhaps it was the forecast of rain on our first day as we made our way up a long trail over a mountain. Or perhaps it was because we were facing 500 miles of hiking in thirty-seven days rather than seventy miles in five days, as these new peregrinos were. Regardless, as we had sat at breakfast as we prepared to start our Camino over a month earlier, we had been far from giddy.

But you couldn't fault these folks for their excitement; they were beginning what, for most of them, would be the adventure of a lifetime.

Possibly because we looked worn and grizzled compared to everyone else in the room, an older American woman hobbled up to our table and expressed concern about not having hiking poles, suggesting that while she didn't have any, she had heard they would be helpful, if not necessary. This exuberant lady walked with some difficulty, appeared a bit overweight and out of shape, and was wearing a jacket that would be far too heavy for hiking the Camino in early October. Bev took some time addressing her concern, explained how hiking poles could be helpful on both the uphill and downhill sections, and tried to reassure her she could make it to the next town (though we both had our doubts). As I thought about this woman as she began a series of walks that would average ten to twelve miles a day, I couldn't help thinking how unprepared she seemed. It was as if she had decided on a whim to "hike the Camino." As I reflected on the beginning of our Camino over a month earlier, I smiled a little inside as I realized how unprepared we had seemed on our first day, and we had devoted a year to researching and training in preparation. We never saw this woman again, but we hoped she could complete her journey in good health.

It was still dark as we left the hotel, and at first, we encountered only a few people on the city sidewalks as we made our way back to the trail. But as we approached the route, the number of people walking with backpacks increased exponentially. In time, as we neared the trail and as the sun continued to rise, the crowd grew enormous, people walking from various directions toward a singular entry point onto the Camino Francés. The hordes of people gave me the feeling of walking into a sports arena or stadium; our days of trail solitude were over.

Then, as we were walking on the street portion of the route, just before it converted into a natural surface, we saw a very animated man speaking in stern Italian to a large group of high school-age students. What we didn't realize but would soon have to deal with, these 100 or so high school kids were getting ready to begin a field trip, a walk on the Camino from Sarria to Santiago. When, a short time later, we took a wrong turn onto an alternative route, this mass of young people got ahead of us. They were typical teenagers, loud and boisterous, and one even had a boombox attached to the top of his pack. None of the students with whom we briefly interacted was anything but polite. But the trail wasn't very wide, and we had to weave our way through and around large groups of kids just to make quicker progress on what would be a fifteen-mile route to the riverfront town of Portomarín. After the relative quiet and isolation of the first 430 miles of the Camino Francés, this was a shock to our systems. By midday, the high school group was behind us, but the congestion on the trail would continue to Santiago.

We walked for a time with an amicable lady and her grown son, who had started in St. Jean after we did but had averaged more miles each day. She had been a counselor at a high school in South Carolina, and we discussed how we had thought our days of chaperoning school field trips had been behind us. It was heartwarming how she and her son were sharing this time together, and they were taking a less structured approach to the journey, reserving lodging just a day or two in advance.

The scenery was nondescript, perhaps because, by this time in our Camino, we were less observant of our surroundings and more focused on simply getting to Santiago. The first nine miles of the route were a steady but subtle incline, and the last six miles into Portomarín were steadily downhill, the trail at times steep. It was a rural area, and the gravel path passed by old churches and through little hamlets and dense forests. Occasionally, the trail weaved around trees on a sunken trail, with the terrain rising several feet on either side of us. When we walked into a clearing, we could often see beautiful green vistas of the region we were passing through.

IN TIME, WE WERE approaching the riverfront village of Portomarín. Situated on a hill overlooking the Río Miño, this village of 1,300, less than a third of its population a hundred years earlier, seemed to have regained some of its vitality with the influx of peregrinos. The original village of Portomarín had been located directly alongside the Río Miño but was submerged when the river was dammed in the 1960s to create a reservoir. Some of the more ancient buildings, including the fortress-like main church, were disassembled and reconstructed in their new locations on higher ground. As a result, the town has a fresher look than comparable villages we visited along the Way.

To reach the downtown area, we crossed a long and impressive ancient Roman bridge across the river. As this was a dry season in northern Spain, the river/reservoir below us was largely dry. After the bridge, we climbed a series of steps to get to a surprisingly robust central business district lined with bars, restaurants, and shops. From a commercial perspective, the Camino de Santiago has been good for this village.

Our hotel for the evening, the Portomono Hotel, was a quarter mile from the main part of town. As we approached the modern building in which we would stay, we saw further evidence that our Camino had changed. Earlier in our time in Spain, we might have picked up our luggage from the handful of suitcases that had been delivered to the hotel. At this, our first Camino stop after Sarria, the room designated for luggage storage was full of suitcases, and the overflow extended out onto the sidewalk. Thank goodness, this modern hotel had an elevator in which to transport us and our garb to our third-floor room.

It had been some time since our early lunch, so we walked back to the downtown area for an early dinner. Sitting in the shade at an outdoor table, we enjoyed selections from the menu del día. We both started with large mixed salads, followed by grilled beef for Bev and a grilled chicken leg quarter for me, all with a bottle of Spanish red wine. Compared to the many other pilgrim's meals we had experienced, this was a pretty good one.

THE NEXT MORNING, WE walked into the large breakfast room at around 7:30 a.m. to find a busy and festive atmosphere. We sensed that many in the room had finished their first day on the trail and were preparing for their second, and their excitement had not abated. After a traditional breakfast of bread, ham, cheese, fruit, and café con leches, we joined the masses and left Portomarín at 8:15 a.m., just after sunrise. Our destination was the small city of Palas de Rei, a hilly sixteen miles away.

The route for the day was varied, the first nine miles a steady climb that was never particularly steep but was still strenuous. After starting the day on a nice natural path through a forested area, the remainder of the route followed a sparsely traveled highway. With Santiago in our sights, it was another day of putting miles behind us on an uninspiring path.

After about five miles, we came across the high school group we had first encountered in Sarria. The group was spread out, with some trailing far behind. Most of these students seemed a little less boisterous, the effect of a long hike the day before followed for many by a night of insufficient sleep. We came across a nice young man from the group who was walking by himself. He spoke very good English, so we asked him about the group and where he was from. He said the group was from Milan, Italy, and that this was a regular trip that students completed before graduating from high school. He was an impressive young man who represented his school very well.

Just up the trail, we passed a group of the high school students who had stopped to watch with great interest a small herd of cows. In Milan, there probably aren't a lot of cows, and these large animals chewing on grass were like a zoo exhibit. The cows would bend over to chomp a mouthful of greens, and one would occasionally look up at the young people staring at them on the other side of a fence as if to wonder, "Why are you watching a bunch of cows?" We kind of wondered the same thing.

The high school kids had spread out fairly quickly, so getting around the slower-moving ones was less of a challenge than it had been the day before. Overall, it seemed like a pleasant group of young people. Sure, there were some obnoxious ones, most notably the ubiquitous kid with the boombox strapped to his backpack, playing rap music loud enough for anyone within a quarter mile to hear it. It's kind of a teenager's job to annoy older people; I'm sure I was quite adept at that skill eons ago when I was that age. But most were working their way down the trail cordially and respectfully. Whether these young people realized it, walking the last seventy miles of the Camino de Santiago as a school field trip was a wonderful opportunity, providing memories and a sense of accomplishment they would carry with them for a lifetime.

EVEN AFTER WE HAD passed the large group of students, the trail was still crowded most of the day. There weren't a lot of bars and cafes along the way, and the available ones were very busy. A couple of hours after leaving Portomarín, we found a table at a bar in a little village where we enjoyed café con leches and glazed chocolate croissants. One of the many little rituals we would miss when our Camino ended was our morning coffee and pastry stops. Then, in the early afternoon, we stopped at another bar where we had excellent bocadillos (omelet with jamón and cheese for Bev and grilled pork tenderloin and cheese for me) and cans of Coke Zero. With the end of long daily walks just a few days away, we needed to transition back to a more normal approach to eating: hence the calorie-free choice of beverage. Time would suggest I didn't transition quickly or decisively enough.

We met the wonderful German family as they passed us on the trail. (The only times we had ever passed them were when they had stopped on the trail.) Since the days after leaving St. Jean Pied de Port, we had seen these nice people every day, usually at breakfast, a time or two on the trail each day, and often at dinner. This older couple with whom we could barely communicate had been such nice travel companions, and the arrival of their daughter in León to accompany them on the remainder of their Camino had raised their spirits. I asked if we could take their photo, and then they took ours, and the daughter took a photo of us and her parents together. These fine folks were part of a cadre of hikers we had shared the trail with almost daily for over a month. Though we had not grown close to any of them, there were several peregrinos we knew we would miss when our Camino concluded.

We walked for several miles with a lady we had met earlier but had not spoken to before that day. She lived in Fredericksburg, a small city in Texas where we had enjoyed a rest day during our cross-country bicycle trip six years earlier. We spoke about her town, grandchildren, and our respective experiences on the Camino Francés. Later in the afternoon, we came across the lady from Australia with whom we had shared a taxi and then a beverage a couple of weeks earlier. She shared with us some of her Camino experiences since we had last seen her and spoke proudly of the new pair of hiking shoes she had purchased (though she didn't think she would wear them on the Camino because she might get them dirty). Again, an entertaining "piece of work."

It was a long day on an undulating trail that offered little scenery of note. By mid-afternoon, we finally made it to Palas de Rei, a surprisingly robust small city of just over 3,000 inhabitants. Our lodging that evening was in the Hotel Leopoldo, a charming little six-room inn that had been converted from an ancient building. We were greeted by the innkeeper, a delightful woman who took obvious pride in the hotel's upkeep and the service it provided. As she checked us in, the innkeeper shared information about the inn, about Palas de Rei, provided a recommendation for an early dinner, and scheduled a time for breakfast the next morning. As the next day's route was eighteen miles, the last long hike of our Camino, we opted for the earliest breakfast time available.

Our last matter of business was laundry. This would likely be our last time getting our clothes washed before we headed home, and the gracious lady at the Hotel Leopoldo was happy to oblige us. Again, for a nominal fee, our clothes were washed, dried, folded, and placed in our room, waiting for us when we returned from dinner. I took a photo of Bev playfully caressing the pile of folded clean clothes as they lay on the bed; it was nice to see her so happy.

Our room was small but interesting, with a fenced-in balcony overlooking the sleeping area, accessible with an odd retractable ladder hanging from the ceiling. It was like our own personal attic. We never climbed up to look at the balcony but decided that Edie and Gus, our only two grandchildren at the time, would have had a great time playing up there. That thought made me a little homesick, but by this time the following week, we would be back home.

With few dining options and an influx of pilgrims on the prowl for dinner, we struggled to find a restaurant that served an early dinner. We finally located the restaurant the innkeeper had mentioned, a little three-table bar that served pizza. We ordered glasses of Rioja wine and then pondered whether two pizzas would be one too many. They were not, as we ate all the first and most of the second. It was far from a gourmet meal, but it was very filling. And as I suggested to Bev, perhaps we could eat healthier the next day.

WE HAD SUGGESTED TO the innkeeper that we would prefer to eat breakfast at 7:30 a.m., the earliest time available. I am a notoriously early riser; in my regular, non-Camino life, I seldom sleep past 5:00 a.m. While walking across Spain, I developed a habit of waking up especially early (say, 3:00 a.m.) and not immediately getting back to sleep. When this happened, with Bev sleeping nearby, I quietly read emails and completed other activities on my phone, which I kept near the bed. When I again grew drowsy, which often happened, I occasionally fell back to sleep for another hour or so. On the morning in Palas de Rei, with one of the longest hikes of the trip ahead of us and needing to get up earlier than usual, after resigning myself to not getting back to sleep, I did just that and woke up at 7:20 a.m. Yikes! With getting ourselves ready, packing, putting on sunscreen, putting tape on problem areas on our feet, getting our water packs filled and our backpacks ready, and the myriad of other tasks required, it took us considerable time each morning before we were ready to leave. On a hike that would require eight hours or more, time wasted in the cool morning meant more time walking in the hot and sunny afternoon. So, oversleeping on this day was no small issue. Plus, we had asked the innkeeper to be ready for us at a particular time.

But she was very understanding (another couple was eating at that time anyway) and provided one of the best breakfasts we had on our trip, a spread that included many of the traditional Spanish menu items and a delicious egg, ham, and potato casserole served in cute little individual dishes. It had been a pleasant stay at the Hotel Leopoldo.

DESPITE OUR (MY) OVERSLEEPING, we left Palas de Rei at 8:30 a.m., perhaps half an hour later than we had planned. As we departed this little hamlet, it was cool and breezy; by early afternoon, it was hot and sunny, with temperatures reaching the mid-80s. According to the locals we spoke to, these were atypical conditions, much warmer and drier than normal. Santiago was almost close enough to see, just two more days away. But with what would end up being a nineteen-mile route in those hot and dry conditions, the Camino still had some challenges for us before we reached our destination.

It all made for a dreadfully long day on a nondescript route, though one that was not without its highlights. In the little village of Casanova, we stopped for yet another of those glazed, chocolate-filled croissants we had grown to love, a simple little treat that, with a café con leche, had become our go-to mid-morning pick-me-up. By this time the following week, we would be home transitioning back to our regular lives. Given my aging metabolism, my days of enjoying these chocolate-filled treats would soon end.

After our mid-morning stop, we traversed a series of long inclines followed by similar downhills, most on a well-worn natural path. Earlier in our journey, we had given much more thought to the terrain we encountered, especially the climbing and descending. Five weeks into our Camino, we simply hiked over whatever obstacles we faced with little thought.

Our guidebook suggested the small city of Melide as a good lunch spot near the halfway point of the route. We also knew that Melide was known for its octopus dishes. So, as we entered the outskirts of town, we came across a nice restaurant with a beautifully shaded outdoor patio. From our table on the terrace, we ordered two large salads and an order of pulpo, or octopus. The salads were welcomed by both of us following our gut-busting pizza dinner the night before.

The pulpo soon arrived, large chunks of octopus served in a wooden bowl. The seafood appeared to have been grilled and then sautéed in olive oil and dusted with a little paprika. Bev thought it tasted fishy, but I thought the flavors were amazing, one of the most memorable meals we enjoyed on this trip.

As we walked through the surprisingly busy small city of Melide, we still had nine miles to get to Arzua, our destination for the day, and it continued to get warmer. Needing a boost of energy, at around twelve miles, we stopped for soft drinks and a couple of bananas. The nourishment was great, but it was especially good to get our packs off and out of the sun. As we continued, with the temperature now around eighty-seven, many of the hordes of people on the trail seemed to wilt. With three miles to go, we stopped at a very busy bar and had ice cream bars, hoping the surge of energy would propel us on.

I don't know if it did, but at 4:30 p.m., after eight hours of walking, we mercifully reached Arzua. This hectic little Galician city of 6,500 has long been a Camino crossroads, the point where the Camino Francés and the Camino del Norte (the Northern Way) meet before reaching Santiago de Compostela. Located a hundred meters off the route, our hotel for the evening was the Pension Boutique La Casona De Nene, a very long name for what was an inn with a small number of rooms. But it was an attractively decorated old hotel that exuded a more modern feel. Our room was on the second floor (which in Spain is actually the third floor, because the ground floor is zero). Bless the staff, because there was no elevator, and the amiable lady who checked us in told us our suitcases were in our room and would be picked up there in the morning. As we made our way to our small but cozy room, we were dirty, sweaty, grimy, tired, and our feet hurt. After checking in, we took some time to get cleaned up before heading out to explore the surrounding neighborhood.

At the innkeeper's recommendation, we walked a short distance to a restaurant that offered early dinner service. With a bottle of Spanish vino blanco, we had the menu del día, one of the last of our Camino experience. Bev started with the ratatouille and I had a pasta salad (really a regular mixed salad with tuna and pasta, but tasty). For the main course, Bev had lasagna (oddly with a coating of mashed potatoes, sort of like a Spanish/Italian version of shepherd's pie) and I had the fish. I asked, but don't recall the type of fish, but it was a grilled whole fish that was very thin and full of pesky little bones. It made for a lot of work for not a lot of fish. While Bev skipped dessert, I had a small piece of cheesecake. Still exhausted from our nineteen-mile day, we went back to the inn and were in bed earlier than usual.

OUR JOURNEY ON THE Camino was a multi-faceted experience, flat days and hilly days, short days and long days, urban days and rural days, etc. But in another respect, our walk on the Way could be divided between the first thirty-two days before we arrived in Sarria and the five days after we departed that city, the start of the Camino for so many pilgrims. After the second day out of Sarria, we never again encountered the high school group from Italy. But the path was still clogged with hikers, most of whom were just starting their journeys. There were, no doubt, some wonderful people in the large group that started sixty or seventy miles from Santiago. But, as we can attest, there were also some knuckleheads among these late starters.

At the risk of seeming arrogant or condescending, the attitude of many of these new pilgrims was simply different. Most of those of us who had been on the trail for over a month had, through weeks of long, hard days, developed a reverence for the Camino and for each other. We had developed a deep respect for what we were doing and for the amazing experience we were sharing. We had developed a sense of awe and reverence for the Camino Francés and for what we were accomplishing, a 500-mile hike across Spain. Despite this sense of accomplishment, most realized that the Camino de Santiago, with its lore and history and the countless peregrinos who had come before us, made the accomplishment of any of us simply like a blip in time.

Completing a Camino that would last only a few days, so many of these new pilgrims had simply not had time to learn these deep, reverential lessons. And though we tried to take their actions in stride, so many of these folks were downright annoying. Starting in Sarria, a party atmosphere descended on the Camino, with hikers talking and laughing loudly without regard for the countless people around them. Seldom did an hour go by that we didn't encounter at least one individual listening to loud music or having a heated conversation on their phone, all without headphones. Large groups of ten to fifteen hikers, something we simply did not see in our first month on the trail, would walk five or six abreast, blocking the passage of faster-moving pilgrims. And it was not uncommon for individuals to simply stop without warning on the narrow trail to take a selfie, oblivious to the fact that thousands of other peregrinos were hiking on the same path. We did our best not to get too bothered by these behaviors, resigning ourselves as we concluded our journey to "walk our own Camino," just as these other folks were apparently doing.

So, the community that developed early in our journey had become increasingly difficult to find as the trail became more crowded. However, there were folks we had met weeks earlier who, as our Camino was ending and after we had assumed they were ahead of us, behind us, or had returned home, seemed to just reappear. There was a nice lady from Florida we had met early on but had not seen for what seemed like weeks. I had mentioned to Bev that I wondered what had happened to her, and then, a couple of days later, as we walked by the patio of a restaurant, there she was having lunch with a group of other folks we had not seen for some time. Then there was the lady from Las Vegas who, in an extended conversation on the trail a week earlier, had shared with me much of her life story and her views on her faith and her church. It was a deeply personal discussion in which she had been completely open to me, an absolute stranger. After a lengthy, fascinating, and largely one-sided discourse, I bid this nice and sharing lady "Buen Camino" because I needed to find a bathroom spot. As an introvert who is guarded in what personal information I share about myself, I was amazed by the openness that had been demonstrated by this new acquaintance. And as I went in search of a secluded spot off the trail, I assumed I would never see this lady again. Then, a couple of weeks later, after checking into our hotel in one of the countless villages in which we stayed, as we walked by yet another restaurant patio, there was our Vegas friend sharing a meal with the lady from Texas. Even as the Camino became crowded after the onslaught of hikers after Sarria, there were still instances in which memorable pilgrims from earlier in our journey would reappear unexpectedly.

Perhaps our favorite example of this was a young woman from Ottawa, Canada. It was during the first week on the trail, as we were climbing a very long and steep hill, that we came across this young woman who was, and I don't want to be insensitive, rather overweight. She was struggling as she slowly ascended that hill. We said little to her as we passed her beyond a quick greeting, and her breathless response showed the extent she was straining on that incline. Bev and I spoke to her a couple of times that week under less trying circumstances, sharing where we were from, where we had started on the Camino, etc. We hadn't seen her in several weeks and wondered if she was still making her way to Santiago, skeptically hoping that she was. Then, a few days before we arrived in Santiago and as we were getting used to the influx of pilgrims on the trail, we passed a bench on the side of the path and there she was. Bev said to me, "Is that the lady from Canada?" I simply said to her as we passed among a throng of hikers, "Is that Ottawa?" She gleefully replied with a glowing smile, "Hey Chicago!" We never learned this beautiful young woman's name, but we were so proud of her for overcoming the extra challenges she faced as she walked the same 500 miles we did.

Bev and I had only a handful of conversations with this young Canadian, and while we will never see her again, we will forever have a bond with her and the countless other peregrinos with whom we shared this transcendent journey. That is one of the many amazing powers of the Camino de Santiago.

WE WERE TWO DAYS of hiking from Santiago de Compostela, and the route from Arzua was twelve miles to the suburban village of Pedrouza. Breakfast for guests of the Pension Boutique La Casona De Nene was provided at a little restaurant a quarter mile from the inn but right on the trail. We packed up and headed to the café at 7:30 a.m., and finished our traditional Spanish breakfast (toast, cheese, ham, salami, fruit, orange juice, and coffee) around 8:00. This part of Spain is in the far western portion of the time zone we had been in since arriving in the country, so sunrise was especially late. It was dark when we left Arzua, which posed few problems as we walked through the outskirts of town, but became sketchy as we entered the countryside. There were again many pilgrims on the trail, so, assuming they all knew where they were going, we had plenty of hikers to follow. It was warmer than in recent mornings, and for the first time in weeks, neither Bev nor I started the day in a jacket.

It was another nondescript day of hiking, with much of the route on a natural path with considerable shade, but also a paved trail alongside a busy highway. Though we made steady progress, we found our minds wandering to our arrival the next day in Santiago when, after thirty-seven days, our Camino would come to an end. It was a day of constant rolling hills with just a few flat sections, but we didn't really care.

After an hour on the trail, we stopped for a café con leche. For the past few days, Bev and I had discussed items and rituals we were going to miss when we returned home, and these amazing cups of coffee were near the top of the list. At around 11:30 a.m., we stopped for lunch at a very nice trailside restaurant. As bars or restaurants located alongside the Camino go, this one was memorably good. Bev ordered a vegetarian burrito and house-made iced tea (with ice!), and I had the "Galicia burger" with fries, a very good burger with special cheese, homemade ketchup, bacon, and grilled onions. It was a luxury, for one of the few times, to have ketchup with the countless orders of fries we had been served. It was an excellent lunch in a very nice restaurant, and we kind of didn't want to leave. But we still had five miles to go and there was a line waiting for a table, so we trudged on.

The travel company app on our phones provided maps and route information, and as our Apple watches passed 10.7 miles, as listed in our guidebook, and then kept going, we knew it was going to be a longer day than expected. The route ended up being almost twelve miles, but that put us a mile closer to Santiago on the next day's last route.

Though it had a history that predated the recent surge in popularity of the Camino, Pedrouza had the feel of a town created to serve the needs of peregrinos at their last stop before arriving in Santiago. Our hotel for the evening was the Pension Residencias Platas, a modern restoration of an older building. Our room was characteristically small for a Camino-focused inn, but in a welcome change on a hot day, it had very good air conditioning. We had stayed in rooms with air conditioning units since arriving in Spain five weeks earlier, especially in larger cities like Barcelona and Pamplona. But on a continent with more focused attention on the effects of climate change, those units seldom provided much more than enhanced ventilation for a stuffy room. This was the first unit that worked well. In fact, despite temperatures in the upper eighties, we got a little chilly by the late afternoon. In the United States, massive amounts of power are used to drastically lower the temperature in homes and other buildings in warm climates. As we prepared to leave Spain, we knew there was much that could be learned from these more eco-conscious nations.

After checking into the hotel, though we were sweaty and dirty from our penultimate day on the trail, we delayed getting cleaned up to walk to a nearby restaurant to have a beer. We sat in the shade of an awning on the outdoor patio and enjoyed watching the countless pilgrims as they aimlessly passed by. Later, after showering, we walked back to that same restaurant and had dinner. It was a "cantina" with a Mexican theme, so I had a margarita. Bev had a glass of vino tinto and we shared a small order of chips and guacamole and then large mixed salads. Cultures are different, obviously, and my margarita came at room temperature with no ice, and the guacamole came with about five tortilla chips. These are small, insignificant issues, no doubt, but the experience provided further evidence that we would need to reacclimate ourselves to the greater American tendency toward excess, with the ever-present "bottomless" baskets of tortilla chips common at Mexican restaurants in the US as just one example.

Our athletic-looking young server spoke very good English and asked us where we were from, and when we said "Chicago," his eyes lit up. He told us his dad was an engineer who had worked on projects in Chicago, and that it was his favorite city. He talked about how much he liked the Smashing Pumpkins, and I told him Billy Corgan, lead singer of the band, lived near where we lived. He was a big fan of American football and said in excited English that he had played safety for a Spanish national team. He even said he had on his phone a photo of Justin Fields, starting quarterback for the Chicago Bears in 2023. (I doubt that anyone actually living in Chicago had a photo of Justin Fields on their phone at that time.) It was a pleasant exchange and provided further evidence that the world is often smaller than we realize.

W E WERE IN A pensive mood the next morning as we prepared for the last leg of our Camino, contemplating how far we had traveled and how, in a few short hours, we would have no more hikes to prepare for. Bev and I were still ready to get home, but a part of each of us knew we would miss the daily routines that had become ingrained over the last thirty-seven days. We had thought about this trip for so many years and had prepared for it longer than the past twelve months. We felt a growing sense of accomplishment at what we were about to achieve. But with that accomplishment also would come an unceremonious ending.

Years ago, during my time as a track coach, I stressed to my athletes that when they finished a race, they needed to keep moving. Throughout the race, the heart and lungs had reached a point where they were pumping huge volumes of blood and oxygen throughout the body. To abruptly stop moving while the body was still working to keep up with the demands of running was unhealthy and, for older folks, possibly dangerous. There needed to be a transition from peak demand to rest.

So it is with a long and arduous journey like walking the Camino de Santiago, though the challenges associated with the inevitable abrupt ending are mental rather than physical. You go and go, day after day, and then you stop. Rather than a pounding heart and heaving lungs, you are left with a sense of, "What do we do now?"

W E LEFT PEDROUZA AT 8:00 a.m., just as it was getting light outside. When we checked into our hotel, we had been given a coupon entitling us to breakfast at a little café next door. The place was busy with only one older lady working frantically to fill everyone's order. When it was our turn in line, we showed her the little coupon from our hotel that entitled us to a complimentary breakfast. In response, she rattled off in rapid-fire Spanish a series of questions about what we wanted. Understanding virtually none of what she said, we just nodded and said "Si." We expected little, but after about five minutes, the server brought out two large plates of food with fried eggs, large slices of Spanish bacon, and a huge slice of toast, all with orange juice and coffee. This overworked lady had provided, on our last hiking day, one of the best breakfasts of our entire Camino. Perhaps there was a message here.

Despite the significance of this last hike of our Camino, and though we would walk through Santiago de Compostela in a few hours, the morning felt much like the previous thirty-three walking days on the trail. The route was listed as a little over fourteen miles but, based on the location of the hotel we were leaving, we suspected it would be closer to twelve. By the time we made it to the cathedral in Santiago and then back to our hotel, our last official Camino hike was around thirteen miles.

Outside of Santiago de Compostela

The Camino still had some challenges for us with a lot of climbing, especially early on the route. As we had suspected, the trail was very crowded, though there were short periods when we found ourselves oddly isolated. The trail was either well-worn or paved, and there were stretches where we walked under a fully enclosed canopy of trees. There were some beautiful sections of this last route, and we consciously tried to stay in the moment and savor our last hours on the Camino. But we found it challenging not to look ahead, to Santiago, to no more hikes, to our flights to Madrid and then on to Chicago, and to our return to our "regular" lives.

After four miles, we stopped for coffee and, for the last time on the trail, one of those glazed chocolate croissants that Bev and I shared. Later, we stopped for a light lunch of a sort of tuna-filled thin pie, something common in Spain that we likely won't want to replicate back in the United States. After countless lunches of bocadillos, Spanish omelets, pulpo, and other treats, our last meal on the trail was less than memorable.

Much of our morning was spent walking around the Santiago-Rosalía de Castro Airport, from which we would depart in two days. Though we knew we were close to the airport, and despite the occasional sounds of planes arriving and departing, dense foliage and well-placed earthen berms prevented us from seeing any terminal buildings or aircraft. We trudged on and were so ready to be finished, but the day seemed to just drag on.

Shortly after our trek around the airport, we passed through the little village of Lavacolla, an unheralded but very significant site on the Camino. For centuries, peregrinos bathed in a little stream here, an act of spiritual and physical cleansing at the end of a long journey before paying homage to the remains of St. James in Santiago. We certainly didn't take a dip in the water and didn't see anyone else completing a ritual bathing. (I would be surprised if many who passed by that day were even aware of the custom.) But in my mind, it brought focus to how far the Camino, and society in general, has progressed. For more than the first thousand years of this famous pilgrimage route, the countless peregrinos who passed by this tiny stream bathed here because that was all that was available. Most were impoverished, and by this time, many were clad in threadbare clothing after weeks of almost continual exposure to the elements. These true pilgrims didn't sleep in a warm bed, didn't have hot showers available to them, and didn't have to worry about a functional air conditioning unit getting their private room too chilly.

IN TIME, WE WERE walking on streets and sidewalks into the center of Santiago de Compostela. All of the official Camino routes end at the Santiago de Compostela Cathedral, the massive and ornate basilica that is the location of the crypt purportedly containing the remains of the Apostle James. On a family vacation to the Black Hills in South Dakota when our children were small, as we were leaving Rapid City, we started looking for Mount Rushmore in the distance. I recall getting a fleeting glimpse of the mountainside sculpture from several miles away, and then not another glance. Then suddenly, we rounded a curve and there it was in all its magnificence. It was the same with the cathedral as we walked through Santiago. The towers of the cathedral are nearly 250 feet tall and dominate the Santiago skyline. As we were following the last miles of the trail, we topped a hill and could view in the distance the unmistakable façade of this enormous church. Then, because of topography and multi-story buildings, we didn't see it again until we were virtually next to it. But somehow, we sensed we were getting close.

There was a rush of humanity as we walked the last few hundred meters of our Camino, and we could sense the energy of the countless people milling around us. We walked through a tunnel to the deafening sound of a bagpipe player, then rounded the side of a huge building and suddenly we were in the Plaza del Obradoiro, the enormous paved open space in front of the cathedral where arriving pilgrims celebrate the end of their journey.

And just like that, our Camino had come to an end.

"EVERYONE HAS TO DO THEIR OWN CAMINO."

*"It's your road and yours alone. Others may walk it with you,
but no one can walk it for you."*

Rumi

"WELL, THAT'S NOT FAIR," I said to myself in an incredulous and judgmental tone. We were early on our first day on the Camino, just a few miles outside of St. Jean Pied de Port. We were making steady progress up the long incline into the Pyrenees, the light rain not yet turning into the deluge that would soon descend on us.

We had encountered a couple of older Dutch men on bicycles, one an amiable gentleman who spoke some English and the other a non-speaker who typically stood by his bike and smiled a lot. We had spoken briefly and had taken each other's photos. Then, although we were walking and they were on bicycles, we kept passing each other, nodding hello or offering the universal "Buen Camino."

I started watching these two cyclists and the recurring routine they followed as they climbed up the mountain. After taking a break on the side of the road, the two would start riding together, and given the steepness of the climb, the English-speaking man would soon start walking his bike. The other rider kept climbing, almost effortlessly, and would ride for a half mile or so before stopping to wait for his riding partner to catch up to him. This went on for several miles, the one rider working hard to get up the hill while the other was seemingly on a relaxed morning jaunt in the Pyrenees. This struck me as strange, as the effortless rider appeared older and rather out of shape, certainly not your typical mountain-climbing cyclist.

After watching this play out a few times, as we walked past the one cyclist as he waited for his riding mate, I realized he was riding an e-bike, a bicycle with a small motor that provided a mechanical boost on the constant uphill sections. The other Dutch rider was riding a regular bicycle that relied solely on his own power to get him up the hill. Perhaps in part because I was already feeling the effects of hiking up this long incline, I started thinking about how this was so unfair to the guy riding the regular bike.

But really, what business was this of mine? Why should I have been so concerned about the fairness of how these two were beginning their Camino? The short answers are it was none of my business and I had no reason to be concerned. The man riding the regular bike seemed undaunted by any disparity in the modes of transportation he and his partner were using, so why should I be?

Like every individual we encountered that day on the trail and for the thirty-six days that followed, these two Dutchmen were doing their own Camino, just like Bev and me.

Like in many areas, there is a certain amount of "snobbishness" among Camino purists, a belief that a trek to Santiago de Compostela has to meet certain criteria or it is somehow diminished. On the Camino Francés, as an example, the journey must begin in St. Jean Pied de Port and continue straight through to the cathedral in Santiago. For the true Camino experience, one must carry everything in a backpack and stay each night in a communal albergue. Unstated is the notion that every inch of the Way must be traveled on foot. (Pilgrims on bicycles were, at best, interlopers, nuisances who had no business on the trail.)

Bev and I bypassed a couple of sections of the trail when it made sense to do so. We stayed each night in a private room and (gasp!) had our suitcases shuttled from one inn to the next. We were walking our own Camino, and our experience wasn't diminished in the least.

Admittedly, I felt a sense of irritation as we were joined by the hundreds of new peregrinos who began their Camino in Sarria. Under requirements established through the Cathedral of Santiago de Compostela, pilgrims must walk at least 100 kilometers (sixty-two miles) on an approved Camino route to qualify for a Compostela, or certificate of completion. On the Camino Francés, the city just beyond that 100-kilometer threshold is Sarria. As a result, for individuals placing importance on earning one of these certificates, this was the logical starting point.

By the time we arrived in Sarria, Bev and I had hiked nearly 430 miles over often-challenging terrain. We had developed a sense of community with a group of hikers we had come to like and respect. And we had gained a sense of reverence for the history and traditions of the Camino that had developed over the past millennium. We respected the Way and had come to understand we were just passing through, that the Camino had been there long before us and would continue long after.

Starting in Sarria, all of that seemed to change in an instant. Where there had often been tranquility and occasional isolation to that point, suddenly we were in the middle of throngs of people. While we had often enjoyed the quiet of the trail, now we were inundated with often obnoxious sounds. Hikers listening to podcasts or audiobooks without headphones, groups of eight or ten pilgrims spreading across the path, talking and laughing loudly. Or the occasional individual stopped in the middle of the trail, talking loudly on their phone. And perhaps most emblematic of this change of atmosphere, the high school kid blasting hip-hop music from a boombox strapped to his backpack.

To the purists who viewed luggage transfers as a blemish on one's Camino credibility, these hikers who started in Sarria were just a bunch of annoying people taking a vacation. To the rest of us who had started on the other side of the Pyrenees, many of them were simply annoying.

But is that fair? These people weren't completing their Camino the way we were. But like us, they were walking their own Camino, finding what worked for them. Bev and I had the time and resources to spend six weeks walking across Spain. Many of those walking from Sarria likely lacked the advantages we did, and hiking sixty-plus miles was the best they could physically, monetarily, and occupationally handle.

Given some of the inconsiderate behaviors we witnessed from these new pilgrims, our occasional irritation was likely justified. But they were walking their own Camino, doing the best they could under the circumstances under which they operated. They deserved our respect, admiration, and grace for their accomplishment in getting to Santiago de Compostela.

But still, we sure could have done without that damn boombox.

EPILOGUE

MAKING SENSE OF AN AMAZING EXPERIENCE

WHAT DO YOU DO when you've just finished an iconic 500-mile hiking journey, when you look up and see the Cathedral of Santiago de Compostela, the symbol of the goal you've been trying to reach for the past thirty-seven days, and much of your adult life?

As the paved path Bev and I were following spilled onto the sprawling Plaza del Obradoiro, we found ourselves among hundreds of pilgrims donned with backpacks, funny hats, and hiking shoes. Most were in a celebratory mood, for good reason, and a festive atmosphere permeated the large crowd.

In *The Pilgrim's Guide to the Camino de Santiago*, the guidebook we had relied on for 500 miles, the late John Brierley writes about the moment you find yourself on the plaza in front of the cathedral, "Take time to *arrive*. We each experience different emotions, from euphoria to disappointment on seeing the Cathedral. Whatever your individual reaction, honor and accept it."

Our emotions at this important moment ran the gamut. There was a sense of pride, no doubt, for accomplishing what we had set out to do. There was happiness, though I'm not sure whether that was because we *had* finished or because we *were* finished. There was certainly gratitude, for each other, for the amazing experience, and for the opportunity to fulfill a longtime goal.

But really, our greatest emotion at this moment was a profound sense of relief.

THE ATMOSPHERE ON THE plaza seemed to include a similar range of emotions. People were hugging in recognition of their accomplishment, and large groups boisterously celebrated their arrival in Santiago. Others seemed dumbstruck by what had just happened, struggling to figure out what to do next. Still others seemed to consider their brief time on the Plaza del Obradoiro to be an obligatory ritual, an informal ceremony to signify the end of their long journey. Bev and I most closely resembled this last group. For us, our brief time in front of the Cathedral of Santiago de Compostela was important but meant far less than the arduous experience that had brought us to this iconic location.

Standing among the hundreds of newly arrived pilgrims in the middle of the plaza, Bev and I shared our thoughts and appreciation for each other, took several photos of ourselves and our surroundings, and asked an amiable young lady standing nearby to take our photo. She took the task seriously, taking my phone and lying on the pavement to get a better angle. We appreciated her efforts, and the photo she took of Bev and me standing in front of the cathedral will remain a special one.

Standing in the Plaza del Obradoiro

We looked around for anyone we knew, but after thirty-seven days of making acquaintances on the trail, we saw no one we recognized. While we weren't sad, a bit of melancholy set in as we couldn't share this moment with anyone else. There was an odd, cacophonous feel among the countless celebrants, and Bev and I moved to the edge of the square where we took off our packs, sat down briefly, and tried to gain a better sense of how we were feeling. Finding the perspective we were seeking would take time, but we had more clarity about what we were feeling; we were ready to move on.

In our decades together, Bev and I have had a few accomplishments, some minor and others more significant. As an example, I have earned four college degrees, each requiring a tremendous amount of work and years to complete. But for the first three, I had no interest in participating in graduation ceremonies. I attended the commencement following the completion of my doctoral degree, in part because of the unique rituals associated with the receipt of such a degree, but also to allow my family to enjoy the moment they had helped make possible with their many sacrifices. But even that ceremony, while very memorable, was much of an afterthought. What counted with those various academic degrees was the work involved, what had been learned, and the opportunities each made available to me and our family. In other words, I was ready to move on.

With our previous adventure trips, including our hike across the Grand Canyon and our bicycle ride across the southern United States, when we finished, Bev and I expressed our appreciation for each other and briefly celebrated with our travel mates, but didn't linger. It was as if the celebrations were a small bonus, like icing on a cake. The real gift was the journey, the preparation, the hard effort that got us through the challenging days. While we certainly don't look upon such celebrations with any disdain, we simply have developed a different mindset.

So, as the hundreds of peregrinos enjoyed their well-earned festive moment on the Plaza del Obradoiro, Bev and I decided we were ready to move on. We were so happy and grateful to have finished our Camino, but we wanted to get off our feet.

AFTER LEAVING THE PLAZA, we went in search of the Pilgrim's Office where we would receive our Compostela, the certificate signifying we had completed our walk on the Camino de Santiago. The office is on a side street near the cathedral. We quickly found the office where we assumed we would return the next day. On the way back toward our hotel, we walked by an outdoor patio and saw the nice young British couple, one a breast cancer survivor and the other a London police officer, we had befriended during our second week on the trail. We hadn't encountered them for at least two weeks and had assumed they were on a different schedule and we wouldn't see them again. Just a brief time earlier, we had lamented that we would not see for the last time some of the great people we had met during our Camino. It was a fortuitous lifting of our spirits to get to say goodbye to this wonderful young couple.

Our hotel for our two nights in Santiago was the Hotel Boutique Capitol, a newer hotel located a few blocks from the cathedral. This was the last lodging included as part of the package we had purchased from the travel company. The prospect of traveling to a foreign country and staying in thirty-two different hotels and inns, sight unseen and reserved by a commercial entity, had initially caused some uneasiness. We had not been sure what to expect. Though some establishments we stayed in were better than others, and some were spectacular while others were meager, all were clean, safe, and serviceable. We had been fortunate, the travel company had done a great job, and the Hotel Boutique Capitol was among the best hotels we stayed in.

Still buzzing from our time on the Plaza del Obradoiro, and even before showering, we walked a couple of blocks down the street from the hotel to have a celebratory beer. We talked just briefly about the day, our journey, and what we had accomplished, Then, we turned to the next day when we planned to visit the Pilgrim's Office to receive our Compostela, do a little souvenir shopping, and tour the cathedral. But our greatest focus as we sat at an outdoor table at this little bar was a little farther into the future. We were ready to get home.

AFTER GETTING CLEANED UP, we walked back to the area near the cathedral hoping to find a restaurant serving dinner at 6:00 p.m. on a Sunday. We did not, but we noticed that the Pilgrim's Office didn't appear to be very busy. We had expected we would need to stand in a long line to have our pilgrim passport verified to confirm we had walked enough miles to qualify for a Compostela. When we walked into the Pilgrim's Office that evening, we were pleasantly surprised to see only a few peregrinos in line. As we were waiting for dinner anyway, we decided to get this last official bit of pilgrim business completed.

The procedure for procuring a Compostela has in recent years been modernized. Historically, when the number of peregrinos was much more manageable, the process had been fairly primitive. When they arrived in Santiago, pilgrims presented themselves at a small office in the Cathedral and someone reviewed the stamps placed in the Pilgrim Passport, perhaps asked some questions, and then hand-wrote the pilgrim's name on the certificate. This simple procedure was dramatized near the end of the movie *The Way*.

Now, peregrinos are required to complete online preregistration with various personal information before arriving at the new, much larger Pilgrim's Office. We had done that a few days before arriving in Santiago, and an email with a QR code was sent back to us. There were just a handful of people waiting in line in front of us, and with several clerks processing the applications, it was soon our turn. The affable young man took a quick glance at our Pilgrim Passports to make sure we had walked the requisite distance, then scanned each of our QR codes and quickly printed out our certificates. There was no charge for the Compostela, but we had each requested an optional distance certificate for an additional charge. We took our certificates to a payment kiosk, scanned our credit card, and were soon on our way. After anticipating a lengthy wait followed by a more onerous review of our documentation, we were in and out in less than fifteen minutes. And with that, yet another aspect of our Camino experience was behind us. It was rather fascinating how something as primitive as the Camino de Santiago was being brought into the modern age.

As we had earlier searched for a restaurant with early dinner service, we had noticed one with a handwritten sign indicating it would open at 7:00 p.m. It was nearly that time, so we walked in and saw a family of four, two parents and a teenage son and daughter, sitting around a table. When we asked if they were open for dinner, the father enthusiastically told us we could pick any table in the restaurant. (We were their first customers of the evening.) With a bottle of Spanish red wine, the ubiquitous vino tinto, we had our last menu del día of our six weeks in Spain. It had always been good to score one of these traditional, three-course pilgrim's meals, an excellent value with food that was usually quite good. In the city, this one was more expensive, but still a splendid meal. Bev started with a bowl of lentil soup and I had the Galician broth, and both were tasty. Then, we both ordered chicken asada with salad, and I finished with ice cream for dessert. It was a good last pilgrim's meal, and we were glad to have provided what appeared to be a fairly new family business with some customers.

As we were leaving, we noticed sitting at a table outside the restaurant the older couple from Seattle we had talked with several times since leaving St. Jean Pied de Port. They had shared with us how they had struggled and how the husband had dealt with severe leg pain. We had not seen them for over a week, so we were happy they had completed their Camino. Impressively, they were planning to continue walking for a few more days, following the trail to the Atlantic Ocean and the little Spanish town of Finisterre. We congratulated them and told them we were amazed by their drive and resilience, but sheepishly shared that we were ready to head home.

When we went to bed that first evening in Santiago de Compostela, Bev jokingly told me she didn't want a wake-up call. She didn't get one, and though I woke up quite a bit earlier, neither of us got up until after 8:00 a.m. While that's late for Bev, it's a form of hibernation for me. But we didn't have to pack our bags, or tape our feet, or fill our water bottles, or get our packs ready. For the first time in thirty-seven days, there were no hikes in our immediate future.

That morning, during my extended time lying in bed, I had a lot to think about, reflecting on what we had finished the day before. I thought with pride about reaching a tough, long-term goal, and doing so at sixty-six. When we had pondered the notion of walking the Camino, the prospect of daily fourteen-to-fifteen-mile hikes in a foreign country with a language we barely understood, the whole thing seemed very daunting. But we persevered, and as a result, we gained yet another life-altering experience. I thought of Bev and how she had endured the particularly difficult times. Though we had dealt with fatigue-driven conflict that had briefly put us at odds with one another, the entire journey was so much more meaningful because we had completed it together. I think Bev would agree with that.

And I thought about home, about our family that we deeply missed, and about spending time with our two grandchildren. In three days, we would be back in the United States, back home, and back to the routines that we had developed during the past few years of our retirement. A part of me wondered if, after spending six weeks traipsing across a foreign country, those routines would provide sufficient excitement to keep us satisfied. (They would.)

This had been the second time since entering our sixties that we had been away from home for a month and a half, completing a strenuous adventure trip. Bev and I discussed this extensively during the last weeks of our Camino, and we agreed about future trips of this nature. While the strenuous part doesn't bother us, being away from home for six weeks does. We had moved to the Chicago area to be closer to our family, to watch our grandchildren grow and develop, and to enjoy time with and be available to help our grown children and their spouses.

There will be adventure trips in our future, at least for as long as we are physically capable. But trips of this length are likely now in our past. And we were not saddened by that realization, just thankful for the opportunities we had been given.

As I lay next to my partner in life and adventure in that hotel room in Santiago de Compostela, I was happy, proud, grateful, and relieved. And ready to go home.

In the hotel restaurant, we had the most leisurely breakfast we had enjoyed in weeks. I had three cups of café con leche and felt a little buzzing in my head as a result. Full and, in my case, a little jacked from the caffeine, we set off to do some shopping. But first, we had a donation to make.

There is an American-based organization called the "Pilgrim House" that has a welcome center in Santiago. The organization supports individuals before, during, and after their Caminos, and the welcome center accepts donations of hiking gear and clothing that could be of use to needy peregrinos. We had some gear that was still in good condition but we didn't want to carry back to the United States.

Our daypacks, which we had bought on a whim during the pandemic and then wondered whether we would ever use them, had served us well.

But day after day of sweating onto the back side of the packs, plus days of trail dust and grime, had made them a bit rank. Both were still in good condition but needed a good cleaning. We hoped some needy pilgrims could use them. We also donated some clothes and a couple of pairs of hiking shoes.

It was an impressive center with a friendly vibe. The helpful young lady who assisted us had an American accent, and when we asked where she was from, she indicated she had been born in Kansas City (near where we lived for decades) but had moved when she was very young. This was quite a coincidence, and we were glad we had connected with another former Missourian.

As we made our way across Spain, we saw countless little shops that offered Camino-focused souvenirs. As we had limited luggage space and didn't want to lug added weight across the country, we had not even looked at their wares. With Santiago as the epicenter of the Camino world, there seemed to be souvenir shops on every street. We purchased some books and little Camino shell coin purses for the grandkids, a map of the Camino Francés, a couple of tote bags (we had used our daypacks as our carry-ons on the flight to Barcelona), and a beautiful dark blue tile with a yellow Camino shell painted on it.

We took our purchases back to the hotel and then headed to the cathedral for the noon pilgrim's mass. The cathedral typically fills up for this ceremony, so we arrived forty-five minutes before noon, got good seats in the center section, and watched as this vast place of worship filled to overflowing.

Like those we had toured in Barcelona, Burgos, and León, the Cathedral of Santiago de Compostela is amazing, huge, and ornate, with the main altar flaked in gold. The effect of the midday sun shining through the many stained-glass windows and reflecting off the shiny gold façade was stunning.

Promptly at noon, a cantor took his place on a little side balcony and several priests walked onto the lectern. The mass was led by one priest (or bishop, or cardinal, or whatever title he had been given), who was differentiated by being the only one wearing a hat. In addition to the cantor, this priest was assisted by five other priests, three nuns, and several other assistants. We understood virtually none of what was said, but the service was warm and rather soothing. Attending a pilgrim's mass is considered a rite of passage for those who have completed a Camino. Though not Catholic, we were glad we had experienced such a welcoming ceremony.

Made popular by the movie *The Way* (and YouTube videos), the most famous symbol of pilgrims' masses in the Cathedral of Santiago de Compostela is the "Botafumeiro." This huge thurible, or incense burner, is only brought out for special occasions (the mass celebrating Bev and me completing our Camino was apparently not one of them), but creates a spectacular effect when it is used. In the Catholic Church and some other religions, a small thurible hanging from chains is used during services to spread incense smoke among the congregants, with a priest or another individual lightly swinging the device back and forth.

The Botafumeiro, on the other hand, is huge, almost five feet tall. When it is used in a service, this large brass and bronze incense burner is connected to a rope attached to a pulley system hanging over sixty feet above the altar. When used during a special mass, the incense smoke-spewing device is lifted by a team of eight men pulling on the rope, who then maneuver the device so it is rapidly swinging over and above the side sections of the cathedral. The effect of this ceremony is spectacular. We would have enjoyed witnessing this spectacle in person, but our pilgrim's mass was still memorable, a warm and oddly comforting experience.

We had hoped to share our goodbyes with some of the great people we had met on the trail, and that afternoon we were not disappointed. As we waited for the pilgrim's mass to begin, we spoke briefly with the nice German family we had encountered every day since leaving St. Jean Pied de Port. Then, after exiting the cathedral and as we were walking around searching for a special restaurant for lunch, we happened upon the two ladies from Michigan and the one from Texas. All three were flying out of Santiago that afternoon. We had enjoyed our conversations with these very intelligent and interesting ladies, and it was good to be able to say our goodbyes. Bev asked if they had seen the couple from Alaska, and they said they were having lunch at a café just down the street. We soon found them and said our farewells, and with them was one of the ladies from Wisconsin we had met during our first week on the trail as well as the young lady from Ottawa, Canada. It was cathartic to have closure with these folks, and though we never became particularly close to anyone on the trail, the emotions we felt as we said goodbye to each of these fellow pilgrims spoke to the sense of community we had developed during our five weeks on the Camino Francés.

We were seeking a restaurant for a special last large meal in Santiago, and we certainly found one. Splurging a little, we had lunch at the Parador de Santiago de Compostela. We walked in and were immediately struck by the splendor of the space, with primitive arched stone walls, recessed lighting throughout, and white tablecloths. Our server was very personable and spoke fluent English. He told us this long-arched space with an underground feel had been converted from an ancient stable. With a glass of the house white wine, we shared a salad that included octopus, white beans, and greens, all tossed in a vinaigrette. Then, Bev had a delicious lamb dish, and I had the monkfish, which came with potatoes and vegetables cooked in a broth. It was the last special meal of our Camino, and it was wonderful.

BEV HAD BOOKED A cathedral tour for 4:00 p.m. The tour had been recommended by one of our Camino acquaintances, but we weren't sure what to expect. The tour focused on the rooftop of the cathedral, with a promise of panoramic views of the city. Those views were delivered but, for me, the most powerful memory of the tour was the odd disorientation I experienced.

To get to the rooftop of this vast building, we started climbing an intricate set of stairways that ultimately led us up to the roof on what was, thankfully, a beautiful, sunny day. The main section of the roof was constructed of concrete tiles, perhaps two inches thick, that were layered like shingles on the slanted roof. The pitch of the roof was not extreme, but still fairly steep, and there were no visible guardrails or other apparent protective measures. As we viewed the Plaza del Obradoiro a great distance below us, I sensed that someone slipping and falling might tumble down the roof and end up splattered among the pilgrims milling about in front of the cathedral.

While I'm not typically frightened by heights, trying to navigate this odd, slanted roof got me disoriented, as if I was experiencing a case of vertigo as I tried to navigate across the different angles. Bev helped me as we moved from one part of the roof to another, and in time, I got better acclimated. But it was a struggle at first, an experience that would never have even been available in the United States given obvious safety concerns.

There were, however, incredible views, of the top of the cathedral, of the plazas surrounding the building, of the entire city, and of the mountains in the distance. The friendly young lady who was our guide kept up a steady flow of information into the headset we had been given, almost all of it in Spanish and virtually none of which we understood. Though we had observed seldom-seen parts of this iconic structure, I was glad to be back on a level surface when the tour ended.

We had hoped the tour included time inside the cathedral, but it did not. We had viewed our trek on the Camino Francés as a walk across a beautiful country that was new to us. But the origin of the Camino de Santiago was as a network of paths to Santiago de Compostela, where peregrinos could view and pay homage to the remains of the Apostle James. Until the past few decades, virtually everyone who hiked long distances along the various Camino routes to this Spanish city did so for religious reasons. Until the Camino gained widespread popularity, such walks completed for adventure or cultural immersion (two of our primary motivations) would have been viewed as silliness if not a sign of insanity. It was exclusively considered a spiritual journey, with pilgrims earning the right to view the remains of St. James.

Though our Camino was in many respects a spiritual journey, neither Bev nor I hold the strong Christian beliefs that draw thousands to this spot each year. But to walk 500 miles on the Way of St. James and then not view his remains seemed at best a lost opportunity, and at worst a sacrilege.

By the time our tour ended, the crowds in and around the cathedral had considerably thinned. We could walk right into the massive basilica and follow the arrows to view the crypt that allegedly holds the relics of St. James. The crypt is located below the main altar, so we followed the signs behind and over the altar and then walked down some steps to the crypt. We passed by an opening and looked in a few feet to see the silver reliquary holding the remains of the Apostle and two of his disciples. While a beautiful container, the entire presentation was rather understated, particularly as this beautifully ornate basilica had been constructed in large part to showcase these remains.

As I stood there viewing this small, ornate crypt, I was spiritually unmoved, as I might have anticipated. I felt like a tourist in the waning days of a long vacation, checking items off a to-do list before catching the inevitable flight home. And I couldn't shake the question of whether this box actually contained the remains of one of Jesus' main disciples. As with the miracle of the chickens associated with the cathedral in Santo Domingo or the flesh and blood transformation associated with the chapel in O Cebreiro, for this to have meaning, one had to accept the veracity of the story.

But really, what was far more important than whether I accepted these legendary tales as fact was whether the true believers, the deeply religious individuals, believed them to be true. Much of spirituality, and virtually all of religion, is, in my mind, based on faith. And if one's faith confirmed that the remains of the Apostle James were in this container, then, in effect, they were. Just as "everyone walks their own Camino," so, too, does everyone determine how they view the stories embedded in their religion, or if they have a religion at all. To Bev and me, the viewing of the crypt of St. James was more symbolic of the end of our Camino journey than anything else.

As we walked out of the Cathedral of Santiago de Compostela for the last time to return to our hotel, our focus shifted to preparing for our return home. After over five weeks, our Camino experience was concluded.

WE WERE UP EARLY the next morning and had a quick breakfast in the hotel restaurant, our last meal included in the package we had purchased from the travel company. With our suitcases packed, we asked the young lady at the front desk to call us a taxi. Nervous about our travel arrangements for the next two days, we waited for fifteen minutes for the car to arrive, a time that seemed far longer. But it eventually arrived, and we were soon on our way to the Santiago-Rosalía de Castro Airport. Because of the limited number of flights departing from this smaller airport, we had booked a flight with a regional airline for the short, one-hour and fifteen-minute flight to Madrid. We had a reservation at a hotel near the Madrid airport where we would spend the night before flying back to the United States the next day.

We had booked this flight months earlier, and it was on what was considered a budget airline among budget airlines. We had paid extra for our two checked bags and even for assigned seats so we could be assured of sitting together. Neither of us is particularly nervous about flying, but this was a little different. We were in a foreign country where we assumed safety measures were taken seriously, but we were flying on an airline for which every little cost-cutting measure allowed the company to eke out a little more profit. It was, of course, an uneventful flight.

We arrived in Madrid ahead of schedule and started looking for signage directing us to the baggage claim area. The Madrid-Barajas Airport is large, the second largest in Europe and the fifth busiest, but we found it surprisingly easy to navigate. Our bags soon arrived, and we quickly hailed a ride to our hotel for the evening.

After a month and a half in Spain, and with just one night left in the country, we likely needed to begin transitioning back to our regular lives in the United States. We started that process at the Marriott Madrid

Auditorium Hotel near the airport. We had stayed in some nice inns, some memorably so, since arriving in Spain. But this had the feel of a modern, upscale American hotel, an ideal setting to begin settling back into our non-Camino lifestyle, for better or for worse.

After quickly being checked in by a friendly young lady at the front desk who, like everyone else we would encounter at this hotel, spoke impeccable English, we headed to our fourth-floor room. As we entered our clean and spacious room, we couldn't help but ponder how different this setting was from what we had been experiencing. Just a week earlier, we were hanging our clothes out to dry and felt okay doing so. Most days we had lugged our suitcases up multiple flights of stairs to our often-meager accommodation. Rather than five different restaurants ready to cater to our needs, like in this hotel, we had to take what limited dining options were available to us, and almost always enjoyed what we were served. Yes, that transition back to our old lives was going to take some time.

After getting settled in our room, we returned to the lobby bar for a glass of wine and a couple of salads, a late lunch following our flight from Santiago de Compostela. It was a very relaxed setting, and the wine, food, and service were all good. But this was an American hotel with prices in line with what we would expect back home. Our days of economical pilgrim's meals and glasses of wine for one euro were behind us.

A few hours later, we had dinner at the Champions Bar located just off the hotel lobby. As we walked in, we gazed around to see a fully stocked bar, countless big-screen TVs broadcasting different sporting events, a pool table, and a loud buzz filling the air. We could just as easily have been in a sports bar back home in the Chicago suburbs. Bev and I both ordered burgers, and mine was a huge slab of ground beef with cheese and bacon on a large bun served with a mound of fries. It was something I would seldom order in my regular life and served as a reminder that the transition back to our regular lives would need to include a return to a healthier diet.

On this our last night in Spain after almost six weeks since arriving, and with a big travel day ahead of us, we went to bed earlier than usual. Given our upcoming international flight and our unfamiliarity with the Madrid airport, we planned to arrive in plenty of time.

THE HOTEL SHUTTLE TO the airport left at predetermined times, and we wanted to check in for our flight at least three hours before its 10:45 a.m. departure. Though earlier than we would prefer, we signed up for the 6:45 shuttle, hoping to get some breakfast at the airport.

We stood outside with our luggage on a very temperate mid-October early morning, and the shuttle bus arrived at around 6:40 a.m. Two middle-aged men were coordinating the shuttle loading process, the first with a Marriott name badge who was checking names off his list. The other was dressed in a green, military-looking outfit whose no-nonsense facial expression made us believe he was in charge of shuttle security. When he started loading suitcases onto the bus, we decided he perhaps had multiple functions. Though still dark outside, the shuttle bus was nearly full by the time we left the hotel.

Other than the use of multiple languages to ask what airlines the travelers were flying on, this short, ten-minute bus ride was just like the countless airport shuttles we had ridden on in the United States, with everyone quiet and either looking at the airport scenery or their phones. And just like that, we were deposited at the terminal where we would check in for our Delta flight. At this early hour, the airport was already buzzing, a likely contrast to the rest of the country at a time when most Spaniards were just getting started with their day.

From check-in through the security screening to getting breakfast sandwiches and coffee, the morning seemed to flow smoothly. Gauging our emotions as we waited for our flight to board, we had surprisingly mixed feelings as we prepared to leave Spain. Just a week earlier, we had both been exhausted and emotionally drained and were so ready to get home and back to our regular lives. But now that the inevitable departure was imminent, we realized there was much about this adventure we were going to miss. In our eagerness to get to Santiago de Compostela, we had been so focused on the everyday grind of our daily hikes that we had lost touch with the significance of our overall journey. Perhaps we were just beginning to gain the perspective of our Camino that had been missing. We realized we had developed a deep reverence for Spain, the Spanish culture and way of life, and the Spanish people. We knew, especially now that it was over, that our six weeks on the Camino Francés had been an amazing experience we would soon miss.

The gate for our flight was located on the edge of an enormous room with high ceilings and seating for hundreds of travelers. We soon realized that most of these folks would board the same plane for the United States that we would, another large Boeing 777 like we had flown on to Barcelona a month and a half earlier. With an hour and a half before the plane would begin boarding, we found a secluded spot in the cacophonous terminal, or at least as secluded as was available. We sat there reading or ruminating about our experiences until we made our way toward our gate around a half hour before boarding was to begin.

There was another security check where airline personnel reviewed travel documents and boarding passes before allowing travelers to proceed into the waiting area around the gate. Bev was in front of me as the line inched toward the four individuals checking travel documents. I was stunned when the screener told Bev she would be required to undergo additional screening and was escorted to a glass-enclosed office in a corner of this huge terminal. It wasn't like a scene from the movie *Midnight Express* or anything sinister, but it was rather unnerving, at least for me. I hadn't overheard the exchange between Bev and this screener, so I wasn't aware of what was really happening, except that she had quickly told me she was being taken for additional screening.

Bev had originally been as concerned as I was until she questioned the screener and was told it was a required random check; Bev had been selected by chance, likely in some computerized manner. This made much more sense because, like me, Bev has to be the antithesis of someone who might pose a security risk on an airplane. As she was escorted to the screening area, her greatest concern was that she was being separated from me.

I knew little of this except that my wife had been detained (not really, as it turned out) in a foreign country for additional security screening, seemingly like she had been flagged on a no-fly list. I was concerned, and after completing my own screening, I walked toward the area where they had taken Bev and found the little office where she was being questioned. A few minutes later, she was walking toward me. They had looked through her small tote bag, reviewed her travel documents, and then allowed her to return to the waiting area. It was no big deal, but a combination of the circumstances and my imagination resulted in much more stress than either of us needed.

In time, the flight started boarding, a lengthy process given the hundreds of passengers. Two jetways were used to expedite the boarding process. We located our seats toward the back of the plane and settled in for the scheduled eight-and-a-half-hour flight to JFK Airport in New York.

We departed on time and were soon in the air on an overcast morning. The flight was uneventful, and after watching a couple of movies, reading a few chapters from our books, and enjoying a surprisingly tasty light lunch, we landed in New York. Our layover at JFK was three hours, but as we were re-entering the United States, we would need to go through customs.

In what felt like the bowels of this massive airport, we secured our suit-cases from the baggage carousel but then almost immediately gave them to another baggage handler before we were processed for re-entry. The customs lines were long, but a few months before departing, Bev and I had completed a comprehensive screening for "Global Entry" clearance. That screening and the card that resulted from it allowed us to move to a separate area, complete a facial scan, and then quickly continue into the terminal for our connecting flight. As I passed by his station, the customs agent said, "Welcome back to the United States, Mr. Leachman." It was the first time we had used our Global Entry cards, and the process was slick.

Because of our surprisingly quick passage through customs, we still had over two hours before we were scheduled to board our flight to Chicago. We had a quick dinner, did some more sitting around, and were soon in our seats on a smaller plane that would take us to O'Hare International Airport in a little over two hours. Other than the unexpected security hiccup in Madrid, it had been a smooth but long travel day.

I often do odd calculations in my head as we move across time zones, what the time will be when we arrive, what the time is where we departed, etc. As we left New York City, the time in Madrid, where we had started our day, was 10:00 p.m. and would be three hours later when we arrived in Chicago. By the time we were scheduled to arrive at O'Hare, it would have been over twenty hours since we had arisen that morning, and we still had to get from the airport to our home. As we settled in for our relatively short domestic flight, we were already tired.

O'Hare International Airport is enormous, and it is some distance from most of the gates to the baggage claim area. It often takes a great deal of time for the bags to be offloaded from the plane and transported to the baggage carousels. But on this mid-October evening, this often-elongated process seemed expedited, and our wait for our bags was much shorter than usual.

Our son picked us up just outside of the baggage claim area, and as we passed by sights and landmarks we hadn't seen in over a month and a half, we soon pulled into the familiar confines of our neighborhood. As we had so desperately wanted just a few days earlier, we were home, back to our bed, our routines, and our family. It was great to be home, but it was like we had brought a little piece of Spain home with us.

And now, our Spanish adventure had truly come to an end.

Or had it?

As we had learned six years earlier at the end of a similar long and strenuous journey, our cross-country bicycle ride, an experience like this one stays with you, maintaining a prominent position in both your psyche and your identity. For weeks after that bike trip, we occasionally relived different memorable episodes from that journey, and there were so many. Though the experience was vastly different, we would find the same to be true with our walk on the Camino de Santiago.

And as the sage older gentleman in Molinaseca had shared with us, we wouldn't understand this journey and what it meant to us until we returned home. That would come with the greater perspective that accompanied being able to detach ourselves from the experience. We had spent five weeks laser-focused on the "trees" that were ahead of us, the day's route, any tough terrain, the name and location of our hotel for the evening, where we might have dinner, etc. As a result, we hadn't concerned ourselves with the "forest" through which we were passing, the magnitude of the totality of what we were accomplishing. As we settled back into our regular routines and had no more "trees" to worry about, or at least different ones to focus on, we began to consider the size and density and beauty of the "forest" we had just experienced.

As I pondered these questions in the days after we returned from Spain, I gained a greater appreciation that our journey had been magnificent, amazingly beautiful, and incredibly challenging. And though I would prefer not to dwell on such accolades, what we had accomplished was rather impressive.

The question that had stared us in the face after finishing in Santiago had been along the lines of, "What did we just do?" The literal answer to that question is that, at sixty-six, Bev and I had spent a month-and-a-half in Spain, a country in which we had been unfamiliar with the culture and non-proficient with the language, and with virtually no outside support, we had fairly easily navigated both. When the rational, logical parts of our brains warned us about the possibility of danger, or worse, failure, if we pursued this dream, we had trudged on. While on the Camino, almost every day, we walked with fifteen- to twenty-pound packs on our backs for an average of between thirteen and fourteen miles every day. Over some very challenging terrain, we walked from the French border, over the Pyrenees, and then nearly 500 miles across northern Spain. This is not meant to be boastful, though it may be perceived as such, but as a way to help attain the perspective we were seeking. We battled accumulating fatigue, emotional highs and lows, and sore legs and feet. Yet we came out of this amazing experience feeling far better and stronger than we could have ever expected. There's a large part of me that's proud of that accomplishment, but an even larger part that's grateful to have had the opportunity to experience this amazing journey.

I came away from this experience especially thankful to have been able to share this experience with Bev, who persevered through unique challenges to the very end. Could I have completed a walk across the Camino Francés without her? Maybe, probably, but I'm sure I wouldn't have even tried.

In time, inevitably, our Camino memories faded into the background, triggered occasionally by happenstance occurrences and, for me, by the writing of this book. The writing process reverted my focus to the details of the trip rather than its overall scope, the "trees" rather than the "forest."

We returned to Barcelona in the fall of 2024 on a sightseeing trip with members of our extended family. It was a wonderful time that renewed our love of Spanish culture, Rioja wine, and the Spanish people. But with family members and tour guides available to guide our exploration and a Mediterranean cruise in our future rather than a 500-mile hike across a foreign country, the feel was quite different. After two nights in this wonderful city and a cruise ship stop in Valencia, we were on to France and then Italy. Our time in Spain had been brief, and our agenda had been much more tourist-based. As a result, our second trip to this wonderful country did little to elicit memories of our Camino adventure.

Bev is the handyperson in our family, using self-taught skills she picked up completing home improvement projects during the pandemic. Over a year after our return from Spain, Bev completed a renovation of a stairway down to the basement of our townhouse. Once completed, her vision included maps of our various adventure trips, including our trek on the Camino Francés. After we placed the beautiful, framed map on the wall, I mindlessly completed my countless trips up and down those stairs, concentrating on other issues or nothing at all.

Then, on one of those trips down to the basement, for some reason, I impulsively stopped and took a long look at this detailed map. On it, I noted St. Jean Pied de Port and the high point in the Pyrenees we passed shortly after leaving that French village. Listed on the map were the wonderful cities of Pamplona, Burgos, and León. Also listed were Carrión de los Condes, where we stayed in a beautiful, ancient monastery, and

Ponferrada, where we shopped like regular Spaniards for a new suitcase. There was Cruz de Ferro, the site of our most spiritual moment on the trail, and Santiago de Compostela, the destination for ours and all Camino hikes.

But as I paused to look at the map of the Camino Francés hanging on our wall, besides the rush of memories that flowed over me, I was struck by the scope of what we had done, the length of our journey. We had walked almost all the way across this wonderful country.

It was all a helpful reminder that yes, this had been a magnificent adventure.

REFERENCES

Brierley, John, *A Pilgrim's Guide to the Camino de Santiago*, Camino Guides, 2023

Foster, Elaine and Foster, Joseph, *In Movement There is Peace: Stumbling 500 Miles Along the Way to Spirit*, PsyConOps, 2013

Kerkeling, Hape, *I'm Off Then: Losing and Finding Myself on the Camino de Santiago*, Free Press, 2006

MacLaine, Shirley, *The Camino: A Journey of the Spirit*, Pocket Books, 2000

McCarthy, Andrew, *Walking with Sam*, Grand Central Publishing, 2023

Shaia, Alexander John, *Returning from Camino*, Quadratos, 2018

Acknowledgements

There are many individuals whose contributions made this project possible:

The folks at **Macs Adventures** and **Tee Travel** for their meticulous planning and assistance as we prepared for and completed this journey.

The wonderful people of Spain, whose spirit and welcoming attitude warmed and comforted us each day during our extended time in this amazing land.

Family members and **Roland and Kathy Colson**, whose watchful presence allowed us to be out of the country for six weeks.

Early readers of the manuscript whose feedback was helpful, supportive, and informative: **Bev Leachman**, **Kassie Leachman**, and **Larry Love**.

Brian Tutko, who skillfully edited the manuscript.

Members of our family, particularly **Jonathan, Kassie, Annie,** and **Nick**, as well as our extended family, for their support before, during, and after our Camino journey and through the completion of this project. And to our grandchildren, **Edie, Gus,** and **Luca,** as well as any others who may bless us in the coming years: always know that you can accomplish virtually anything you set your mind to.

Bev, my partner in life and adventure: without you, our Camino experience, and this book, would have never become a reality.

About the Author

Rob Leachman is the author of *The Long Walk to Compostela: Life Lessons Learned on the Camino de Santiago* and the award-winning *One Ride at a Time: Life Lessons Learned on a Cross-Country Bicycle Ride*. A writer, educator, speaker, and self-described "occasional adventurer," Rob draws inspiration from the long miles and deeper moments of his travels with his wife, Bev. Together, they've completed a series of "ageless adventure" journeys—from biking across Missouri and hiking across the Grand Canyon to cycling coast-to-coast across the southern United States and walking the 500-mile Camino de Santiago.

A retired school administrator and university instructor, Rob holds a doctoral degree from the University of Missouri and now writes from his home in the Chicago suburbs. His work explores themes of goal setting and leadership, resilience, and purposeful living, especially in life's later chapters. When not writing, he and Bev can often be found hiking or biking their favorite Midwest trails.

Learn more or get in touch at *RobLeachman.com.*